CHILD CARE FOR THE '90s
An Owner's Manual

CHILD
CARE
FOR THE
'90S

AN OWNER'S
MANUAL

1st Edition

ALFREDO SANTESTEBAN, M.D., F.A.A.P.

A B C & F PRESS
Bedford, Texas

CHILD CARE FOR THE '90s: An Owner's Manual
ABC & F Press - January 1993

Copyright 1993, by Alfredo Santesteban, M.D. F.A.A.P.

First Printing 1993

Library of Congress Cataloging-in-Publication Data

Santesteban, Alfredo, 1936-
  Child Care for the '90s: An Owner's Manual / Alfredo Santesteban
  -- 1st ed.
  p.   cm.
  Includes bibliographical references and index.
  ISBN: 0 - 9634035 - 0 - 8
  1. Pediatrics--Popular works. 2. Child Care. I. Title
RJ61.S325   1992
649' .4--dc20   92-33306
                                                          CIP

Printed in the United States of America

To my wife Celia, and my two children: Ariel Roberto and Martina Raquel. Without their patience and understanding I could not have done it.

Special thanks to my parents for giving me space to grow during my young years and for having faith in me.

January 1993

AUTHOR NOTES

The information in this book is not intended to substitute for the advice of your child's doctor. Do not start any treatment without first consulting with his physician, especially if your child seems to have something serious. By contacting him or her in advance, he or she can tailor the treatment to your child's individual needs.

I chose to use both the pronouns he and she, alternating with each chapter, rather than use only he as other books do. I do not think that this method will cause any confusion and will be well received by those readers of the feminine gender.

I have tried hard to research all the subjects in this book for accuracy and correctness. The latest information has been included here. However, remember that your child's physician knows your child first hand. Therefore, do call his or her office as I explained above, and call again if your child is getting worse. Both the publishers of this book and myself as the author disclaim responsibility for any harm that may ensue due to misapplication or misinterpretation of advice or information contained in this manual.

ACKNOWLEDGEMENTS

The author wishes to thank the American Academy of Pediatrics for permission to reproduce the sections titled *Choking*, *Cardiopulmonary Resuscitation* and *Child Safety Seats*.

The Metropolitan Life Insurance Company graciously allowed the reproduction of the section titled *Child Safety*.

Several people helped in the preparation and revision of this book. My heartfelt thanks to Rebecca Paisley, an excellent author herself, to Wendy Stackable, who edited a large portion of the manuscript and offered sound advice.

To Ruben Rendon I am thankful for creating a cover that exactly represented what I had in mind, and for his patience working with me.

My office personnel had to endure my grumpiness many times when things weren't going well with the book, or I had spent a whole week-end working at this second job.

TABLE OF CONTENTS

PART I
BASICS OF NEWBORN CARE

Chapter 1
Before Your Baby
is Born

Chapter 2
The First Month of Life

Chapter 3
After the First Month

PART II
ILLNESSES, PROBLEMS, ETC.

Chapter 4
Fever

Chapter 5
Stomach and Bowel
Problems, etc.

Chapter 6
Respiratory Illnesses

Chapter 7
Infections and other
Problems

Chapter 8
Your Medicine Cabinet, etc.

Chapter 9
Toilet Training, Bedwetting,
Discipline, etc.

Chapter 10
Growth and Development, Hearing, Vision, Speech

Chapter 11
Accident Prevention, Poisons, Safety, etc.

Chapter 12
Children and TV, Toys, Don'ts for Parents, etc.

§§§

INTRODUCTION

Dear Parents:

You are about to embark on a wonderful but sometimes scary journey...The joy and happiness you find as a parent are mixed with a tremendous sense of responsibility.

This tiny human being has been entrusted to you... All of a sudden, you may feel scared. Doubts may overtake you... What if something happens to my baby ...? Will I be able to know what to do? Will I be able to be a good parent? and so on.
Every parent has felt those same fears. Every parent makes mistakes along the way. You are NOT alone however. You *can* be prepared. I hope this BOOK and your CHILD'S DOCTOR will help you be the best parent you can.

I have divided the book into two parts: the first is dedicated to the care of the newborn. Parents of newborns can choose to only read this first part, which is not very lengthy. It should give them good information on the most common situations or problems encountered with a newborn.

The second part, entitled "Illnesses and Other Problems" describes the most common medical problems, some useful preventive measures and emergencies.

The glossary covers other problems which are not an everyday occurrence but that nevertheless I feel are deserving of consideration, especially for those parents who desire to become more knowledgeable. A section titled Hotlines and Resources should be helpful I hope.

A few final words: Relax, use your common sense, and enjoy the trip! Don't be afraid to ask for help from your relatives, from your friends, but *most of all from your child's doctor*. Above all, trust yourself and push any negative feelings aside. I am talking not only to Moms, but also to Dads! And to Dads especially I say: "Don't pass up this great opportunity to get to know and love your child. The rewards will be worth it, believe me!"

Good luck -- and happy parenting!

Alfredo O. Santesteban, M.D. F.A.A.P.
Bedford, Texas, January 1993.

How to use this book

Dear Parents:

When searching for a subject, an illness, etc., look first in the Index. If not there, search the Glossary. For medical emergencies I strongly recommend that all parents keep this book handy: *A Sigh of Relief*. (see section Hotlines and Resources).

A word of caution:

Many well-intentioned people will volunteer lots of child rearing advice, especially when parents are inexperienced. This advice may be correct, but often it is not. It may even lead you to make a mistake in caring for your child.

This advice sometimes comes from a respected, older person such as a parent. It can be tough *not* to do what a mother-in-law recommends!

Before you accept or refuse suggestions concerning your baby, listen carefully, use your common sense and, if it is not an urgent matter, look up the item in question in this book or ask your child's doctor.

Communicating with your child's doctor
(I use the masculine below for simplicity)

Following are a few of my personal suggestions about how best to communicate and work in harmony with your doctor's office so that the best interests of your child are served. To function effectively, doctor's offices like any other offices or agencies must have certain rules.

Most doctors and their staff are dedicated, caring individuals and have the best intentions toward the people they serve. When they set office rules or policies they do it so that everybody, especially the patients, benefit from them. On the other hand, these people have families, other obligations and a need for leisure time.

Remember these are my personal suggestions. You should check with your pediatrician or family doctor about his policies and rules.

- **Calls after hours or week-ends:**

Don't call him after hours unless it is for a problem that you truly think cannot wait until the next morning. Especially if your child's illness began two or three days ago, and his condition is not worse now that it was earlier in the day! Try to anticipate your future reactions. For instance, is 10:00 a.m., your child is coughing some but has no other complaint. Ask yourself: "Even if he doesn't get worse later in the day, come the evening, will I panic and want then the doctor's advice?" If the answer is yes, then call in the morning when the doctor or his nurse can better advice you on what to do. They will have your child's record in front of them and will give you the best advice. If he is allergic to a certain medicine they can see that information in his chart, etc.

Please! DO NOT CALL FOR PRESCRIPTION REFILLS AFTER HOURS OR ON WEEK-ENDS. Try this test: put yourself in the place of the doctor's wife. You and him are having a nice, quiet dinner, and a call like the one I mention above comes in! How would you feel? A little upset, may be? Or maybe he is coaching his son's soccer team. Or attending a function at his daughter's school.

Most pharmacists will give you at least a small quantity of the medication your son has run out of if you explain the problem. Of course, the ideal situation should be for parents to call for refills before they run out of medication.

A not infrequent situation: Your child is pretty sick, you believe. You called and told the answering service to have your doctor call you back as soon as possible. You don't hear from him after what you consider a reasonable amount of time. Please! Do call again, because your message might have gotten lost, misplaced or the doctor got somehow the wrong number and has been trying to call you unsuccessfully.

• **Don't call asking for antibiotics or other strong medicines to be prescribed over the phone** without the doctor examining the child first. Few things upset physicians more than this kind of calls! Why? First, the child might not need these medications. Secondly, the medication might be harmful. Even if the doctor has known your child for a long time, an examination is always advisable before he is medicated. Also, let's face it, prescribing over the phone puts the physician in legal jeopardy also.

• **Office Rules, etc.**

Please follow the office's rules about appointments, payments, i.e., "at the time of service", etc., follow-up visits, compliance with medications and other matters. Does your doctor want you to go to the emergency room of the hospital after hours? Or does he prefer that you always call him first?

When unable to keep an appointment, please cancel it as early as possible so another patient can be scheduled then.

• **Be prepared to explain your child illness**

When your child is ill, before you call, try to be prepared and calm. Go to the point. Avoid irrelevant details. Your objective is to get your message across. The receptionist can then make a decision whether to let you talk to the nurse or directly give you an appointment, etc. If your child has fever and is vomiting, then say so and wait for the office clerk's questions. If he looks sick, weak, etc. state so. If on the other hand he seems active, with good color, etc. say it. Avoid rambling. The receptionist or nurse may be very busy at the moment you are talking to her, so again, try to be clear, straightforward.

• **School health physicals**

Please do not ask your child's doctor to sign a school health examination form if he has not had a complete physical in a long time. Even if the doctor saw him several times in the last few months but these were sick visits, these do not qualify as well exams, because they are not usually complete. A complete physical examination involves more than looking inside the ears, or listening to the heart or lungs. Signing the school form without a proper physical examination puts both the doctor and the child in jeopardy, both legally and medically. Thus: avoid getting a negative answer or engaging in a dispute with the office personnel.

- **Should he be seen today or tomorrow?**

If the doctor's office considers that your child is not sick enough for him to be seen that same day, do not demand the contrary unless you honestly believe that your child's condition warrants it. I train my nurses to work-in the same day any patient whose parent feels strongly that he must be seen. However, sometimes a mother panics and after I do see the child in the office I feel bad because the child is not very sick and the office visit was probably unnecessary. This is an uncertain, subjective situation. How does one decide if a child is sick enough to be seen the same day or not? Many cases are clear cut, but others aren't. Follow your doctor's policy on this. Probably every doctor will handle these in a different way.

- **The panicky or the demanding parent**

Doctor offices' personnel understands that we all can lose our temper when a loved one, especially a child, is ill. It is easy to panic. You become irate if the nurse or the doctor doesn't come to the phone right then or if they don't give you an appointment immediately! This is a plea to all parents: We understand and we'll bend over backward to fit you in the schedule. Even if sometimes we don't surmise from your account of the child's illness that he is very sick. But please: Do not do it over and over again. You'll be like the shepherd in Aesop's fable. You have to trust that the doctor's personnel is on your side. We do care and will always try to do what's best for your child's health.

- **Other common situations to avoid:**

If your child is coming in for a recheck visit, for instance for an ear infection, most doctors do no like it if you ask them to do right then a well baby check up -a full check up- "just because he is or will soon be due for one anyway". The reasons: Most rechecks require a short amount of time. A full check up requires a longer amount of time, i.e., the child must be weighed, his height and temperature must be measured, etc. When the receptionist schedules your child for a recheck she does not allocate enough time for a full check up. This causes the doctor's schedule to fall behind.

Another problem that also disrupts the office schedule: Please don't ask your doctor to "just look into Joshua's ears since he is here ..." (Joshua didn't have an appointment, his sister Lisa did).

• How to choose a doctor for your baby:

Choosing a doctor for the new baby is an important decision for prospective parents. Above all, Mom and Dad want to feel confident in their physician's ability to care for baby in illness and emergency situations, as well as in routine checkups.

It is best if parents make this choice well before the baby is born, preferably during the seventh or eighth month of pregnancy. Usually, physicians will be happy to schedule prenatal consultations with expectant parents.

Starting the search for the right doctor before delivery allows the parents to focus on their prenatal interview with him. This way you can talk without the distractions that will be present once the baby is born. It also will serve to put nervous new parents at ease with the doctor when they bring baby in for his first checkup.

Observe Doctor "In Action"

If possible, the parents should schedule this prenatal visit during regular office hours so they can see the office "in action." They can observe office procedures and get to know the physician simultaneously.

This is a good time to discuss typical hospital procedures, routine tests and any other concerns parents might have about the baby's stay in the hospital. Arrangements should be made for parents or hospital staff to notify the doctor once the baby is born.

Many factors go into choosing a doctor, such as his qualifications, location and accessibility and comments or recommendations from friends. Most will provide reading materials to help answer many questions before people ask them.

Some "must-know" subjects will include his ideas on breastfeeding, circumcision, feeding schedules, etc. Once parents and physician have met, discussed policies on childcare, on-call and emergency procedures, fees and hospital affiliations, Mom and Dad will have the information they need to make a choice.

Information Exchange

Other questions parents might want to consider asking during their prenatal interview include:

1. Where did you train and how long have you been in practice?

2. Is your practice a solo, group or shared practice?

3. How often are routine checkups scheduled?

4. When is our baby's first visit, and how far in advance should we call to make an appointment?

5. How can we reach you after hours?

6. Who covers for you when you are out of town?

7. What are your ideas on the use of medications, breastfeeding, etc.

8. What are your views concerning discipline?

Also, the doctor will have some questions for parents that will help him be better prepared to care for their baby. He will ask about the course of the pregnancy, whether you know the gender of the baby, whether delivery might be vaginal or caesarean, whether parents have taken Lamaze classes and if the father will participate in the delivery.

He also will try to find out if the parents have any specific fears or concerns about the birth of the baby. He probably will ask for the parents' medical history. He may even want to know whether the baby will be cared for in the home or if the mother plans to work after delivery. In the latter case he will ask about child care plans associated with that decision.

Pediatrician or Family Practitioner?

Finally, if the couple is confused about whether to use a pediatrician or simply to take the baby to their family doctor, they should understand the difference between the two. Pediatricians treat babies and children exclusively while family practice physicians manage a general medical practice that may include obstetrics, gynecology, surgery etc.

Board-certified pediatricians train to recognize and handle unusual pediatric situations because they have spent at least three years in an approved residency training program beyond medical school and have passed appropriate written examinations.

There are many dedicated, qualified physicians in both categories, and parents must ultimately choose the one whom they are confident will best meet the healthcare needs of their child.

When you need a new pediatrician or general doctor for a child older than a newborn -for instance, if you move from one state to another- you can get recommendations from your new neighbors, co-workers, etc. Usually "word of mouth" plus the tips I explain above are the best way.

CHOKING

If your child is choking and is unable to breathe, begin the procedures explained below. If he is coughing, crying or speaking, DO NOT do any of them, but call your doctor for further advice.

FOR INFANTS UNDER ONE YEAR OLD (A)

• Call for emergency services or 911
• Place infant face down over your arm with head lower than the trunk. Rest your forearm on your thigh.
• Deliver four blows with the heel of the hand, striking high between the infant's shoulder blades.
• If blockage is not relieved, roll the infant over. Lay the child down, face up, on a firm surface. Give four rapid chest compressions over the breastbone using two fingers. Repeat back blows and chest thrusts until the foreign body is expelled or the infant becomes UNCONSCIOUS.
• If the above measures have not removed the blockage, and the child becomes UNCONSCIOUS, open mouth with thumb over tongue and fingers wrapped around lower jaw.
• If you can see the foreign body, remove it with a sideways swipe of a finger. (Never poke your finger straight into the throat). Be careful, though, because finger sweeps may push the object further down the airway.
• If the blockage is not relieved and the child cannot breathe, begin the technique of pulmonary support as outlined in figure D.
• Rapid transport to a medical facility is urgent if these emergency first aid measures fail.

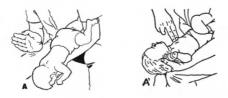

FOR CHILDREN OVER ONE YEAR OLD (B,C)

• Call for emergency service or 911.
• Place child on his back. Kneel at the child's feet. Put the heel of one hand on the child's abdomen in the midline between the navel and rib cage.
• Place the second hand on top of the first (B).

- The older, larger child can be treated in a sitting, standing or recumbent position (C).
- Press firmly, but gently, into the abdomen with a rapid inward and upward thrust. Repeat six to ten times. The abdominal thrusts -- called the Heimlich maneuver-- should be applied until the foreign body is expelled.
- If the above measures have not removed the blockage, follow the same instructions as above (from the fifth dot downwards).

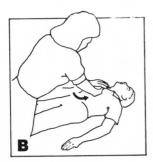
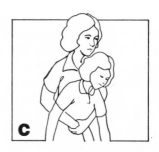

CPR
(CARDIOPULMONARY RESUSCITATION)

This technique is to be used in situations such as drowning, electric shock and smoke inhalation or when breathing or heartbeat stops.

TECHNIQUE OF PULMONARY SUPPORT (D)

If the child is not breathing and unconscious, begin the following:

- Place victim on back.
- Straighten neck (unless neck injury suspected) and lift jaw.
- Give 2 full breaths into infant's nose and mouth or into larger child's mouth with nostrils pinched closed.
- If chest doesn't move --the air is not entering the lungs-- go back to "Choking" and then move to (D), and so forth.
- Breathe at 20 breaths per minute for infants and 15 breaths per minute for children, using only enough air to move the chest up and down.

TECHNIQUE OF CARDIAC SUPPORT

Begin the following if the child has no pulse:

• Place the victim on his back on a firm surface.
• In the infant, using two fingers, depress the breastbone 1/2 to 1 inch at the level of one finger's breadth below the nipples (E).
• Compress at 100 times/minute.
• In the child, depress the lower 1/3 of the breastbone with the heel of the hand at 80 compressions/minute. There should be five compressions to one respiration (F).

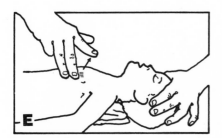 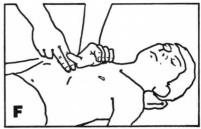

Learn and practice CPR

(This section published here with permission of the American Academy of Pediatrics (modified). Copyright 1989)

GOING HOME DAY
(Last-Minute Recommendations for New Moms)

Feedings:

• Feed your child on demand, day and night, but at least every three to four hours.
  • If breastfeeding, mother should R E L A X !
  • Pacifiers are O.K.
  • HOLD HER, LOVE HER (No, you won't spoil her!)
  • DELEGATE! Enlist help around the house.
  • REST. Nap when she does. Disconnect your phone.
• If breastfeeding, give the baby vitamins and fluoride. Mother should not eat chocolate, cabbage or cauliflower.

Bathing:

• Bathe her two to three times per week. Sponge bathe until the umbilical cord falls off. Ask your doctor about lotions, oils or powders.

Umbilical Cord Care:

• Apply alcohol four to five times per day until it falls off and the area is dry.

Diapers:

  • Use warm water on soft washcloth to clean her bottom.
  • Change her often.
• Apply A & D ointment and/or zinc oxide early if a diaper rash appears.

Circumcision:

• Wash carefully with soap and water whenever diapers are changed. No special care is required usually.

Do Not Cover Baby Too Much!

No, babies do not catch colds more easily, but:
  • Avoid crowded conditions or sick people.
  • Keep other kids away as much as possible.

Watch For Jaundice:

(yellow skin). Call doctor.

Normal Events:

• Sneezing, hiccups, spitting up, the "rash" of the newborn (red blotches, like hives, anywhere on the body).
• Fast breathing, followed by periods of slow breathing.

Normal Discharges:

• Yellow, mattering from the eyes.
• Yellow, foul-smelling discharge from the umbilicus.
• Yellow, pus-like discharge near the tip of the recently-circumcised penis.
• White discharge from swollen breasts or vagina. The discharge from the latter may be bloody, like a menstrual period.

Prevent Falls:

• Newborns can roll off beds, sofas, etc., if left unattended.
• Use safety car seats at all times when driving!

It is ok to fly or to go out—but avoid extreme weather conditions.

The PKU Test: Also called "Neonatal Screen," this test is usually conducted in the nursery before baby leaves for home, and again at two weeks of age in a doctor's office or in the hospital outpatient area. This test is performed on all newborns throughout the country to detect five serious metabolic illnesses that can cause serious illness and/or mental retardation. By discovering them soon after birth, treatment can be started early thereby preventing disease.**THIS TEST IS VERY IMPORTANT. DON'T SKIP IT!**

If in doubt about any medical problems, call your baby's doctor!

PART ONE

Basic

Newborn

Care

##

CHAPTER 1

BEFORE YOUR BABY IS BORN

Infant Mortality: A national disgrace

Every hour, nearly five babies die in the United States of America.

America ranks 19th among industrialized nations in the number of babies who die before their first birthday.

Prenatal care can cost as little as $400-but keeping a low birthweight baby alive can cost as much as $400,000.

The leading cause of infant deaths, high rates of chronic and disabling illness and costly medical care is low-birthweight-babies, those born weighing less than five-and-a half pounds.

Early, comprehensive prenatal care is the most effective way to make sure that all babies have the best chance to be born healthy.

All women should schedule a visit to their physician or other health practitioner as soon as they think they are pregnant. Prenatal care should begin as early as possible and continue on a regular basis throughout the pregnancy.

America has the best medical technology on earth. Shouldn't we also have the healthiest babies in the world?

Every baby should be a healthy baby!

For more information, contact your local health department or the National Commission to Prevent Infant Mortality, Switzer Building, Room 2006, 330 C Street, S.W., Washington, D.C., 20201.

If You Smoke during pregnancy

Your unborn baby doesn't breathe before the moment of birth, but it practices some motions of breathing by exercising certain chest muscles. The effects of cigarette smoke are so immediate --and so

1

muscles. The effects of cigarette smoke are so immediate --and so powerful-- that your baby's practice movements slow down after you smoke just two cigarettes. The more cigarettes you smoke, the more you interfere with your baby's preparations for life outside the womb.

When you smoke, some of the harmful gases and poisonous substances in smoke actually pass from your blood through the placenta and into the baby's blood.

One of these gases is carbon monoxide, which forces oxygen out of the red blood cells -- both yours and your baby's. Another powerful poison, nicotine, adds to the damage of narrowing blood vessels, including those in the placenta itself. This means not as much oxygen and food is delivered to your developing baby.

The babies of mothers who smoke during pregnancy are more likely to be born undersized. And these babies have a greater chance of dying soon after birth.

Studies show that women who smoke during pregnancy also have more stillbirths, spontaneous abortions and premature deliveries than women who don't smoke.

After the baby is born

It's always important for you, your husband and the baby to stay away from cigarettes.

Babies have little lungs and very small airways. Breathing smoke-filled air causes those tiny airways to get even smaller, and breathing can be blocked or impaired.

Babies in their first year have a higher rate of pneumonia and bronchitis if their parents smoke at home.

And, if you smoke while your children are growing up, you have enormous influence on their behavior. Parental smoking -- by both fathers and mothers-- is a major factor in motivating youngsters to smoke. Few, if any, parents want their children to take up a habit that can cripple their lungs and shorten their lives.

Your Own Health

Even if you feel fine, smoking makes you a slow time-bomb. But, if you quit smoking now, you'll increase the possibility of your being around to see your child grow and develop.

2

Cigarette smoking is the major cause of such lung diseases as emphysema, chronic bronchitis, and lung cancer. Smoking constricts blood vessels, increases blood pressure and damages the heart. Even one cigarette upsets the flow of blood and air in the body.

Your family wants you alive and well. Cigarettes don't keep you that way.

Stop Smoking!

If you stop smoking this minute, you'll be giving your unborn baby the smoke-free environment both of you need to be healthy. It's more than a gift. It's a matter of life and breath.

For more information on how to quit smoking, check with your local lung association. They care about every breath you take.

Alcohol Drinking and the Two of You

It has been proven that alcohol ingestion by a pregnant woman is bad for the unborn child.

Babies have been born with anatomical defects and mental retardation. This condition is called *Fetal Alcohol Syndrome*.

The more a pregnant female drinks, the worse the effects on the fetus. However, drinking in moderation (i.e., one to two glasses of wine or beer a day) is absolutely safe. Scotch, vodka, and other liquors are the ones to avoid.

If you want to quit taking alcohol or other drugs, call a local agency, i.e. Alcoholics Anonymous, Narcotic Anonymous, your local health department, etc. or call 1-800-662-4357.

PRE-NATAL VISITS

A pre-natal visit to a pediatrician is desirable, especially during the first pregnancy. Call to set up an appointment with pediatricians in your area. You will thus make a more informed choice of doctor for your soon to be born child.
You will also get to know him or her, his office policies, philosophy about child rearing, nutrition, etc.

There are pre-natal classes available in most areas also, and you could benefit by attending them.

A useful list of supplies which should be available at home when baby comes follows:

- "Wet wipes"
- Cotton and swab sticks
- Unscented soap
- Mineral oil (not scented baby oils)
- Cornstarch (instead of powders)
- Petrolatum (Vaseline)
- Zinc oxide ointment with cod liver oil
- Diapers (36) or diaper service
- Shirts (4-6), cotton, half-sleeves
- Nightgowns (4-6), cotton, light-weight
- Blankets (2-4), cotton, washable, 2-3 light synthetic ones
- Sheets (6)
- Pads (4), absorbent cotton
- Waterproof sheeting
- Mattress-firm, waterproof covering
- Crib: large enough for 2 years
- Prepared formula in six-pack for breast feeding "emergency"
- Formula with Iron 6-8 (8 ounce) bottles and nipples.
- Vitamins:with Fluoride (prescription)
- 4-ounce red rubber ear syringe (for stuffy nose)

RECOMMENDATIONS FOR BED AND CRIB SAFETY

Safety literature should include: basic federal regulations in simple terms; how to check second-hand cribs for dangers; and safety precautions to be taken in sleeping environments. The following safety checklist could be used as a model to be distributed by health professionals.

Safety Checklist: If you can answer "yes" to any of the questions below, your child's crib is unsafe in its present condition.

A. Mattress:

1. *Size*: Is there a space greater than 2.5 cm (1 inch) between the mattress and the crib sides or ends?
2. *Support*: Does the mattress sag in any spot when the baby is on it? (Check both the middle and edges.) Can the plastic mattress cover be removed?

B. Crib Sides and Ends:

1. Are there any splits, cracks, toe-holds or old paints visible?
2. Can the rails be pulled out, away from the side of the crib?
3. Are the spaces between the slats more than 6 cm (2 3/8 inches)?
4. Can the rails fall down accidentally? (Shake them and apply pressure to the top.)
5. When the mattress is in the lowest position and the rails are up, is there less than a 66 cm (26 inch) difference between the two?

C. Accessories:

Are there rope or string-like objects in the crib, such as a cradle gym, a pacifier hung around the child's neck or medals on chains?

D. Positioning:

Is the crib positioned beside any other furniture such as a chair, bureau, radiator or another bed that the baby could use to climb out?

RECOMMENDATIONS FOR CARE OF INFANT IN CRIB

1. The infant should never be left alone when the side rails are down.

2. The mattress should be lowered before the baby can sit unassisted and set at its lowest position as soon as the infant can stand.

3. No toys or other articles which can be used as steps for climbing out should be left in the crib.

4. Crib toys should not be hung within reach of the infant.

5. The infant should no longer use the crib once the height of the side rail is less than three-fourths the child's height.

6. The crib should be placed away from windows and from other furniture that the baby could use to climb out.

ACCIDENTS IN CHILDREN

We call them "accidents" but most childhood injuries can be predicted and prevented.

The five leading risk areas are:
- Traffic accidents
- Drownings
- Burns and scalds
- Choking and poisoning
- Falls

Applying basic safety steps can save thousands of children from death, and hundreds of thousands more from being disabled for life.

ACCIDENTAL INJURIES KILL 8,000 CHILDREN (ages 0 to 18 years) PER YEAR, OR ONE CHILD EACH HOUR IN THE U.S.A.

"If a disease were killing our children in the proportions that accidents are, people would be outraged and demand that this killer be stopped"

C. Everett Kopp, M.D. Sc.D.
Former U.S. Surgeon General

LEARN CPR
SIGN UP FOR A COURSE
TODAY

CHAPTER 2

THE FIRST MONTH OF LIFE

Caring for your baby during the first four or five weeks can be an easy task or a very difficult one. Sometimes all he or she wants to do is sleep. Some babies sleep 20 or even more hours a day. When they wake up they usually cry. What this means is: "I'm hungry. Give me something to eat." Feeding and changing his diapers, will be all you will have to do during the first four or five weeks with this kind of baby.

Some babies, on the other hand, can be very difficult to care for: they seldom are satisfied. They want to eat frequently or they are restless for long periods of time
This is a very difficult, trying time for both mother and father. Fortunately, this is a phase babies go through until they are five or six weeks old. After that they usually start a more predictable pattern of feedings and sleep longer between feedings.

Feedings: Feedings must be given *on demand.* This means that whenever the baby wakes up and starts crying --especially during the first weeks of life-- he must be fed. Most experts recommend not to feed infants more often than every two hours. But they give no reasons why this should be so. I am of the opinion that if a small infant were crying less than two hours after a feeding, and a pacifier or being held in Mom's arms did not console him, and if he drank eagerly from the formula bottle and shut up afterwards then he WAS HUNGRY, and he needed to eat!

How much should he be fed? Until he seems to be satisfied: i.e., he falls asleep or stops sucking or turns his head away from the nipple. Feeding time varies. Some infants are quick, some are slower. Some babies need only five or ten minutes to drink the total amount they need. The following are averages formula feedings for infants:

First month: 5-10 feedings/day; 1-1 1/2 oz/feeding. Total: 10-15 oz/day.

Second month: 6-8 feedings/day; 2-3 oz/feeding. Total: 12-24 oz/day.

Third month: 5-6 feedings/day; 4-5 oz/feeding. Total: 20-30 oz/day.

Fourth month: 4-5 feedings/day; 5-7 oz/feeding. Total: 20-35 oz/day.

Fifth month: 4-5 feedings/day; 8 or more oz/feeding. Total: 32-40 or more oz/day.

Six to eight mos.of age: 3-5 feedings/day; 6-8 oz/feeding. Total: 24-35 oz/day.

Eight to ten mos. of age: 3-4 feedings/day; 5-8 oz/feeding. Total: 20-32 oz/day.
10-12 mos. of age: 3-4 feedings/day; 4-6 oz/feeding. Total: 16-24 oz/day.

When you are ready to feed the baby, sit down and hold him as much in an upright position as possible --about a 45 degrees angle-- so that the milk, as it flows from the bottle into his mouth and throat, goes directly down into the stomach. The likelihood of the milk going toward the respiratory airway and causing the baby to choke is decreased. Never feed a small baby in a completely horizontal position.

The size of the nipple is also important. You should always invert the bottle before you give it to see how the drops fall. If the drops take a long time to form and fall, the nipple hole is probably too small. The drops should fall at about one per second.

Another important point to remember when feeding your baby is to burp him as often as possible. This should be a minimum of about three times per feeding. As a rule, you can burp the baby after you have given him one ounce, again in about the middle of the feeding and at the end of the feeding. The reason for burping is to get rid of air bubbles that could have been sucked by the baby in his eagerness to eat.

Propping The Bottle: This should not be done until the baby is older: at least six months but preferably eight to ten months, when he can hold it by himself. A younger baby should be fed by his mother or caretaker in her arms, in touch with her chest as described elsewhere in this book.

Propping the bottle has another bad effect: milk can trickle from the throat into the eustachian tubes (see "Otitis Media" below) and then into the middle ear. Result: otitis media.

Types Of Formulas: There are basically two types of milk. The infant formulas which are especially made up to resemble the composition of mother's milk and the regular whole milk that adults drink. The latter is too strong for a small baby.
Formulas are sold in powder, concentrate and ready to feed. The powdered formula is the least expensive but most cumbersome way to feed the baby. You must use a special measuring teaspoon especially provided with the cans and you must pack the powder in this spoon. Follow the directions which are written on the side of the cans. The amount of powder used depends on how much formula you want to prepare.

8

The ready to feed is expensive, more so than any of the others. It is convenient, especially when you are traveling.

The concentrated formula is the most widely used. The price is intermediate, and the preparation is not so complicated. It comes in 13 ounce cans and all you have to do is mix it with another 13 ounces of boiled or tap water. You stir it and you are ready to put it in the bottles.

As for the bottles, you may use the regular plastic or glass bottles, or you may use the type of bottles that have a plastic pouch inside. They are more expensive but convenient.

Some Do's and Don'ts in formula feeding:

It is not necessary to sterilize bottles and nipples or to boil the water used to prepare formula anymore.

Discard any formula remaining in the bottle after a feeding. Prepare a new bottle for the next feeding.

Do not warm your baby's bottle in a microwave oven.

Better not use well water to prepare baby formula. If you must, have the water tested to make sure it is safe.

Babies fed exclusively with ready to feed, or formula prepared with bottled water may need fluoride supplements. Check with your child's doctor.

After you heat a bottle, always test the temperature of the formula before you give it to the baby to drink. Actually, I feel it is a myth that cold formula is harmful or will cause stomach ache in babies. Letting the bottle warm itself at room temperature after pulling it out of the refrigerator is probably the most practical way.

Iron in infant formulas: Formulas are manufactured with a low and a high concentration of iron. It is common for some people to blame minor medical problems such as colic, diarrhea, "spitting up", etc on it. The iron in infant formulas, even those with the higher concentration, is not responsible for those difficulties as was proven in an excellent study performed a few years ago.

Cow's Milk Allergy: About 3% of all infants are truly allergic to cow's milk. To be truly allergic to milk a child must get better (be symptom free) after milk is discontinued from his diet, and must have his symptoms recur after he is challenged with milk again. This challenge test is better done in a doctor's office and under his or her supervision.

9

Most children outgrow their food allergy by age one or two. Others much later or never. Some food allergies are never outgrown. Examples are: peanuts, egg, soybean, wheat, etc. Also, the older the child is when his food allergy starts, the less likely that he will outgrow it.

Breastfeeding babies may be allergic to a food that their mother eat. Its elimination from mom's diet should improve the child's condition.

The family history is important when evaluating a child for possible food allergies. If parents or older siblings have been allergic to some foods, then the child stands a good chance of also being allergic. Eczema, respiratory allergies, etc. often run in these families.

Watch out for hidden sources of milk/dairy products: Butter, cheese, cheese sauces, chocolate, ice cream, creamed/scalloped vegetables, soups, gravies, some margarines and some salad dressings --check the label-- waffles, pancakes, biscuits mixes, white sauces.

Any dishes requiring milk may be made by using an equal amount of a soybean formula.

Breastfeeding: Breast milk is the best milk. Nowadays, about 50 percent of mothers breastfeed. Breast milk is superior to formula. However, this does not mean that a bottle-fed baby won't grow and develop as well as a breast-fed baby. Of course, they do. However, breast milk does have antibodies which are useful in fighting infection. It is a good and natural milk for the baby.

All breast milk is good. There is no such thing as bad breast milk. What does happen at times is that some mothers have more milk than others. However, it rarely happens that a particular baby will not be satisfied with his mother's milk. If this should happen, it is not because the breasts are defective. Some mothers have some inhibitions which interfere with her production of milk.

Milk is produced by the breast glands, and the outpouring of the milk is due to a reflex which starts in the brain. If something is bothering you, if there is an emotional problem or you are not convinced that you want to breastfeed for some reason -- this can suppress the secretion of milk. That is why you do have to be relaxed and you have to feel confident.

Any woman can breastfeed. You should not have any feelings of inadequacy at all. If you do have these feelings or if there is any emotional burden in your life at that particular time, you probably should not breastfeed.

Don't worry during the first two or three days if the baby doesn't seem too interested in eating. It is OK, but try to offer the breast as often as he wants it. Babies can be offered some sugar water or just plain water after each time at breast until your milk letdown happens.

However, he should be breast-fed even if the milk has not come yet. There is a secretion from the breast called colostrum which is also rich in protein and is similar to breast milk. You should feed this to the baby on demand, preferably by rooming in with him soon after birth, unless you or him is sick.

Frequent feedings are important because they prevent nipple soreness and cracking.

Other tips to prevent sore or cracked nipples: avoid the use of soaps, lotions or ointments. Position your baby properly. Make sure his mouth covers most of your breasts' areolae (the brown area around the nipples).

If pain is severe, you might have to discontinue breastfeeding. Pump milk from your breasts and feed it to your baby in a bottle. Do not use a breast shield! You might also substitute a bottle of formula for one of your breastfeedings.

At the same time the baby gets used to the breast, the breast nipple gets used to the baby's mouth. In a way the baby's mouth does help the nipple, trying to shape it to accommodate his mouth so that feeding can proceed normally.

How do you know you have enough milk and that your baby is getting it? You might say: "my breast leaks a lot...." or "milk comes out of my baby's mouth" These things do not mean that you have an adequate amount of milk.

Good Clues That Your Baby Is Getting Enough Milk Are The Following:

1. Breast-fed babies should have two or more stools per day. This is a good indication that enough breastmilk is being ingested. Check with your child's doctor for advice.

2. You can usually hear gurgling sounds coming from baby's throat. These indicate that he is swallowing milk.

3. After he is satisfied, your baby falls asleep in your arms. Not even burping will awaken him sometimes.

4. Most of the time your baby sleeps three to three and a half or even four hours, following feedings. (He might sleep much less during the first month.)

5. Later on, around four to eight weeks of age, he sleeps about eight hours after the 10 or 11 p.m. feeding.

A controversial issue: *Should breastfed babies receive supplemental sugar water feedings?* Some purists object to this because they feel this practice may interfere with breastfeeding. I and many other pediatricians feel that there is a real danger of an occasional baby dehydrating or developing low blood sugar --and convulsions-- if sugar water is not supplemented.

Sometimes the production of the breast milk may decrease, especially in the early evening hours. The baby might not get enough milk. Some doctors recommend to bottle feed him instead of brestfeed him at those times. This has an advantage in that your husband can be the one who gives this feeding. This can be a source of satisfaction for him. It gives him something to do and he probably won't feel so left out. He will be contributing to the care of the baby also.

While breastfeeding, avoid spicy foods, chocolate and cabbage. Use cigarettes and alcohol in moderation, or preferably not at all. Drink freely, or at least half a quart of skim milk or whole milk daily, and eat a balanced diet. You should continue to take the vitamins and iron supplements you took during your pregnancy.

Stools of breast fed babies differ from those of formula babies. The early (transitional) stools are yellow-green and liquid, with small curds which resemble broccoli seeds. This usually occurs three to four days after birth and are likely to cause irritation of the baby's buttock. Application of A & D cream or zinc oxide generally controls this irritation. Initially, bowel movements occur after each breastfeeding; but after a week, your infant will pass each day two to four large, very soft, bright yellow stools.

How long should you breastfeed? This is up to you. Two months are better than one, three are better than two, and so on. Since the amount of milk a baby drinks should decrease after four to six months of age, you could feed until the baby is ready for the cup (six months of age) and at that time you start substituting a cup of formula for one breast feeding. A month or two later, you substitute another breastfeeding, and so forth.

For any problems with breastfeeding, consult your local La Leche League. This organization could help you in finding a mother who is experienced in breastfeeding and lives close to you. She can give you helpful advice and literature about breastfeeding.

It is very important that breastfeeding mothers be well-rested, eat well and be emotionally stable. When you go home from the hospital, many duties await you. If you want to breastfeed successfully, I strongly encourage you to concentrate on the baby and yourself. The laundry, cleaning the house, etc., even time with your husband are all secondary to successful breastfeeding. Don't try to be a "nice lady": if neighbors, friends or relatives keep calling or coming to your house when you should be resting don't try to smile and socialize. If you are sleepy, excuse yourself, ask these neighbors or friends to come some other time, and rest.

This is especially important during the first month because some babies want to eat frequently. They may be up several times during the night, and nobody can feed the baby but you, so that you might not be able to sleep well during the night. If the baby naps during the day, you should also nap. You cannot count on being able to sleep during the night.

If you do not follow this advice, you will find yourself tired all day, edgy, nervous. You probably will not eat well, etc., and all of these factors will reduce the amount of milk you produce. The baby will notice this, will want to eat frequently, will cry a lot, etc. This will make you more nervous, suppress more of your milk production which in turn will make him more unhappy and so on. The result is that your breastfeeding will fail.

If you have to unplug the phone, do it. If you don't want to answer the doorbell, don't. Your well-being and your baby's success with breastfeeding are number one.

I must warn you of something that happens with breastfeeding babies. As said earlier, babies should be fed on demand. However, for some strange reason some babies sleep for many hours and awake, for instance, only every five to six hours. These babies may become undernourished because of the infrequency of their feedings and if this is not detected early, they could even die of malnutrition. Nobody knows why certain babies don't have a desire to eat more often. Fortunately, only very few babies behave in this manner. Do

13

not allow this to happen with your baby. If he doesn't wake up after three-and-a-half or four hours, then you should awaken the baby and put him to the breast. Do this especially during the day. During the night, you may or may not want to.

Another thing to remember in breastfeeding babies is that, some of them may develop jaundice. (See below under Jaundice of the Newborn)

DRUGS THAT CONTRAINDICATE BREAST FEEDING

1. Atropine
2. Anticoagulants
3. Antithyroid drugs
4. Antimetabolites
5. Cathartics
6. Dihydrotachysterol
7. Iodides
8. Narcotics
9. Radioactive preparations
10. Bromides
11. Ergot
12. Tetracyclines
13. Metronidazole (Flagyl)
14. Isoniazid
15. Chloranphenicol

DRUGS THAT MAY BE HARMFUL IF TAKEN CONTINUOUSLY

1. Steroids
2. Diuretics
3. Oral contraceptives †
4. Nalidixic acid
5. Sulfonamides
6. Lithium
7. Reserpine
8. Diphenylhydantion
9. Barbiturates

A lot of research is currently being conducted. In the near future, much better information will be available on this subject.

Smoking & Atropine decrease milk flow.

† Very controversial: may decrease milk production.

BREASTFEEDING RULES:

1. *Good Diet:* Adequate intake of proteins, vitamins and fluids is very important.

2. *Sufficient Rest*: Housework can wait. Daytime naps are refreshing.

3. *Appropriate Breast Care*: Washing with water is sufficient for cleanliness. A breast cream with lanolin is helpful for dry or sore nipples. Never use alcohol on your nipples.

4. *Frequent Nursing*: From right after birth, frequent stimulation and emptying of the breasts is absolutely necessary for the development of full milk production. For this reason, nursing should be on demand and, at least in the beginning, supplementary formula should be avoided. Pumping milk from your breasts also enhances milk production.

5. *Correct Knowledge*: All the following are normal: (a) mild breast discomfort between and during feedings; b) nipple pain at the beginning of feedings; c) leakage of milk between and during feedings; (d) uterine contractions, painful or pleasureable, during feedings.

6. *Patience*: It takes two to five days before the milk 'comes in' (begins to flow well). Until then, follow rule 4, pump your breast once or twice a day to further stimulate your breasts and above all try to relax and be patient.

BREASTFEEDING AFTER A CAESAREAN BIRTH

Breastfeeding may be somewhat more cumbersome after a caesarean, but very much possible and desirable.

Even although a Caesarean is a surgical procedure and you might have to get general anesthesia, your output of milk will not be affected. The brain mechanisms for triggering the release of hormones which control the production and release of milk are no different after a cesarean than after a vaginal birth.

How soon after birth you can start breastfeeding will depend on your condition and the baby's. If you had a "spinal" (actually the right name is epidural) anesthesia, you will be awake and could nurse your baby at any time, even in the delivery room, but of course your obstetrician probably will have to OK this. After a general anesthesia you can probably begin to feed after you wake up.

If your baby needs to be placed in a special care nursery, or a neonatal intensive care unit (NICU), you might be separated from him for 24 or 48 hours. In this case, you could, with the help of the nurses in the hospital, pump your breasts to get and maintain a good milk supply. The milk can also be given to your baby in a bottle until you can start to actually nurse him.

Nursing will probably be uncomfortable and cumbersome at the beginning. Sometimes, the pain is quite severe. Also, you might experience cramping pains due to contraction of your uterus triggered by the breastfeeding. Pain medication might be started by your obstetrician, usually intravenously. These medications belong to a category of drugs called "narcotics" and may pass through your milk

15

to the baby. Because of this, some doctors forbid breastfeeding in those situations.

You will need and should get help from the nurses to position the baby and yourself in a comfortable way. Initially the baby probably will be placed on your chest while you lie down on your back. Later on you can lie on your side, with baby next to you, a pillow supporting your back. To switch breasts, you hold the baby on your chest while you roll over slowly. Again, a nurse or your husband can physically help you do this.

By the second or third day, you most likely will be able to sit in a chair to nurse. One or two pillows in your lap will give you support and protection. You might also wish to try the "football hold." In order to do this, you hold baby under your right arm to feed from your right breast, pretty much like a football player carries the football, and vice versa. Your baby should be lying on your arm or on a pillow, cradled against your side.

Weight Gain: All babies lose weight after birth. This loss represents mainly excess water loss. By the fifth to seventh day, the birth weight is regained. From then on the average daily weight gain is one half to one ounce until about three months of age.

CIRCUMCISION

Circumcision, which means "cutting around", is the surgical removal of the foreskin, or prepuce. This foreskin is similar to a fleshy hood that covers the head of the penis or glans. Part of is fixed to the glans and the distal part overhangs it. In uncircumcised older children and adults, this foreskin is loose, and allows expansion of the penis during erection.
In newborns, the foreskin is fixed to the glans or head of the penis. When the prepuce is circumferentially excised (removed), it leaves the glans exposed.

Q. How Did The Practice Of Circumcision Get Started?

Circumcision apparently started in Egypt, where royalty, nobility and priests were required to be circumcised, generally between the ages of 6 and 12.
The Mongol, Finnish, Hindu, Hungarian, Oriental, Hispanic and Germanic people do not perform circumcision. In Scandinavia, routine circumcision is rare. In general, the vast majority of the world's population is uncircumcised. It is estimated that only 25 percent of all males are circumcised.

Q. In What Countries Or Groups Of People Is Circumcision Performed Nowadays and Why?

Moslem and Jewish boys are routinely circumcised after birth. Jews consider circumcision to represent a fulfillment of a covenant between God and Abraham in which God required every male child to be circumcised as a sign of their loyalty to Him.

16

Circumcision did not become commonplace in the U.S. until after World War II where battlefield conditions prevented good hygiene and infection of the penis was relatively common, often necessitating circumcision.

In 1974, the Committee on the Fetus and Newborn of the American Academy of Pediatrics (AAP) stated that there were no valid medical indications for circumcision in the newborn period. In 1990, however, the AAP partially modified its statement. (see below)

It should be noted that there are potential health hazards for uncircumcised males, including the following:

Phimosis is a narrowing of the preputial orifice with resultant inability to retract the foreskin. The child cannot urinate without pain and swelling. The treatment is circumcision. *Paraphimosis* is the retention of the retracted foreskin "below" (proximal) to the coronal sulcus (the groove around the glans). This squeezes the shaft of the penis and swelling of the glans follows. It is usually due to forceful (unwarranted) retraction of the foreskin in efforts to clean the inside. Severe pain, difficulty in urination and swelling of the glans and even gangrene may occur! Treatment is circumcision. *Balanitis* is inflammation of the glans, and *posthitis* is inflammation of the prepuce; these conditions usually occur together (*balanoposthitis*). The sequence seems to be:
Poor hygiene leads to infection (balanoposthitis). This in turn leads to phimosis.

Circumcision prevents phimosis, paraphimosis, and balanoposthitis.

Q. Is Circumcision Necessary For Penile Hygiene?

Penile hygiene of the uncircumcised male includes the retraction --pulling back--) of the foreskin to remove the thick, white material that collects underneath ("smegma"). But, this retraction cannot and should not be done forcefully. (see above: paraphimosis)..
Unless personal hygiene is extremely poor no problems will result. In industrialized societies, with virtual daily bathing, penile hygiene can be achieved effectively.
While circumcision makes it easier to keep the penis clean, it is not an absolute requirement for good penile hygiene.

Q. Will Newborn Circumcision Prevent Cancer Of The Penis?

Although cancer of the penis is rare, it does occur, and circumcision protects against it. Penile cancer occurs exclusively in uncircumcised males. Since 1932, in the English-speaking world medical literature, all the men reported to have penile cancer had not been circumcised during the newborn period.
However, circumcision may not be the whole story. Hygiene (or the lack of it) seems to be also very important.

In developing countries, where there are low standards of hygiene, the incidence of cancer of the penis in uncircumcised men is three to six times greater than in the United States.

The AAP says: *"THE DECISION NOT TO CIRCUMCISE AN INFANT MUST BE ACCOMPANIED BY A LIFETIME COMMITMENT TO GENITAL HYGIENE TO MINIMIZE THE RISK OF DEVELOPING PENILE CANCER."* Poor hygiene, lack of circumcision, and certain sexually transmitted diseases all correlate with the incidence of penile carcinoma.

Q. Will Newborn Circumcision Prevent Cancer Of The Cervix?

There seems to be a strong correlation between cancer of the cervix and STDs (sexually transmitted diseases or infections: viruses, syphilis, etc.) EVIDENCE LINKING UNCIRCUMCISED MEN TO CANCER OF THE CERVIX IS INCONCLUSIVE. The same can be said with regards to STDs; more studies are needed.

Q. Are Urinary Tract Infections (UTIs) Less Common In Circumcised Males?

Several recent studies seem to support this possibility. As a matter of fact, these new findings have prompted the AAP to review its previous stand against routine circumcision. It now states that..."newborn circumcision has potential medical benefits and advantages as well as disadvantages and risks...".

Q. Is AIDS Less Common In Circumcised Males?

A study in Kenya showed an incidence of 7 to 8 times more AIDS infections in uncircumcised versus circumcised men. However, this was an isolated study and needs to be duplicated by other researchers.

Q. Does Circumcision Hurt?

It certainly does. There is a method of local anesthesia (penile nerve block) nowadays. However, a recent review by the AAP stated: "The block is not without risk" and "more study is needed to determine it's usefulness, safety...". The AAP (1989) states "Local anesthesia adds an element of risk and data regarding its use has not been reported in large numbers of cases."

Q. What Are The Contraindications Of Newborn Circumcision?

Circumcision is contraindicated in sick "unstable" newborns, infants with genital anomalies (hypospadias,etc.). If there is a family history of bleeding disorders (hemophilia), appropriate tests should be performed before circumcision. In small premature babies, circumcision may have to be postponed due to small penile size.

Q. What Are The Complications Of Newborn Circumcision?

Risk of complications is very low, approximately two to six out of 1,000 babies, but firm figures are lacking. Local infection and bleeding are the most common, but usually not serious. Loss of penis (destruction) due to being burned by the use of electrocautery has occurred, but it is an extreme rarity. Deaths due to bleeding, infection or anesthesia are also extremely rare. There

18

was one death in 1973 and a review of the medical literature showed only two more deaths in the previous 25 years.

Commonly, skin adhesions develop and may sometimes have to be surgically removed.

Meatal stenosis (narrowing of the urinary opening) can result from irritation to the meatus (meatitis) after the foreskin, which serves to protect it, has been removed. Commonly, irritation can be caused by the ammonia in urine in combination with the diapers rubbing the glans. This is perhaps the most common complication.

Q. What Are The Psychological Effects Of Circumcision During The Newborn Period?

There seems to have been no studies done (how could they be done?) about this. Any opinions are conjecture.

Q. What Are The Psychological Effects If Circumcision Is Performed After The Newborn Period?

The psychological effects of the procedure are determined by many factors. Important considerations include the age of the child and his developing body image, as well as the convictions expressed by the parents.

In toddlerhood, surgery involving the genital can be very traumatic. The boy becomes very aware and protective of those parts that make him different. He may even express concern and fear of any injury to his penis, especially if he has had negative experiences related to his genital development, such as parental punishment for masturbation.

In the late preschool years, the situation is probably worse, so that circumcision should not be a routine procedure. It should be done only if absolutely necessary for health reasons.

Q. Are there any other considerations in the decision to circumcise or not?

Social pressure may influence parents regarding whether they decide to have his son circumcised or not. For instance, if the father was circumcised, he most likely will want his son to be too. Maybe they feel that it is the thing to do, that they want their son not to be different than the majority of boys. Or maybe they think that the circumcised penis will look better, etc. Besides, other circumcised male siblings within the family may also have some bearing on the decision. These factors should be taken into consideration when discussing circumcision.

Q. What can one expect to happen after the circumcision?

Usually the area operated will look red and raw. Some degree of swelling of the penis is also common and not a cause for concern. If the plastibel method was used, this contraption will separate and fall off after four or five days. Minor bleeding is common. You see a few red dots on the diaper. This usually stops in 24 hours or so.

Commonly, a yellow-greenish secretion may be seen at the base of the glans. This is normal. It is not an infection.

Penis after circumcision. Note the rim of the Plastibell and the string knot (top of picture)

Penis after the Plastibell has fallen off

Note: Permission to reproduce this copyrighted material has been granted by the owner, Hollister Incorporated. Plastibell® Circumcision device.

Less commonly, the plastibell may remain in place after a week or longer. As a general rule, if by the tenth day or so the bell has not fallen, parents should call the doctor who performed the surgery. Most likely, the bell will be cut off with scissors and removed, a procedure that is simple and almost painless.

Bleeding more than just a few drops on the diaper, as explained above, must be also brought to the attention of the surgeon. If you see the blood oozing or dripping constantly, apply pressure with a clean towel or gauze and call or go to the emergency room. He might have to have one or two stitches in order to stop the bleeding.

Another uncommon situation is when the plastibell drops down the shaft of the penis. If you notice this, notify the doctor, don't be alarmed. He will easily cut the bell as explained above.

Q. How do I care for the penis after the circumcision?

If the Gomco method (no plastibell) was used: Do not wash for six or seven days, when the wound will most likely healed. Apply vaseline and a gauze to protect the area. With the plastibell method, just wash the area as you normally would with soap and water, but only after the first week.

Conclusions:

Circumcision remains the most common surgical procedure in the United States. Most doctors personally favor it for the following reasons:

- Circumcised males have less chance to develop urinary tract infections..
- The penis is easier to clean.
- The procedure is simple and considered quite safe.

20

• The child will not suffer embarrassment in the "locker room," because most of the other boys are circumcised. Also he will not be physically confused because is physically different from his father.

• If the decision to circumcise a boy is postponed until toddlerhood, or later, there could be psychological trauma, as explained above.

Fingernails: To prevent baby from scratching his face and body, keep fingernails trimmed. Use blunted baby scissors for this purpose.

Teething: Baby's first teeth (usually the lower front ones) will probably begin to appear at six months. Teething will, of course, cause your baby some discomfort, but do not make the mistake of attributing symptoms of illness (diarrhea, fever, convulsions) to teething without first checking with your baby's doctor. Variations in the order of appearance of the teeth are common and no cause for alarm.

The Diapers: Checking to see if diapers need changing should be done as often as possible. As a matter of fact, it should be done at least every time you feed baby and if he wakes up at other times between feedings, consider that he may be wet. Feel inside the diaper with your hands.

With every diaper change you should use soap and water. Any mild soap is OK (Ivory, etc.), along with thorough rinsing. Use any bathroom soap and wash well, especially the crevices; rinse well so that there is no soap left in contact with the skin; dry well. Again, take particular care with the crevices. Apply either baby oil or baby powder.

If there is a rash, you can apply Desitin ointment, A & D ointment, Diaperene, etc. A baby's skin is very sensitive. It is difficult to have a baby free of diaper rash during his entire infant life. At one point or another most babies do have a rash. However, if you take the measures mentioned, the usual run-of-the-mill diaper rashes will be controlled without any great difficulty.

Cloth diapers or disposable diapers? Both are equally good probably. Cloth diapers are less expensive unless you use a commercial service. Disposable ones are convenient. Environmentally they are about even. Which one to use then depends on personal reasons.

Bathing: Until the umbilical cord falls off, which happens about the second or third week of life, you should bathe the baby with a wet towel and not immerse him in the bathtub. The umbilical cord is very susceptible to infection and, certainly, if bathed and covered by dirty water, the chances are that it might become infected. After the cord falls off, put the baby in the bathtub and bathe him in the usual manner. If the scalp is scaly (cradle cap), use Cradal. Shampoo frequently and comb very gently with a fine-tooth comb.

Skin: If much dryness is present, use plain mineral oil or lotion. Powder may be used, but avoid excess in body creases.

Eyes: Clean gently with water and cotton if any excess secretion is present. Secretion may be present for several days because of irritation from the silver nitrate instilled in baby's eyes at birth.

Face: Bathe with plain water.

Nose and Ears: Cleanse outer areas only with a moist Q-tip. Do not attempt to clean the inside of the nose or ears.

Mouth: Do not cleanse. Put only clean sterilized nipples in the mouth.

Never use bubble bath soaps. They may cause vaginal irritation.

Care Of The Umbilical Cord: How do you care for the cord? It is simple. Several times a day, wet a cotton ball with alcohol, touch with it the umbilical cord area, and rub it gently. Before the cord falls off, there is usually some oozing of a yellowish-green, foul-smelling, sometimes bloody material. This should not be of any concern unless there is a lot of blood oozing from the cord stump. Usually, it is just a little and nothing to cause undue concern. Continue cleaning this as explained above. In a few days the oozing will stop and the cord will be completely healed.

If the skin immediately surrounding the cord is red and/or swollen, call your doctor right away. Your baby's cord might be seriously infected.

Care of the Uncircumcised Penis: Until the age of five or six years, the foreskin of the child's penis is tightly attached to the head, also called glans. NOBODY should try to pull down the foreskin in an uncircumcised penis! Under no circumstances. Why? It will hurt a lot, it will bleed, the foreskin might not be able to go back over the glans again --*paraphimosis*-- and emergency circumcision might have to be done. Finally, it is NOT necessary to clean inside the penis. Just wash the outside of the penis with soap and water, in the same manner that you wash the rest of the body.

After age five or so, the foreskin usually slides back and forth easily over the glans. At this time, it will be O.K. for you to clean the inside, but never use force. Observe your son's reaction. If he cries, you are hurting him and should stop pulling.

Events You Should Not Worry About: Let me tell you now about some events which might happen to your baby which are usually normal.

One of these is that the *breasts will become swollen* in most babies -- whether they are boys or girls. Sometimes the swelling is considerable. Just relax; this is a normal physiological phenomenon and it should not cause any concern. It may take many weeks, but the swelling will eventually disappear. This does not mean that the baby has a tumor, abscess or infection. It usually is just the normal skin color. It is not necessary to do anything about it; certainly, you should not squeeze the breast because it might become infected. Sometimes a small amount of a white liquid may ooze from the breasts. This is called *"witches' milk."* Again: Don't worry.

Sometimes during the second, third, or fourth week, you might see a *bloody discharge* coming from the baby's vagina. This should not cause concern either. It is perfectly normal. Both this and the breast swelling are due to the influence of maternal hormones during pregnancy.

Birthmarks, usually the "strawberry" kind, should not cause any major concern, except when the birthmark occurs in certain areas of the body like immediately next one eye or close to the anus, mouth, etc.. In these areas, a birthmark could be dangerous. About 99 percent of the babies who do have one birthmark or another have them on the nape, behind the head and on the face-close to the eyebrows. However, these are usually the flat type; they are not raised or bumpy. These should cause no concern at all.

Sneezing: When a baby sneezes, he is trying to get rid of particles of dust or secretions. Babies usually don't have a cold during the first four weeks -- so don't worry. Of course, if there is a nasal discharge, that is a different story, but simple sneezing is no problem.

Hiccupping: In newborn babies, this is a perfectly normal phenomenon. No treatment necessary.

Spitting up, also called regurgitation, is normal. It is important that we make a differentiation between this and vomiting.

23

Regurgitation or spitting up is when the baby -- usually at the end of the feeding or right after it -- drools some of the formula. This does not come forcibly but slowly drips down. Vomiting is when the baby throws the formula or mucus out at a distance from where he is. This, certainly, is a cause for concern -especially if it happens more than once. If it happens only once or twice a day, don't worry as it may be a perfectly normal thing. However, if it happens after every feeding, you should call your child's doctor right away.

The skin of the baby, as I said before, is very sensitive and you will see a lot of different spots and rashes. These are usually of no consequence. We have already mentioned diaper rash. There can also be *heat rash.* These are very tiny, bumpy spots which are usually a yellowish or pink color surrounded by a red area. These usually appear in areas where there is more perspiration, like in the fold of the neck, under the arms and on the back of the head, etc.

One cause of heat rash, in addition to hot weather, is over clothing the baby. Just a diaper and gown or shirt is enough if the temperature inside the house is comfortable for everybody. If it is a little cool, of course you should use a sleeper or cover the baby a little more. But, certainly, if adults around the baby are wearing only a shirt and the temperature is comfortable, the baby should not be overdressed. Overdressing the baby can, by itself, raise baby's temperature and can cause heat rash.

Acne of the newborn: most male infants develop transient acne-like pimples on their cheeks. They are due, like true acne, to inflammation of the sebaceous glands of the skin because of the stimulation of maternal sex hormones during pregnancy.

Drooling rash: it is common to see pink or red "bumps" on the chin of babies who are teething and therefore drooling profusely. It doesn't hurt babies and heals when drooling decreases.

Granuloma of the Umbilicus: Not infrequently after the umbilical cord has fallen, the navel continues to ooze a yellowish liquid. Your child's doctor will show you a small inflamed area inside the navel which is responsible for this oozing. It is not known why this happens. It is not an infection. Your doctor will likely apply silver nitrate on it, and this granulation tissue will heal and shrink.

Clogging of the tear ducts: Infants very frequently develop "mattering" in their eyes. This is due to clogging of their tear ducts. These ducts, which have soft, pliable walls, get obstructed because the walls stick together. Treatment: wash eyes with a wet cotton ball, as often as necessary. If the baby has not outgrown this problem by the age of six to eight months, then surgery by an ophthamologist (eye doctor) may be necessary.

Diarrhea in a 1-2 week old infant: Babies at this age have a "normal diarrhea." The stools are mushy or plain liquid, green-yellow in color. You should not worry about it unless it persists for more than three or four days.

WHAT TO DO WHEN BABY CRIES

Crying is the only way that your baby can tell you he needs something. Thus NEVER LET A SMALL INFANT CRY unless you tried everything in the following list first:

1. HUNGER: This is by far the most common cause of crying in babies. Feed him right away. If he still cries, then:

2. DIAPERS ARE DIRTY: Check these often and change them right away.

3. HE NEEDS LOVING!: Hold him close. Remember that babies need attention, LOVE. Touch him, talk to him and kiss him often.

4. THIRST: If he still persists in his crying, try one to two ounces of water in a bottle.

5. PACIFIER.

6. OTHER, LESS USUAL CAUSES:
   • he may be teething (rarely before four months of age).
   • he may be sick, check his temperature.

A Few Facts About Crying:
   • Mothers who respond consistently and promptly to their babies' crying have babies who cry less in later months.
   • Babies cry a lot until about the age of seven weeks, and then begin a gradual decrease.

Persistent Crying: (i.e., for several days in a row, etc.) A thorough physical examination should be performed. Call your doctor's office for an appointment. If nothing wrong is found, baby may be having abdominal pain due to intolerance to the formula, solid foods or vitamins. A formula change or a discontinuation of the solid foods or vitamins might help.

COLIC

A baby with colic usually is:
1. Constantly crying or fretting, as if in pain.
2. Always squirming, restless, even during sleep.
3. Legs are drawn up while screaming.
4. Passes a lot of gas by rectum (debatable, see below).
5. Doesn't stop crying when picked up or if fed.

It most commonly occurs in first-born babies; in bottle-fed much more than in breast-fed. Colic usually disappears by age three to four months.

Cause: unknown. There are several theories, but no agreement as to the cause or causes of colic.

"Gas trapped in the baby's bowels" was an explanation that people accepted for many years. Research done recently denies any role for gas in colic because both colicky and non-colicky babies produce the same amount of gas.

Food allergies is another explanation. There are other theories. None has proven itself.

Treatment: (Before you assume your baby has colic, consult his doctor.)

There is no single good treatment. You may have to try several methods: Give him lukewarm water to drink, or place a hot water bottle under his tummy (careful not to burn him), or insert a glycerin suppository in his rectum. This may help baby expel gas or stools through his rectum, thereby alleviating the pain.

Preventing "gas trapping": Follow these guidelines:

1. Burp correctly, especially soon after the baby has quickly gulped a good deal of milk, the time most likely for the baby to swallow an air bubble. If you do not and keep feeding him, the bubble of air will be covered by more and more milk. When he finally burps, it will not be expelled through the mouth.

To expel this "trapped bubble", shift his position: hold your baby gently, but firmly. Slowly lower him and lay him on his back across your lap. Wait two to three minutes. Raise him again. The bubble would have now come up on the surface of the milk, and it can be expelled by burping gently.

2. The nipple holes should be large enough so that the milk flows freely.

3. Hold the baby in an upright position (about 45 degrees) while feeding.

4. Medications: Don't use unless your doctor recommends them. They help sometimes, but not always. They may also cause constipation. Do not give oil of wintergreen. It may cause salicylate poisoning.

Other Suggestions For Colic:

• If you are breastfeeding, do not eat chocolate, cauliflower, cabbage or broccoli! This might be a myth, but it seems to work sometimes.
• Solid foods do not help, **ever**, and may do more harm.
• Carrying the baby in your arms or in a "carrier" strapped around your body DOES NOT seem to help (recent research). It won't hurt to try it though.
• Decrease the intake of milk or milk products in your diet if you are breastfeeding your baby. Trial use of soy bean formula may be recommended if your baby is bottle-fed.
• Take the baby for car rides. For some reason, colicky infants seem to respond to vibrating motors. The same effect can be achieved by placing the baby on top of a running washing machine or dryer, or by simply letting the vacuum cleaner run.
• Walk the baby face down, placing the baby's body across your arm with your hand under the abdomen to apply gentle pressure.
• Try a wind-up swing, preferably one that runs 20 minutes before rewinding is required. This can sometimes allow you to get through dinner.
• Mylicon drops (OTC): 0.3 ml three times a day after meals. It is a safe antiflatulant medicine.
• Try a pacifier previously immersed in a sugar solution: i.e., dissolve two teaspoonfuls of table sugar in four ounces of water.

IF NOTHING HELPS, REMEMBER THAT :

• IT IS NOT YOUR FAULT THAT YOUR BABY HAS COLIC.

• IT WILL PASS AND HE WILL NOT SUFFER PERMANENT DAMAGE.

EVENTS YOU SHOULD WORRY ABOUT

The following problems necessitate a call to your child's doctor. One is *vomiting.* As I mentioned before, if the baby vomits -- not just once, but two or three times in a row -- call right away.

Fever: If the temperature (rectally) is more than 103, you should call. A temperature up to 100 is perfectly normal. Temperatures between 100 and 101 are low grade fever and usually should not be of great concern. Observation is all that is needed. In case of doubt: call.

Constipation is something else that should worry you. By constipation I mean hard stools. If the baby moves only once a day or maybe only once every two days, but the stools are soft, this is not really constipation. The problem is when the stools are hard. Call your child's doctor.

Diarrhea occurs, but only rarely in the first four or five weeks of life. We all know that diarrhea is when there are too many stools or they are too loose, and so forth. If you're not sure, call up.

If a *diaper rash* does not seem to clear up after three or four days, with the use of Desitin, Diaparene and so forth, call up. There is a type of rash which is due to yeast. Yeast is similar to a bacteria, and it has to be treated with a special type of ointment. Desitin or A & D ointments won't take care of it.

Jaundice in the Newborn

Many new parents have brought their healthy newborn baby home from the hospital only to panic when the little one's rosy complexion turns a ghastly yellow. This skin discoloration—or jaundice, from the French word *jaune* meaning yellow—is fairly common and harmless in most cases.

Jaundice in the newborn often affects two out of three normal, full-term babies to some degree. Though it can be frightening for the new parent, jaundice is simply an adjustment the baby's body makes to allow it to function on its own instead of inside its mother.

Physiologic Jaundice

The human body makes a yellow-red pigment called BILIRUBIN (pronounced billy-roo-bin). This chemical is a breakdown product of hemoglobin, the oxygen-carring red pigment present in red blood cells (RBCs).

After birth, babies don't need as many RBCs as they did in the womb; therefore many are destroyed quickly. A heavy breakdown of RBCs combined with a too sluggish, immature liver allows a buildup in the bloodstream of enough bilirubin to stain the skin yellow.
In normal newborns, this condition is called "physiologic jaundice." It is self-limited, causes few symptoms and does not harm the infant. It has no relation to liver disease. The baby's liver is perfectly healthy!

Your pediatrician will usually be the first to notice the jaundice in the baby. He will want to perform a test to determine the level of bilirubin in the blood. He may or may not repeat the test the next day or sooner, depending upon the results of the first one.

A blood level of 8 or 9 milligrams of bilirubin per 100 deciliters of blood is common in the first stages of physiologic jaundice. Over the next 2 to 3 days, it usually increases to 10 or 12, then begins to decrease gradually.

Occasionally, the bilirubin may reach higher levels— 14, 15 milligrams per 100 deciliters of blood or more. If this happens, the doctor will most likely recommend a fluorescent light (phototherapy) for the infant. This special wavelength light will act through the skin, breaking down the bilirubin and "curing" the jaundice.
A new phototherapy device, the Wallaby, is now available for treatment of jaundice. It consists of a sheet of fiber-optic material which is wrapped around the baby to provide the necessary light. Moms may hold and feed their babies without discontinuing phototherapy, as is the case with the older fluorescent lighting method.

If the bilirubin level rises higher than 20 or 25 mg/100 dl, bilirubin could THEORETICALLY form deposits in the baby's brain cells causing brain damage, also known as *kernicterus*.
However, *there is no proof* that bilirubin levels greater than 25 mg/100 dl cause brain damage in full-term, otherwise healthy newborns. The key factor here is to ascertain the cause of the jaundice: physiologic or non-physiologic. Only the child's physicians can tell for sure and manage him accordingly.

Parents should not worry about brain damage with physiologic jaundice. The chance of any occurrence of brain damage is almost zero. Of course, you should follow the medical advice of those professionals who are caring for your baby.

On the other hand, it is known that brain damage does occur when high levels of bilirubin (more than 20 mg/100 dl) are found in babies who are Rh incompatible. For this reason, babies with physiologic jaundice were, and some still are treated with phototherapy when levels reach 14 to 15 mg/100 dl just to be on the safe side. Nowadays some experts recommend to wait until highers level of bilirubin, although no total agreement exists on this.

Other Causes of Jaundice

Fortunately, blood group incompatibility (Rh negative Mom with an Rh positive baby) is rare today, thanks to the vaccine Rhogam which prevents it. *Blood incompatibility* means that a pregnant woman produces an antibody against her baby's red blood cells because these and the mother's RBCs have different blood group factors. This antibody destroys baby's RBCs—a process called *hemolysis*—and this in turn causes more bilirubin to form.

ABO incompatibility is common (Mom is usually O+ and baby is A+ or B+). This situation rarely causes severe jaundice. Certain drugs, infections and other rare diseases may cause jaundice in the newborn.

For reasons that are not yet clear to medical experts (possibly a chemical found in breast milk), some breastfed babies tend to have higher levels of bilirubin, and the resulting jaundice seems to last longer than in formula fed babies. Whereas formula fed babies' bilirubin level returns to normal in a few days, about one to two percent of breastfed babies have higher levels for long periods of time.

For these infants, it may be necessary to discontinue breastfeeding for 24-48 hours. The bilirubin level goes down and usually does not go up again even after the resumption of breastfeeding. If the bilirubin level does not go down, the physician will proceed with treatment as necessary.

Premature babies develop jaundice with greater frequency than full-term babies. Infants born four or more weeks early are treated earlier and more aggressively because they can suffer brain damage at lower levels. One out of four preemies will require either phototherapy or possibly even exchange transfusions.

Color Check

How can baby's color be checked to determine whether or not he is developing jaundice? First, examine baby's eyes (the "white" of the eyes) and skin under adequate lighting (fluorescent bulbs or sunlight).

To detect the yellow color, blanch his skin by pressing on one spot for a few seconds with one of your fingers. Lift your finger and check for yellow color on the spot.

Parents understandably have many questions about jaundice and its potential effects on their baby. Below are some of the most common questions and answers:

"What symptoms can I expect my jaundiced baby to have?"

If your baby has physiologic jaundice, and the bilirubin levels are below 20 or 25 mg/100 ml, your baby will not have any symptoms at all.

"Jaundice frightens me. Can my baby suffer any damage even if the bilirubin level is less than 20 mg/100 dl?"

No! If the bilirubin level is less than 20 or 25 (except in premature infants) your baby will not be ill or suffer any damage.

"Should I place my baby next to a window under the sunlight?"

No, for the following reasons: 1) Baby may overheat, begin to sweat and dehydrate; 2) He may be sunburned; 3) Sunlight likely will not help the jaundice at all; 4) You could be wasting valuable time, thinking you are doing something positive for the baby when you should be contacting the baby's doctor for advice.

"Should I try to give my jaundiced nursing four-day-old lots of water to 'flush' the bilirubin away?"

No. Actually, it is best to breastfeed often during the first few days after birth—unless your doctor thinks the breast milk is causing the jaundice. Giving water to the baby to 'flush' the jaundice out of her is LESS effective than breast milk.

31

"My baby is several weeks old and still jaundiced. What should I do?"

Notify your pediatrician. If the bilirubin level is less than 20 (and especially if it is below 12 or 15), he or she will reassure you. He may ask you to discontinue breastfeeding for 48 hours, to call him back if the baby's skin becomes more yellow or he may want to take another blood test.

While it is not known why some normal babies continue to be jaundiced for weeks after birth, it is certain that prolonged low-bilirubin jaundice is harmless. With levels less than 20, observation by your baby's doctor is all the treatment needed.

Summary and Recommendations

Physiologic jaundice is normal, but it should not be ignored. Only a doctor is qualified to determine its severity and prescribe appropriate treatment. If jaundice develops after leaving the hospital or worsens once the baby is home, parents should contact their pediatrician immediately.

GOING HOME

Not very long ago, mothers were confined to bed for two weeks or longer after their babies were born. Today, we know that it is much better for the mother to get up sooner and avoid a weak, bedridden feeling. If your baby was delivered normally in a hospital, you will probably go home in two to four days. Do not forget, however, that your body needs time and care to readjust itself and be careful not to tire yourself by attempting to do too much, too soon.

It is only natural to be a little nervous at first about caring for your newborn, but keep in mind that he is not as fragile as he looks.

His major needs are food, warmth, comfort and love. Take care not to overdress or hover about him, and you'll soon find that you feel comfortable with your new responsibility.

Holding The Baby In Your Arms: Questions about this come up frequently. Some parents feel if they hold their babies in their arms "a lot", they will become spoiled. My answer: babies need LOVE, lots of it. Therefore, hold your infant in your arms! Don't be so afraid of spoiling him that you end up keeping him most of the day in his crib. Babies need to feel the warmth of mommy's chest and arms. They need to be comforted in this way.

If you don't know how long you should hold your baby, I will tell you this: Better spoil your baby than neglect him. Of course, you have things to do around the house. During those times, the baby may be left alone in his crib or a "Swingomatic" or you can carry him in a baby carrier.

When holding your baby, always support his back and head firmly with your arm and hand. He cannot hold his head up alone until he is about three months old because his neck muscles are still weak, and his head must be supported during this time. However, do not discourage the natural movements of his arms and legs. After the first several weeks, the "football hold" leaving one hand free is often a helpful way to carry your baby.

Your Baby's Health: Complete cooperation with your doctor is of great importance. Regular monthly check-ups are recommended. We can help you keep your baby healthy, happy and safe from any childhood diseases. We will tell you when to have your baby immunized against tetanus, diphtheria, whooping cough, polio, measles, German measles (Rubella) and mumps.

Keep your baby away from all persons with colds and other communicable diseases. Never permit visitors to kiss him on the mouth. Small children should tactfully be kept from coming too close. Avoid over-excitement and taking him into crowded areas. If you are in doubt about any health problems, consult his doctor's office.

Taking His Temperature: If your baby is restless, fretful or gives other indications of possible illness, his temperature should be taken. If you do not know how to use the thermometer, have the office nurse show you how to do it. Be sure that the mercury is well below normal before taking baby's temperature.

The easiest and perhaps safest way to take a baby's temperature is to place the thermometer along the baby's groin (crease between upper leg and body). Fold baby's leg against his body, covering thermometer. Hold it there for three minutes, then take thermometer out and read it. The mercury will not slip down until you shake it down, so put the thermometer in a safe place while you diaper him and put him back in his bed.

Baby's temperature may also be taken by rectum, using a rectal thermometer (distinguished from the oral thermometer by its thick bulb). Put some cold cream or petroleum jelly on the bulb for easier insertion. Lay your baby on his back on your lap or on a table or bed. Holding his ankles, raise his legs and carefully insert the bulb of the thermometer into his rectum about an inch. Or, with a towel on your lap, lay baby on his stomach. Holding the thermometer in one hand, press down on his legs gently, but firmly with your forearm, separate the buttocks with the other hand and carefully insert the thermometer. Do not leave your baby alone or let go of his legs or of the thermometer while it is in his rectum. Hold it there for three minutes, then take it out and read it.

Your Baby's Sleep: When putting your baby to bed, lay him on his stomach with his head turned to the side where he will get the most air. We doctors used to advise against babies sleeping while lying on their backs. Recent research in Europe shows that the latter may be safer. Do not disturb him with unnecessary noise or bright light or by going into his room and checking him.

He will sleep for most of the day (18 to 22 hours) during the first month or so, and for the rest of the first year about 14 to 16 hours a day.

Babies should have their own room. They should never be put to sleep in your bed. Not only is it a bad habit, but you could fall asleep on top of him and smother him.

Nursery: The room temperature should be kept near 72-74 degrees Fahrenheit. Ventilation should be provided with the top window to avoid drafts.

The baby's mattress should be firm and flat. No pillow should be used. Protect the mattress with a waterproof cover. Next comes a soft baby sheet and one or two cotton blankets. Do not wrap the baby in a blanket because this interferes with his freedom to move and kick.

Pacifiers: If you follow my instructions in the paragraphs about feedings, that is, if you take as long as necessary for each feeding, the baby will usually satisfy his "sucking needs". However, some babies need a lot of sucking. In those cases, then, try the pacifier. A pacifier is preferable to thumb sucking, because at a certain age, you can discard it and stop the habit. You cannot do this with the baby's fingers, and therefore, you have to wait until the child discontinues this habit on his own, sometimes at a quite late age. However, many times a baby will accept only his fingers as the sucking object. In these cases, just resign yourself. Don't try to change this habit. You will not be able to. Just relax. Accept this as what it is: a normal phase in the baby's development.

Baby's Eye Color: Usually the color of your baby's eyes will become permanent at age six months to one year.

Can babies see at birth? Yes, they can, but their vision is not perfect: they see as a person who needs glasses. By three to four months of age, they see well.

Tears: Usually after the second month, sometimes before.

Mattering of the eyes is something that occurs very commonly in small infants. The cause is lack of complete development of the tear ducts. Tears cannot proceed down the ducts and over flow in a pus-like fashion. Wipe eyes daily with a cotton ball wet with lukewarm water. If the white part of the eyes become reddened, call your child's doctor. Occasionally some babies have to have an operation to open the tear duct, but in most babies the ducts will open by themselves by age four to five months.

OFFICE VISITS

Routine Check Ups:

Your best safeguard against serious disease is periodic visits to your doctor. Many problems can be identified early in this way.

At these visits we will measure your child. A complete physical will be done as well as screening, simple tests (blood count, urinalysis, etc.).

Take him to the dentist six months to one year after appearance of first tooth. Preferably, take him to a Pedodontist (dentist who specializes in children).

1st Visit: (NOTE: Your child's doctor may have a different schedule.)
2 weeks old: for "first" babies, preemies, etc.
4 weeks old for all others.

Subsequent Visits As Follows:
2 months   Checkup -- DPT (diphtheria, whooping cough, and tetanus); Polio (oral) and Hib vaccines.

4 months	Same.
6 months	Same
9 months	Check-up & TB test.
12 months	Checkup -- CBC.
15 months	Check-up -- MMR vaccine, HIb booster
18 months	Check-up -- DPT & Polio booster.
2 years	Complete Check-up -- CBC, TB test.
3-10 years	Yearly checkups -- CBC, TB tests.
5 years	DPT & Polio booster -- TB test
12 years	Complete check-up -- CBC, MMR booster, TB test.
14 years	Complete checkup -- Td booster and TB test, CBC.

From 5 Years On: Measure blood cholesterol, triglycerides, etc., especially if there is a family history of heart attacks.

11-18 years: Same, but every 2 years.
After 10 years, we measure the blood pressure. Vision testing: ask us to do it if not done in school by age 5 or so.

Please call your doctor's office for your child's appointment or more information. See also later on in this chapter for new vaccines.

DIPHTHERIA, TETANUS, PERTUSSIS AND DPT, DT, AND Td VACCINES

What is Diphtheria? Diphtheria is a very serious disease It can cause an infection in the nose and throat which can interfere with breathing. Sometimes it causes heart failure and paralysis of some nerves. About one person out of every ten who get diphtheria dies of it. Presently only a few cases are reported per year in the U.S.A.

What is Tetanus? Tetanus, or lockjaw, results when wounds are infected with tetanus bacteria, which often live in dirt. The bacteria in the wound make a poison which causes the muscles of the body to go into spasm. Three out of every 10 persons who get tetanus die of it in this country. Only 50 to 90 cases occur per year in this country since 1975.

What Is Pertussis? Pertussis, or whooping cough, causes severe spells of coughing which can interfere with breathing. The disease is especially serious in children less than one year of age. *16 out of 100 babies with pertussis get pneumonia. 2 out of 100 may have seizures. Approximately 1 out of 200 babies with pertussis develops brain damage* that may be permanent, and **about 1 out of every 200 babies with pertussis dies of it.**

Before vaccines were developed, these three diseases were all very common and caused a large number of deaths each year. After they became available, the number of cases has decreased considerably. Unfortunately, because of recent adverse publicity, many people are failing to immunize their children properly. This has led to an increase in the incidence of these diseases, especially pertussis

DTP, DT, And Td Vaccines: Immunization with DTP vaccine is one of the best ways to prevent these diseases. DTP vaccine is actually three vaccines combined into one to make it easier to get protection. The vaccine is given by injection starting early in infancy. Several doses are needed to get good protection. Young children should get three doses in the first year of life and a fourth dose at about 18 months of age. A booster dose is important for children who are about to enter school, and should be given between the ages of four and six.

The vaccine is very effective: Tetanus vaccine is 95% effective if all the recommended number of shots are given --95 out of a 100 children vaccinated will not get the disease if exposed to it-- Pertussis is 90% effective and Diphtheria is 85% effective.

Because pertussis is not very common in older children, those seven years of age and over should take a vaccine that does not contain the pertussis. Also, because reactions to the diphtheria part of the vaccine may be more common in older children, those seven years of age and older should take a form of the vaccine that has a lower concentration of diphtheria. This vaccine which contains no pertussis and a lower concentration of diphtheria is called Td vaccine. Boosters with the Td vaccine should be given every ten years throughout life.

The Risks of the Vaccines: Most children will have either no side effects at all or mild symptoms such as a slight fever, irritability or sleepiness for 24 or 36 hours after taking the shot. Soreness and swelling in the area where the shot was given may also occur.

The following side effects occur with an incidence of between 1 in a 100 shots to 1 in a 1,000 shots:
• Crying loud continuously for three hours or longer

• Fever of 105 degrees Farenheit or higher
• Unusual high-pitched cry

After 1 shot in 1,750 a child may develop:
• A convulsion or seizure --thought to be due to the high fever.
• So-called "shock-collapse": child becomes limp, blue or pale, unresponsive. Child does recover without late effects.

The question of brain damage secondary to the DPT shots: At the present time, experts agree that DPT cannot be proven to be the cause of it. DPT vaccine also does not cause SIDS as was implied by some people. DT, Td and T cause fewer problems and less frequently than DPT.

It is the consensus of medical experts that the benefits of the DPT vaccines, as well as of the other vaccines available, far exceed the risks involved. New vaccines, such as the acellular DPT vaccine are being tested and are becoming available.

DPT vaccine should be postponed in children who:

• Are sick with more than just a simple cold at the time they are due for the vaccine.
• Have had convulsions or other brain ailments and the doctor has not given his permission.
• Are not developing mentally in a normal way and the doctor has not given his permission.

DPT Should not be given in the following situations:

• Convulsion, onset of brain damage within 7 days after DPT
• Serious allergic reactions, i.e., serious swelling of mouth, throat, face or difficulty breathing, within a few hours after DPT.
• A previous brain ailment that gets worse after DPT.
• Fever of 105 degrees Farenheit or more within 2 days after DPT
• Shock-collapse within 2 days after DPT
• Seizure within 3 days after getting DPT
• Uncontrollable loud crying that lasts more than 3 hours occurring within 2 days after DPT.

POLIO AND POLIO VACCINES

Polio is a viral disease that often causes permanent crippling (paralysis). Death may occur, depending on the medical technology available. There used to be thousands of cases and hundreds of deaths from polio every year in the United States. Since polio vaccine became available in the mid-1950s, polio has been nearly eliminated. In the last five years, fewer than 25 cases have been reported each year. It's hard to say exactly what the risk is of getting polio at the present. Even for someone who is not vaccinated, the risk is very low. However, if we do not keep our children protected by vaccination the risk of polio will go back up. Also, people from other countries visiting ours may carry the virus and expose those not properly vaccinated.

Polio Vaccines: There are two types of polio vaccines. The most used is the oral vaccine (OPV), in drops, a "live" vaccine, meaning that the polio virus in the vaccine is alive, but it has been made very weak. The "inactivated" vaccine or IPV, contains killed virus and is given by shot.

Polio vaccines are very effective: 90 or more people out of a 100 who get three or more doses of either OPV or IPV will be protected against polio. Four doses are the ideal number of doses for everyone.

Young children should get two or three doses in the first year of life and another dose at about 18 months of age. A booster dose is important for children when they enter school or when there is a high risk of polio. An example would be during an epidemic or when traveling to a place where polio is common.

The risks of the Polio Vaccine. OPV: The person who gets the vaccine drops, may, very rarely, get polio himself. After the first dose, the chances are of 1 in 1 1/2 million doses. After later doses: 1 in 40 million doses.

Persons who have not been properly vaccinated against polio and are in close contact with the vaccinated person may get paralysis. Their chances are of 1 in every 2 million doses after the first dose of OPV, and 1 for every 14 million doses given.

IPV vaccine risks: other than mild soreness or redness on the site where the vaccine was injected. No other serious adverse effects have been reported.

Every medicine and vaccine has risks as well as benefits. It is the belief of the CDC and most experts that the benefits of the Polio vaccines far exceed that of its risks.

The Oral Polio vaccine should not be given in: (give IPV instead)

- Those who are sick right now with something more serious than a cold.
- Those with cancer or leukemia or lymphoma.

39

• Those with diseases that lower the body's resistance to infection, i.e. AIDS and other immunodeficiency diseases.

• Those taking drugs that lower the body's resistance to infection, such as cortisone or prednisone or anti-cancer drugs.

• Those who live in the same household with any of the above persons.

• Children who live with persons with the above situations.

Pregnant women may receive the OPV if needed, because the vaccines do not harm the fetus.

MEASLES, MUMPS, RUBELLA AND MEASLES, MUMPS, AND RUBELLA VACCINES

What Is Measles? Measles is a serious common childhood disease. Usually it causes a rash, high fever, cough, runny nose and watery eyes lasting one to two weeks. Sometimes it is more serious. It causes an ear infection or pneumonia in nearly one out of ten children who get it. One child out of every 1,000 who get measles has an inflammation of the brain (encephalitis). This can lead to convulsions, deafness or mental retardation. One child in every 500 to 10,000 who gets measles dies of it.

Before measles vaccine shots were available, there were hundreds of thousands of cases each year. Nearly all children got measles by the time they were 15. Now, because of the wide use of measles vaccine, a child's risk of getting measles is much lower although recently it has increased due to lack of adequate vaccination.

What Is Mumps? Mumps is a common disease of children. Usually it causes fever, headache and inflammation of the salivary glands, that causes the cheeks to swell. Sometimes it is more serious. It causes a mild type of meningitis in about one child in every ten who get it. More rarely, it can cause inflammation of the brain (encephalitis) which usually goes away without leaving permanent damage. Mumps can also cause deafness. About one out of every four adolescent or adult men who get mumps develops painful inflammation and swelling of the testicles. This usually goes away and rarely makes them sterile.

Before mumps vaccine shots were available there were more than 150,000 cases each year. Now, because of the increasing use of mumps vaccine, the risk of getting mumps is much lower. However, if children stop getting vaccinated, the risk of getting mumps will go right back up again.

What Is Rubella? Rubella is also called German measles. It is a common disease of children and may also affect adults. Usually it is very mild and causes a slight fever, rash, and swelling of glands in the neck. The sickness lasts about three days. Sometimes, especially in adult women, there may be swelling and aching of the joints for a week or two. Very rarely, rubella can cause inflammation of the brain (encephalitis) or cause abnormal bleeding.

If a pregnant woman gets rubella, there's a good chance that she may have a miscarriage or that the child will be born crippled, blind or with other defects. The last big rubella epidemic in the United States was in 1964. After it was over, about 25,000 children were born with serious problems such as deformities, heart problems, deafness, blindness or mental retardation because their mothers had rubella during pregnancy.(*congenital rubella syndrome*)

As stated for measles and mumps, rubella was very common before the vaccine was available and now is infrequent.

Since rubella is a mild illness, many women of childbearing age do not recall if they had rubella as a child. A simple blood test can tell if a person is immune to rubella or is susceptible to the disease. Overall, about 85 percent of women of childbearing age are immune to rubella.

Measles, Mumps And Rubella Vaccines: The vaccines are given by injection and are very effective. In about 90-98 percent of people, one shot will give protection, possibly for life. Since protection is not as likely to occur if the vaccines are given very early in life, these vaccines should be given to children after their first birthday. The recommended age is 15 months. Measles, mumps, and rubella vaccines can be given as individual injections or in a combined form by a single injection. A booster MMR is now recommended at age five or age twelve or thirteen.

Experts recommend that women of childbearing age who are not known to be immune to rubella should receive the vaccine if they are not pregnant and should not become pregnant for three months after vaccination.

Risks of the MMR Vaccine: About 5 out of every 100 children who receive this vaccine will get a *rash* or *fever of 103ºF* lasting for a few days about 1 or 2 weeks after getting *measles* vaccine. Occasionally there is mild swelling of the salivary glands after *mumps* vaccination. Although experts are not sure, it seems that

41

children who get these vaccines rarely have a more serious reaction, such as inflammation of the brain (encephalitis), convulsions with fever or nerve deafness.

About one out of every seven children who get *rubella* vaccine will get a rash or some swelling of the glands of the neck one or two weeks after the shot. About 1 out of every 100 children who get rubella vaccine will have some aching or swelling of the joints. This may happen anywhere from 1 to 3 weeks after the shot. It usually lasts only two or three days. Adults are more likely to have these problems with their joints--as many as one in four may have them. Other side effects, such as pain, numbness or tingling in the hands and feet have also occurred but are very uncommon. With any vaccine or drug, there is a possibility that allergic or other more serious reactions or even death could occur.

MMR vaccine should not be given to:

- Those who are sick with something more serious than a cold.
- Those with allergy to an antibiotic called neomycin.
- Those with cancer, leukemia or lymphoma.
- Those with diseases that lower the body's resistance to diseases.
- Those taking drugs that lower the body's resistance to infection such as cortisone or prednisone.
- Those who have received gamma globulin within the preceding three months.
- Those who are *severely* allergic to eggs. (check with a doctor)
- Children who have a history of seizures have five times greater risk of having a febrile convulsion following the measles vaccine. Your child's doctor should be consulted before giving it.

Pregnancy: Measles and mumps vaccines are not known to cause special problems for pregnant women or their unborn babies. However, doctors usually avoid giving any drugs or vaccines to pregnant women unless there is a specific need. To be safe, pregnant women should not get measles or mumps vaccine. A woman who gets measles or mumps vaccines should wait three months before getting pregnant.

Vaccinating a child whose mother is pregnant is not dangerous to the pregnancy.

Immunization Schedule:

Below is the immunization schedule recommended by the American Academy of Pediatrics:

RECOMMENDED SCHEDULE OF VACCINATIONS FOR ALL CHILDREN							
Vaccine		2 Months	4 Months	6 Months	12 Months	15 Months	4-6 Years (Before School Entry)
DTP		DTP	DTP	DTP		DTP [1]	DTP
POLIO		POLIO	POLIO			POLIO	POLIO
MMR						MMR [2]	MMR [3]
HIB Option 1 [4]		HIB	HIB	HIB		HIB	
Option 2 [5]		HIB	HIB		HIB		
Vaccine	Birth	1-2 Months	4 Months	6-18 Months			
HB Option 1	HB	HB		HB			
Option 2		HB	HB	HB			

DTP: Diphtheria, Tetanus, and Pertussis Vaccine
Polio: Live Oral Polio Vaccine drops (OPV) or Killed (Inactivated) Polio Vaccine shots (IPV)
MMR: Measles, Mumps, and Rubella Vaccine
HIB: *Haemophilus* b Conjugate Vaccine
HB: Hepatitis B Vaccine
[1] Many experts recommend these vaccines at 18 months.
[2] In some areas this dose of MMR vaccine may be given at 12 months.
[3] Many experts recommend this dose of MMR vaccine be given at entry to middle school or junior high school.
[4] HIB vaccine is given in either a 4-dose schedule (1) or a 3-dose schedule (2), depending on the type of vaccine used.
[5] Hepatitis B vaccine can be given simultaneously with DTP, Polio, MMR, and *Haemophilus* b Conjugate Vaccine at the same visit.

New Vaccines:

A safe new vaccine that prevents the most common, life-threatening bacterial disease of young children is now available. This new vaccine prevents diseases caused by the germ known commonly as *"HIb" (Haemophilus Influenza Type b)*.

HIb diseases affect about one child in 200 before the age of five years. HIb diseases, which include spinal meningitis, are serious in nature. Many result in hospitalization, and up to ten percent can be fatal. This new vaccine is 90 percent effective in children between the age of 15 months and six years.

The United States Public Health Service recommends that children 15 months of age and older receive this new vaccine. Because of their increased risk, children 15-23 months old who attend day care centers should also be vaccinated.

Hepatitis B vaccine, although not new, this vaccine is now starting to be recommended for routine immunization of all babies in this country. It is to be given at the following ages: First shot at birth or at two months of age, second at four months and then a third one between the ages of six and eighteen months.

Acellular DPT vaccine: This new, japanese vaccine appears to be an improvement over the previous, cellular types presently available, because the incidence and severity of side effects are less. At the present time it is being recommend for use at ages 18 months and 4-6 years. A combination acellular DPT and HIb and Hepatitis B vaccine is certain to be used in the near future.

The *Varicella vaccine:* (Chicken Pox vaccine) It is still being tested but should be released soon.

Summary of Usual Side-Effects of Vaccines:

The common side-effects of a DPT (diphtheria-tetanus-pertussis) vaccination are:

- fever
- irritability for up to two days
- soreness and swelling at the injection site

Less common reactions, which warrant your calling your pediatrician, are:

44

- constant, inconsolable crying for more than three hours
- unusual, high-pitched crying
- excessive sleepiness or difficulty waking the child
- limpness or paleness
- a temperature of 105 degrees F. or higher
- a convulsion

Most vaccine side effects are mild and will go away within a few days after your child has been vaccinated. Acetaminophen (Tempra, Tylenol, etc.) every four to six hours will lower the fever, the most common side effect of the vaccines.

The HIb vaccines are quite safe. Fever, localized redness and swelling are the most common side effects. No serious side effects have been reported with the hepatitis B vaccine in children so far.

A calm, unhurried atmosphere at mealtimes helps children develop positive attitudes towards food.
American Academy of Pediatrics.

CHILDREN ARE LIKE WET CEMENT. WHATEVER FALLS ON THEM MAKES AN IMPRESSION.
PSYCHOLOGIST HAIM GINOTT.

PARENT ALERT!

Choking is the fourth leading cause of accidental death in young children, especially those under the age of 3 years

45

SHOULD INFANTS SLEEP ON THEIR ABDOMENS OR ON THEIR BACKS?

It is customary in this and other countries to recommend that infants sleep on their tummies. This advice is based on the belief that in this position it is less likely that babies will aspirate and suffocate during their sleep if they happen to vomit.

However, some studies are showing that babies in the prone (face down) sleeping position may be more likely to aspirate than those who slept on their backs, although other factors were also identified which could have made a difference in the results. Thus, among those who died suddenly during their sleep, the majority were found wrapped heavily and they were sleeping in a rather warm room (overheating). In one of these studies, many deaths happened in babies who had a small weight at birth. In New Zealand, investigators found that the prone position, maternal smoking and bottle-feeding were factors that favored the occurrence of SIDS. Also, the incidence of SIDS is higher in western countries where the custom is to have babies sleep face down, than in other parts of the world like Asia where babies are usually placed on their backs to sleep.

Even although the governments of some countries, and the American Academy of Pediatrics are strongly recommending to change the sleeping position from prone to supine (on the back) or to the side, there are many experts who are not yet convinced that the supine position is best.

SOME DO'S AND DON'TS FOR SAFE SLEEPING
- Do not let your infant sleep in your bed with an adult (co-sleeping).

- Do not place your infant to sleep in a water bed, beanbag, other cushions, sheepskin rugs,etc.

- Only use cribs that comply with the 1974 federal regulations i.e. crib slats should be close to each other, no space between the mattress and the side of the crib, firm mattress, etc.

- Keep baby's room warm, not hot. Do not cover baby with heavy blankets which could restrict his movements or suffocate him.

- Place baby to sleep on his back, or ask your child's doctor about his recommendations.

- Do not smoke or let others smoke in your home.

CHAPTER 3

AFTER THE FIRST MONTH

The "Scheduled Feedings" and Sleeping through the night:

At four to eight weeks of age, most babies should be able to switch from "demand feedings" to "scheduled feedings" which take place every four hours, approximately, during the day with eight hours of uninterrupted sleep at night. The main goal is to eliminate the two or three a.m. feeding. The baby should sleep from about 10 or 11 p.m. until 6 or 7 a.m. (straight 8 hours).

You may ask right away: How can I get my baby to sleep through the night? I don't think you can *make* a baby sleep through the night. Most babies will themselves stretch the interval between feedings so that they feed less often, falling into a more predictable schedule and eventually getting about eight or more hours of sleep during the night. Parents can make mistakes regarding night time sleeping and feeding. If you can avoid them, you will probably rest better at night.

- First, don't let your infant take long naps during the day. A long nap would be defined as longer than one hour. If you cannot wake her up, then you are out of luck. But it does make sense that, if a baby sleeps a lot during the day, she is more likely to wake up at night.

- Second: It is bed time. Your baby fell asleep in your arms. You proceed to place her in her crib for the night. What happens? At 1 or 2 a.m. she awakes, finds herself in a strange place, a place she doesn't recall falling asleep in and panics! You'd do the same if you were to awake one night and found yourself lying on the kitchen floor!

We all awake during the night, more than once. We fall asleep again because we recognize that we are in our bed and things are O.K. Babies after the age of two to four months learn also to fall asleep again, UNLESS parents come running to their beds at the first whimper.

-Third point: This follows where the second point above left off. When your two, three or four months old baby awakes at night, WAIT!, listen for a while. She might go back to sleep. Unless she is screaming, stay away from her room. If you must go to her, try to do as little as possible, i.e.: don't turn on the lights, don't pick her up, don't feed her. Talk to her in a firm, clear voice and reassure her everything is O.K. that she must go back to sleep, and then leave quickly.

For more advice on this subject, get the excellent book by Richard Ferber, M.D. titled *Solve your Child's Sleep Problems* ($ 9.95 paperback).

-Fourth: *co-sleeping.* Letting your children share the parental bed, is, in my opinion, a terrible mistake. Lack of space prevents me from expanding on this subject. If you are considering this, think and research the matter carefully before you do it or discuss it with your child's doctor.

See the *Hotline and Resources* section at the end of this book for more information on the subject of sleep.

Solid Foods: (See chart on page 56)

The American Academy of Pediatrics recommends that you not start solid foods before four months of age. Reason? Early introduction of solid foods may cause allergies, obesity or digestive problems. Fruit juice, if started too early may produce diarrhea, rashes, etc.

DO NOT RUSH SOLID FOODS! Do not engage in a competition with friends or relatives to see who gets to raise a fatter baby. FAT IS NOT AN INDICATION OF HEALTH. As a matter of fact the opposite is true: fat babies may become fat adults with all the complications of hypertension, diabetes, coronary disease, etc.

If you and your husband are short or average and slim, do not expect to have a large baby. Do not compare her to other babies.

The ideal time to start solids seems to be between four and six months.

Some babies are tremendous eaters. If a baby is taking eight ounces of formula every three to four hours and still seems hungry, then start the solids. This will rarely happen before age two or three months.

Begin with rice cereal, followed by barley, rye or oatmeal. Vegetables or fruits are next. You may want to start with fruits instead of cereals, and that is OK, too.

Start slowly: one or two tablespoons mixed with formula twice a day. Increase daily until you give it before every bottle.

Cardinal Rules: **Always start one new food at a time. Give it for four to five days.** If the baby is allergic to that particular food, he will develop a rash, or vomit, etc. Then it is easy to identify the offender, which should then be withheld.

Some mothers give solid foods at say 8 a.m., and then at 10 a.m. they give a bottle. At 12 noon they again give solids, and then at 2 p.m. or so they give another bottle. I don't think this is good. It encourages the baby to eat at any time of the day. Remember, she should be eating about four meals a day by six months of age. Feed at one time, for instance, 8 a.m., 12 noon, 4 p.m., 7 to 8 p.m., and give the solids first, the bottle second. How much cereals, vegetables, etc., should the baby eat? As much as she wants. You start slowly, but then build up until you eventually give as much as she will take.

Honey: Because of the danger of botulism, never give honey to an infant less than 12 months of age.

Up until four to six months of age, milk is the most important or only food the baby gets. After that, however, it is no longer enough to satisfy the growing child's daily requirements of proteins, carbohydrates, etc. That is why the solid foods are then introduced. Milk is poor in iron, a metal necessary to form red blood cells. Babies fed almost exclusively with whole milk become anemic (low blood). They may be fat, but they are pale, anemic. If this goes untreated, they can become very ill.

How do you get your baby to cut down milk intake? By offering solids before each bottle. Since she is hungrier at the beginning of the feeding, she will fill up with solids and then not drink as much from the bottle.

By one year of age, the baby should be off the bottle. She should be drinking exclusively from the cup. Besides the total daily amount of milk should not be more than six to eight ounces. Instead, the baby should be eating lots of solid food. The cup can be introduced by six months of age.

One way you can start the cup is by giving your baby a regular empty cup for her to play with. This will allow her to accept this object as part of her environment. Later, have her drink one or two ounces of water, juice or milk from it at different times of the day.

The next step is to substitute a cup drink for a bottle feeding. Start this meal as usual with solid foods, and then, instead of giving the bottle, give her two to three ounces of milk in the cup. Most likely the baby will accept the cup and forget about the bottle from then on. If, however, she refuses the cup and cries, be firm and adopt a "take it or leave it" attitude. Let her cry. After a few days she will finally forget about that bottle feeding.

Other bottle feedings during the rest of the day remain the same. A couple of months later you take away another bottle, and you do the same a couple of months from then and so on until the baby is weaned from the bottle.

Once the baby is able to sit in a high chair, (six to eight months of age), let her experiment by feeding herself with her own hands or with the spoon. She could use the cup also at this time. She will mess up your kitchen floor for a while, but eventually she will learn to develop good eating habits.

To ensure your baby the best nutrition, breast milk or a full-year infant formula, like Similac, SMA, Enfamil, etc., is recommended for the entire first year of life. Although cow's milk whole, two percent, or skim -- is fine for older children and adults, it is not good for babies. In fact, cow's milk can cause some problems if it introduced too soon.

Why Not Whole Milk For Infants?

The problems with feeding cow's milk during the first year are related to several important nutrients. They are:

Protein: Too Much

Cow's milk has far too much protein for babies. The protein in cow's milk is three to four times higher than that in breast milk and infant formula. Too much protein can strain the infant's kidneys.

Also, the type of protein provided by cow's milk is not well-suited to babies. It forms a tough, difficult-to-digest curd in the stomach.

Cow's milk protein has also been linked to intestinal blood loss and allergies in infants.

Iron: Not Enough

Cow's milk contains a very low level of iron, and the iron in cow's milk is poorly absorbed.

This low level of poorly absorbed iron, coupled with intestinal blood loss that occurs in some infants, has been linked to cow's milk protein and associated with iron-deficiency anemia -- one of today's most common health problems among infants.

Sodium: Excessive Amount

The sodium level in cow's milk is far too high for babies.

The high level of sodium in cow's milk, which is about three to four times higher than that in infant formula or breast milk, can strain a baby's delicate system.

Other Nutrients:

There are also other problems with cow's milk. It doesn't provide enough vitamin C, copper or zinc. Also, the fat in cow's milk is poorly absorbed by babies. And, the overall caloric distribution of cow's milk is not compatible with an infant's needs.

```
BABIES SHOULD BE FED FORMULA UNTIL ONE
                 YEAR OF AGE
          NO COW'S MILK UNTIL THEN
```

A Final Word About Good Infant Nutrition:

Because there is more known now about the importance of good infant nutrition, and because big advances have been made in food production technology, babies today have a far better chance than ever of receiving the best possible nutrition.

Parents sometimes say, "Is my baby's nutrition really that important? After all, my diet wasn't that strict when I was a baby, and I grew up OK."

Although you may have grown up "OK," you should not settle for anything less than "state-of-the-art" nutrition for your baby.

Good infant nutrition is important -- especially since what your baby eats has important implications for your baby's health now and later in life.

WATER

I am always asked: how much water does a baby need? I answer that it is not necessary to give extra water to a baby unless she perspires a lot (summer, heating is too high, etc.). The reason is that 90 percent of the milk the baby gets is water. So no extra water is needed. The baby satisfies both her thirst and hunger at the same time with the same means: milk. However, if baby cries and nothing seems to calm her, try giving her water.

Never use the bottle as a pacifier! One often sees mothers who stick a bottle in their baby's mouth to make them stop crying. Try to avoid this. It is a bad habit. These are usually the babies who cannot be weaned from the bottle even though they get to be 18 months, 2 years or older. (See below: *Nursing Bottle Syndrome*).

VITAMINS and FLUORIDE

Who needs vitamins? Breast-fed babies do, and they also need fluoride because there is no way to know how much fluoride breast milk contains. Fluoride supplementation prevents cavities.
Ask your child's doctor about this.
Always remember that vitamins do not increase a child's appetite.

Summary On Feedings:

Choose an infant formula as recommended by your child's doctor. Give until one year of age (has vitamins, iron, and is better digested than regular milk).

At one year, switch to regular cow's milk or 2% milk. Your child should then receive a multivitamin preparation (OTC).

Cereals   )
Fruits   )   Start at four to six months.
Vegetables)

Fruit juices)
Meats   )   At age five or six months or later.
Egg yolk   )

Whole egg)
Beets   )   Age one year or later.
Spinach)

Sterilize and boil water until age four months. (Note: many doctors feel these procedures are no longer necessary at any age.)

Six Months: Begin cup. At first, give it empty, so baby plays and becomes familiar with it; then give fluids in it.

Baby should be off the bottle by 10 to 18 months, preferably around one year of age.

Nuts, popcorn or pumpkin seeds are not to be fed to small children.

Do Not Feed Honey To Babies Less Than Twelve Months Of Age.

WARNING TO PARENTS

FROM THE AMERICAN SOCIETY OF DENTISTRY FOR CHILDREN

Allowing a child to nurse for long periods of time on milk, juices or other liquids containing sugar can have a destructive effect on the child's teeth. The effect on these teeth, which are so important to the normal growth and development of the jaws and permanent teeth, starts as soon as the primary teeth begin to erupt. If nursing is allowed to continue, it can result in a condition so serious that some teeth will need crowns, treatment of pulps (nerves), and often extractions because of extensive breakdown and infections. This condition is called *Nursing Bottle Syndrome.*

Most children fill all their nutritional requirements at mealtime. For those children who nurse for long periods of time while sleeping or between meals, parents are urged to change the contents of the bottle to a liquid which does not cause decay. This can be water or, after consulting with your physician, an artificially sweetened drink. If your child has been nursing for long periods of time, arrange for a dental examination as soon as possible. Teeth affected by prolonged nursing remain highly susceptible to decay long after the nursing stops.

The Milk Bottle, Your Baby's Nutrition & Teeth...

Do not feed a baby older than 12 months from the bottle....

There are several reasons: first, it means you are giving too much milk to your baby, who should be feeding more on solid foods by that age. Secondly, since most babies at that age are on regular milk, which is poor in iron content, the baby might develop "iron deficiency anemia." Thirdly, a baby who is still drinking three or four bottles of milk or juices a day at age one or older, may develop cavities due to sugar in milk and juices (See Warning above).

Sugar + plaque (a film of bacteria in mouth) = acid.

Acid attacks tooth enamel. The end result is tooth decay.

```
MOMS .....PLEASE!
DO NOT USE THE BOTTLE AS A PACIFIER!
DISCONTINUE BOTTLE FEEDINGS
BY 12 MONTHS OF AGE!
```

Tooth Reimplantation:

If your child (usually as a result of a fall) loses a permanent tooth, follow these rules:

• Gently rinse the tooth of gross debris (dirt) using tap water (do not scrub!).

• Place tooth gently but firmly into the socket and hold it in place.

If immediate reimplantation is not possible, place tooth either under her tongue or in her cheek or transport it in mild, moist towel or paper tissue and of course go to a doctor's or a dentist's office right away!

How about PRIMARY TEETH?

Primary teeth should also be reimplanted, except for front teeth. There is no need to replace them.

Teeth Staining:

Iron medications do stain teeth, but this lasts only while the medication is being given; therefore it is not a cause for concern. Antibiotics are, for the most part, safe. The only antibiotic which may cause tooth staining is tetracycline. Pediatricians have not used it for children under the age of eight for a long time.

The Symptoms Of Teething:

Babies who are teething will exhibit one or more of the following: fussiness, low grade fever (not over 101 rectally), runny nose, spitting up, diarrhea, slight cough.

The # 1 health hazard in the USA
is not: AIDS,
MEASLES OR
CHOLESTEROL

INJURIES ARE!
150,000 - 200,000 deaths/year
due to injury

PREVENTION IS THE **KEY**

THROUGH **EDUCATION &**

NATIONAL CAMPAIGNS

QUIT SMOKING FOR YOUR
KIDS' SAKE!
Tobacco smoke contains 4000 chemicals,
some very toxic. If you smoke, your children also inhale these
chemicals (passive smoking)

Did you know than 1 in 5 children in the
United States lives in poverty?
That more of these children are white than black?
That although parents work, they still cannot
make ends meet?
To find out how you can help, write to the
Children's Defense Fund
122 C Street, N.W.
Washington, D.C. 20001

SOLID FOODS CHART FOR INFANTS

AGE	CEREALS	VEGETABLES	FRUITS	FRUIT JUICES	PROTEIN FOODS
4-6 months	None or rice barley infant cereals. (iron-fortified).	None or strained or mashed, cooked. About 1/4 cup/day. (1 cup = 8 oz.)	None or strained or mashed. About 1/4 cup/day.	None or 100% infant juices (no orange or tomato). (1) 2-4 oz./day	NONE
6-8 months	Most cereals (iron-fortified) oven-dried toast, teething biscuits.	Same as above About 1/2 cup/day. Uncooked avocado is OK.	Same. About 1/2 cup/day.	Infant 100% fruit juice. (no orange or tomato juice) (1) 4 oz./day	Strained meats (or wait till age 8 mos.) Plain yogurt Ice cream.
8-10 months (2)	Infant cereals or plain, hot cereals; toast, bagel, crackers, teething biscuits.	Cooked, mashed vegetables.	Peeled soft fruit wedges (bananas, peaches, pears, apples).	100% fruit juices, including orange and tomato. 6 oz./day or more.	Cooked dry beans. Ground or finely chopped lean meats (bones, fat & skin removed); egg yolk, yogurt, cheese (plain, mild).
10-12 months	Infant or cooked cereals, unsweetened cereals, whole wheat bread, rice, noodles, spaghetti.	Cooked vegetable pieces; some raw vegetables (tomatoes, cucumbers, carrots).	All fresh fruits, peeled & seeded; canned fruits packed in water.	All 100% fruit juices. 6 oz./day or more.	Small tender pieces of lean meats; whole egg, cooked, yogurt, cheese beans.

(1) May dilute 1/2 + 1/2 with water initially.
(2) Junior or chopped foods can be introduced at this age.

PART TWO

Illnesses
and
other
Problems

##

CHAPTER 4

FEVER

Rectal temperature: more than 100 degrees F. (R)
Oral or axillary: more than 99 degrees F. (O)

(Never mind the arrow in the thermometer. The above are the figures you should follow in deciding whether your child has fever or not.)

- Low Grade Fever (1)   100-101 degrees F. (R)
- Mild Fever: 101-103 degrees F. (R)
- Moderate Fever: 103-105 degrees F. (R)
- High Fever: 105-107 degrees F. (R)

(1) Exercise, hot weather, excessive clothing, etc. may cause low grade fever.

When should you call your child's doctor (based only on fever)? In the following circumstances:

1. Moderate or High fever if it persists overnight. (Except in infants less than three months old. See below.)
If for instance your child has a temperature of 105 º F. (R), and it is 5 p.m., you don't really need to call yet. Give Tylenol and/or sponge her every four hours. If she still has fever the next morning (high or moderate), then call your doctor's office . I know that many of you, if your child has 104 or 105º F,. are going to call right away, no matter what time of the day it is, and that's OK. If you are worried or scared, CALL! I'm sure your pediatrician will be glad to discuss the situation with you.

2. Low grade or mild fever which persists beyond two to three days.

3. 106 degrees F. (R) or more: Call doctor right away. I say this mostly for your own peace of mind, because doctors know that although 106 degrees F is high fever, there is no immediate danger. Discuss the situation with your doctor. He or she will advise you.

4. If fever is accompanied by other symptoms (serious ones) such as vomiting, labored breathing, lethargy (excessive sleepiness), crying a lot, crying when you move her, stiff neck.

5. Infant less than three months of age: regardless of how high the fever is, call right away. It may be a serious problem.

Remember: Fever is a symptom. A high fever does not necessarily correlate with a serious disease. Some children have a tendency to develop high fevers at the most minor illness. Others behave in the opposite way.

High fever does not "cook" the brain. It does not cause brain damage, unless it reaches more than 107 degrees F. (R). Sometimes a severe illness like meningitis or encephalitis (both can cause fever) may leave a person's brain damaged, but not the fever.

Seizures can occur in a few children. However, those seizures are usually very mild, and they themselves do not impair the brain.

ALSO: High fever does not necessarily indicate a serious infection. When your child has fever, always watch him/her for other symptoms and signs, which might be more important than the fever. For instance, if your child has fever and respiratory difficulty or fever and pain, you might want to call the doctor, not so much for the fever, but for the other complaints. In appendicitis, the fever is usually low. The abdominal pain should make you call, however.

Never cover the child excessively. All you will accomplish is to raise the temperature even more. Dress him lightly and keep the room cool. Give cool liquids frequently.

IMPORTANT WARNING

BECAUSE ASPIRIN MAY POSSIBLY TRIGGER A SERIOUS CHILDHOOD ILLNESS CALLED "REYE'S SYNDROME," IT IS RECOMMENDED THAT YOU DO NOT USE IT TO COMBAT FEVER. You may use it to relieve pain in case of teething, etc.

If the child refuses medication by mouth, try:
1. Children's Tylenol crushed and mixed with applesauce or juices.
2. Acetaminophen suppositories (Feverall, etc.)

If your child has fever and is also vomiting, you shouldn't give him Tylenol by mouth because it may cause more vomiting. Use acetaminophen suppositories instead, to bypass the stomach.

Acetaminophen is the drug in Tylenol, Tempra and Panadol. You buy these suppositories over the counter (OTC). They come in three strengths: 120, 325 and 650 mgm. DOSE: See the chart below.

• Use antipyretics (anti-fever medicines) only if fever is more than 102 degrees F and preferably only if the child is uncomfortable.

• Low-grade temperatures do not require antipyretics. Light clothing and additional fluids are sufficient.

• Remember that the main reason for treating fever is to help the child feel comfortable, not to prevent harm to the child.

Sponging:

Use sponging with tepid water (98.6 degrees F.) only if temperature is higher than 104 degrees F., or if the child has not responded to antipyretics and is uncomfortable. Always sponge after an antipyretic is given (about one hour later). Put the child in a bathtub with two inches of water in it and apply a large wet towel to his head, body, etc. You should sponge until the fever comes down, even if it takes you 15 to 30 minutes. Alcohol sponging: Never! It is dangerous. Also, never use ice water enemas.

Remember, the body has a thermostat for the purpose of controlling fever. This thermostat generally keeps the body temperature below 107 degrees F. The temperature will not climb upwards relentlessly.

BE CALM, FOLLOW THE ABOVE GENERAL RULES AND ALSO MY RECOMMENDATIONS BELOW. REMEMBER THAT IF THE FEVER DOESN'T COME DOWN AFTER TYLENOL OR COMES DOWN ONLY SLIGHTLY, THIS DOESN'T INDICATE A SERIOUS INFECTION, ESPECIALLY IF SHE IS ALERT, ACTIVE, PLAYFUL, ETC. THUS, IT'S NOT THE HEIGHT OF THE FEVER THAT IS IMPORTANT, BUT HOW SICK THE CHILD LOOKS, WHAT OTHER SYMPTOMS SHE HAS, ETC.

Do not keep giving antipyretics every four hours unless you are sure she has fever again. It is better to check the temperature before giving more medication.

Antipyretics should not be used for more than two to three days without consulting a physician. Remember that these are drugs and as such they may do harm if used improperly.

To reduce fever follow this chart. Doses are every 4-6 hours

ACETAMIN-OPHEN* (Tylenol, Tempra, etc)	Drops 80 mg/0.8 ml Dropperful	Chewable Tablets 80 mg tabs	Elixir 160 mg/5 ml	Junior Strength/160 mg Caplets/ Chewables	Suppositories
0-3 mos/ 6-11 lbs	1/2 dppr†				1/2 (120 mgm)
4-11 mos/ 12-17 lbs	1 dppr†	1 tab	1/2 tsp		1 (120 mgm)
12-23 mos/ 18-23 lbs	1 1/2 dppr†	1 1/2 tab	3/4 tsp		1 (120 mgm)
2-3 yrs/ 24-35 lbs	2 dppr†	2 tab	1 tsp		1 or 1 1/2 (120 mgm)
4-5 yrs/ 36-47 lbs		3 tab	1 1/2 tsp		2 (120 mgm)
6-8 yrs/ 48-59 lbs		4 tab	2 tsp	2 cap/tab	1 (325 mgm)
9-10 yrs/ 60-71 lbs		5 tab	2 1/2 tsp	2 1/2 cap/tab	1 (325 mgm)
11 yrs/ 72-95 lbs		6 tab	3 tsp	3 cap/tab	1 1/2 (325 mgm)
12-14 yrs/ 96 lbs and over				4 cap/tab	1 (650 mgm)

Note: Since acetaminophen pediatric products are available without a prescription, parents are warned on the package label to consult a physician for use by children under 2 or for use longer than 5 days...and to contact a physician or poison control center immediately in case of accidental overdosage.

*Do not exceed 4 doses in 24 hours.

†0.8 ml dropperful. Dosages may be titrated up or down based on professional judgement.

A calibrated dropper or dosage cup is included in each package.

A New Anti-Fever Medicine: Ibuprofen (Pediaprofen or Advil Suspension) is a new medicine useful for fever. It requires a prescription and cannot be given to infants younger than six months. Ask your doctor about it in these situations:

1. Your child has a tendency to have febrile seizures.

2. Fever is high and/or does not "budge" after Tylenol.

High Fever: What to do until you call doctor the next morning:

Let us say it's 3 a.m., your 7-month-old baby has a fever of 104 degrees F. rectally: Give Tylenol (0.8 ml.) and then one hour later, if your baby is still hot, sponge him with lukewarm water; or: give him ibuprofen suspension.

When Not To Use Tylenol: When a child has a cold (runny nose, some cough), but NO FEVER OR PAIN. I'm amazed at the number of people who still use Tylenol for a cold. TYLENOL DOESN'T HELP A COLD AT ALL UNLESS FEVER OR PAIN EXIST.

Question: "How long should my child's fever last when the cause is a viral infection (diagnosed by a doctor)?"

A. Very hard to say! From one to three days is the usual length of time. However, a week or more is not all that infrequent. In a child less than three years of age, I would call your doctor's office if the fever persists (even in the absence of other symptoms) more than three or four days, maybe even sooner.

Question: "Why does his breathing become faster? Why does his heart pound harder and faster?"

A. This is due to the fever and therefore inconsequential. However, since he might be having a respiratory or cardiac ailment, you might want to consult your child's doctor.

Question: "My child's fever doesn't respond to Tylenol. What can I do?"

A. Continue giving Tylenol or switch to Advil or Pediaprofen suspension (see above). We don't know why fever sometimes doesn't "budge" after acetaminophen. However, it doesn't matter. IT IS NOT AN INDICATION OF A SERIOUS ILLNESS BY

61

ITSELF! Of course, make sure you're giving the right dose and not less.

Question: "My child has a fever of 101 to 102 degrees F. all day, but now (at 10 p.m.) it is 105 degrees F! I'm worried that he is getting worse."

A. Again, how high the fever is MEANS NOTHING! Many parents become frantic when night falls. Be calm. Continue giving Tylenol every four to six hours, etc. Call the doctor's office in the morning if the fever persists.

Question: "I can't stand seeing my child with this high fever. I'm afraid he'll have a convulsion . . . Can't you give him a "shot"?

A. There are no shots available for fever. Convulsions due to fever are usually not serious; they're brief, mild and usually you don't even notice your child has had one. Yes, one in a thousand could be severe. The child might stop breathing. Learn CPR. All hospitals have good courses.

Question: "What is the amount of fever at which one would push the panic button? "

A. 107 degrees F. In other words, you don't have to push the panic button just because of fever. The other symptoms are more important.

RETURN TO SCHOOL AFTER AN ILLNESS

Before sending your child back to school after an infectious (contagious) illness, he or she should have had no fever for at least 48 continuous hours. Remember that: there is no fever if temperature is 99°F. or less (orally) or 100°F. (rectally).

If your child is on an antibiotic, he should continue taking it until it is all gone. Upon returning to school, and in order to obviate the trouble of taking the medicine with him, he can take it during breakfast, immediately after he is back home in the afternoon, after supper and at bedtime. Some antibiotics are only given three times a day, which is even easier to administer.

Again, make sure that your child takes the antibiotic until it is all gone. Some people try to save some to use it some other time. Please, don't do that. The infection may recur, and worse than before. Results: more trouble, more expense. Also, never use the bottle prescribed for one child to give to another child.

CHAPTER 5

STOMACH AND BOWEL PROBLEMS, ETC

DIARRHEA

If stools are liquid and frequent, the child has diarrhea. The smaller the child, the more serious the problem can be.
What to do:

1. Very watery, large and frequent stools: (more than 15 per day)

   a. Call your child's doctor or give ONLY CLEAR FLUIDS such as Pedialyte, plain water, etc., for 24 hours. If diarrhea improves:

   b. Follow with the clear liquids plus a Soy Protein Formula diluted in equal parts by water. Continue all day .

   c. On the third day, start cereals, crackers, toast, banana, applesauce. Of course, the type of food you give will also depend on the age of your child.

   d. Add more and more foods from the fourth day on, but no fruit juices for at least one week. You must call your child's doctor in case of very watery stools.

2. Diarrhea is not as bad as in 1.

We have recently changed somewhat the way we treat diarrhea. Unless the child is having 15 or more very watery, large stools, follow this diet:

   a. DO NOT PUT BABY ON ONLY CLEAR LIQUIDS, like Pedialyte®, etc.

   b. Give the usual, regular diet, except the following:

   c. Juices, other sugary liquids (Kool-aid, fruit juices).

   d. Green vegetables, high fiber-content foods, etc.

   e. Spicy foods, ketchup, mustard.

If you have followed the steps mentioned above for one or two days and there is no improvement in the diarrhea, then call your child's doctor.

You should also call your child's doctor in the following situations:
• If after several hours since you started the steps mentioned above, the diarrhea gets worse.
• If on top of the diarrhea getting worse, she starts vomiting.
• The child has a high fever or looks sick, listless, etc.
• If you are very concerned or worried, call your child's doctor even though none of the above circumstances is taking place. Your physician will probably be glad to discuss the problem with you.

Ricelyte or Pedialyte (plain or fruit-flavored) are best to replenish the fluids in the baby's body. Jello water and Kool-aid are too sugary and may aggravate diarrhea. If you must give them, prepare them very diluted. Gatorade, diluted and "flat" 7-Up are OK.

The color of the stools: it is not important what color the loose stools are, however if there seems to be some blood in them, make sure you call the doctor's office and inform him of that fact.

VOMITING

Vomiting is the forceful expulsion of gastric contents through the mouth. When just a small amount of food comes up to the child's mouth and is slowly released, we call it "spitting up" or regurgitation. Regurgitation, mainly in babies, is common and you should not be concerned.

If your baby or child is vomiting, the best thing to do is to stop all feeding (solid or liquid) for two or three hours (not any longer) and then start **cold, clear liquids,** in **small amounts** and **frequently** (i.e. Pedialyte®, water, Gatorade, three to four teaspoonfuls every 15-20 minutes for infants) for several hours. Alternatively, you could give crushed ice, popsicles, etc., depending on the age of your child. A toddler might need 1 tbsp every 15 minutes, etc.

If the vomiting stops, check with his doctor to get further advise with regards to feedings, or gradually increase the amount of liquids and start some solid foods until he is back on his regular diet.

Most people, confronted with a vomiting child think: "I must give him fluids so he does not dehydrate." What happens? The child proceeds to throw up. If he is given more fluids, he vomits again and again.

When a child vomits, his stomach is inflamed, irritated. Unless you allow for it to "rest" for a couple of hours, the child will continue to vomit if you persist in feeding him. A short fasting will not further dehydrate him. However, the persistent vomiting will, because he will lose not only the fluid ingested, but also his stomach and intestinal juices. All oral medications must be stopped too. If he has fever, use acetaminophen suppositories (see Fever above), to bypass the stomach.

If, in spite of following all the above instructions, your child continues to vomit, call his doctor's office right away.

DEHYDRATION

A child who has persistent vomiting, or severe, persistent diarrhea may get dehydrated (dry).

Signs of possible dehydration: dry mouth, decreased tears, decreased urination, lethargy, listlessness. If severe: sunken fontanel (if under age 18 months), etc. If not treatment is began to correct dehydration, a child may go into shock and die.

If your child is having persistent vomiting and/or diarrhea, contact his doctor's office even if he does not appear dehydrated to you. Do not wait until he becomes too sick.

DIAPER RASH

What Causes Diaper Rash?

A combination of factors:

• Pre-disposing factor: Wet skin weakens natural defenses. Digestive agents (enzymes) in stools attack and weaken skin even more.
• Urine.

• Bacteria in stools --->breakdown of urine = ammonia. Ammonia in turn enhances the stool enzymes. Now the skin is very "weak" and is easily irritated by:
- friction of the diaper
- irritant chemicals in urine/stools
- germs

RESULT -----> DIAPER RASH

Disposable Diapers Or Cloth Diapers?

It is not clear which one is best. I personally think that the most important factor in decreasing the severity of diaper rashes is the frequent changing of the diapers.
Keep his bottom as dry as possible. Let him stay bare-bottomed at different times. Rubber pants may increase the rash, because they keep humidity in. If the rash is very red, your pediatrician might have to see it. A yeast infection is a common condition and requires a special medicine. Also, other infections and conditions may cause diaper rash.

When Is Diaper Rash Most Likely To Happen?

Based on the latest research, it is possible to characterize diaper rash as follows:

- It happens when babies are not kept clean and dry.
- It occurs more frequently as infants get older, peaking at eight to ten months.
- It happens to most babies. More than 60 percent of babies between 4 and 15 months get diaper rash at least once in a two-month period.
- It happens more often to babies who have more frequent stools, especially when the stools are retained in their overnight diapers.
- It happens less often to breast-fed babies; there is less protein activity in their stool.
- It tends to happen more when babies begin to eat table food.
- It tends to happen more frequently when babies are taking antibiotics.

What Can Be Done To Reduce The Chance Of Diaper Rash?

- Bathe the baby frequently and clean the diaper area with water and cotton, especially after a bowel movement.
- Reduce skin exposure to wetness.

• Avoid the mixing of urine and stool by changing the diaper immediately after a bowel movement.

• If diaper rash develops despite your preventative efforts, apply a bland ointment, such as zinc oxide, to the affected area. Consult your pediatrician if the rash does not disappear within 48 to 72 hours.

• How about cornstarch or talcum powders? Some people warn not to use them because a very irritating paste forms when baby urinates.

• Caution: Some creams used to treat "yeast infection diaper rash" contain steroids. If used too long (weeks for instance), the skin may atrophy (it thins until an ulcer develops). Thus, check with your doctor after a while if rash does not improve.

CONSTIPATION

In Babies:

Remember that infrequent but soft stools are not an indicator of constipation. Constipation = hard stools.

Hard stools may be harmful. They may produce bleeding from baby's rectum.

Put one teaspoonful of Karo syrup (dark) in each bottle. Wait two or three days. If the stools are still hard, increase to two teaspoonfuls. Wait three more days. If the stools are still hard, go up to three, four, five, six teaspoonfuls in each bottle. Most of the time you will eventually reach an amount of Karo syrup which will produce softer stools.

Until this happens, use glycerin suppositories every day or every other day especially if he is straining a lot.

If Karo syrup fails, get in touch with your child's doctor.

Fruit juices are useful for constipation. However, if your child is very young (less than four months) do not give them to him unless his doctor tells you to do so.

In Children:

Toddlers and older children usually are "too busy" to bother to go to the bathroom, therefore they often become constipated. When this happens, the best treatment consists of reestablishing the "defecation reflex." This reflex acts in the following way:

After we eat, as the food reaches the stomach, through a nervous reflex our body tells us that we should go to the bathroom. In some people this reflex is very active. In others, it is not. Children who are constipated become so in general because for weeks, months and sometimes years they do not heed this call from the body to move the bowels. They are busy playing, or some children are shy and they do not want to ask their teacher to go to the bathroom when they feel they need to, for instance, in school.

One way to reestablish the defecation reflex is to have the child sit on the toilet for 15 to 20 minutes every day at least once, preferably twice, a day. The best time is after a meal, for instance after breakfast and then after supper. He can take a comic book with him or if he is too young, one parent can read a story or magazine to him.

This should be an obligation for the child and it should be done on a daily basis. Even if the child does not move his bowels for several days at these particular times, eventually it will happen and then will continue to do so. Laxatives will make the bowels move, but it is not a good idea to use them long term.

NOSEBLEEDS

Recurrent self-limited nosebleeds in otherwise healthy children is normal. They can happen at any age, most commonly around five to seven years of age. No treatment is necessary. It is extremely unusual for a child to bleed so much that she develops anemia. When the bleeding starts, pinch your child's nose and hold for at least five minutes. Preferably, she should be sitting up. If, after several attempts, the bleeding does not stop, call your child's doctor.

LUMPS

Lumps around the neck or behind the head (occiput) are commonly found in children. They usually represent swollen lymph nodes. If they are relatively small (about pea-size or slightly larger), non-tender and easily movable, they are normal. If they seem to be large, tender or non-movable, let your child's doctor know.

LACK OF APPETITE

Infants eat a lot. From about 7 lbs. at birth they go to about 24 pounds or more at 12 months. From about 20 inches they grow to be 30 inches at 1 year. All of a sudden, around the age of one to two years the child decreases his appetite. Parents become very concerned. If they don't, grandmother does. Thus the pediatrician is asked: "Why doesn't my baby eat as she used to?"

The reason is that children don't need to eat as much from one-and-a-half to two years until six or eight years (the "lull period"). They do not grow very much during that period, and this is a normal, physiologic phenomenon which cannot be altered by forcing the child to eat. If one looks at the weight curve for normal children, one notices that from birth to two years, weight increases according to a line with about 45 degrees inclination. From 2 to 8 years the inclination is much less: about 15-20 degrees, and then from 8 through puberty the angle is higher again: 45-50 degrees. So it is OK for a two to eight-year-old child not to eat every single meal, as adults do, and it is OK if their weight does not continue to increase as it did before she was two years old.

How to Develop Good Eating Habits: Avoid between-meal snacks. Let her come to the table hungry so that she will eat better. The only thing I would let her eat or drink outside of mealtime is water or fruits.

Children should eat with the rest of the family as a rule. Since her appetite is smaller, let her excuse herself from the table if she has finished her food.

Mealtime should be a pleasant moment for the whole family. Keep the conversation relaxed. Let her eat at will. Serve attractive, nutritious food.

Let your child feed by herself as early as possible. Don't worry if she messes up your kitchen. She has to learn.

Serve a balanced diet. Be sure to include high-protein foods like meats, cheese and eggs. Serve also a good variety of foods.

DO NOT: Force or bribe your child into eating. The only thing this accomplishes is making her dislike mealtimes. I always tell mothers: Be happy if during the "lull period" she eats a good meal every three or four days, with very little in between. Mothers worry and say: "But how can she survive on so little food?" The fact is they do, as I explained before.

DO NOT prepare special foods only for her.

DO NOT discipline her during meals: "Take your elbows off the table," "use your napkin," "don't gulp your food," "don't kick the chair," etc.

DO NOT push her to eat: "Eat your soup," "drink your juice." Another method not to be used is "waiting her out": "We'll sit here until you finish." The child's response? Dawdling, daydreaming, squirming, etc.

If a child's actions at the table interfere with other members of the family's enjoyment of the meal, then she should be corrected. For example, if she comes to the table with dirty hands, you send her back to wash them. Do not belittle her though. Just send her to wash her hands, period.

If she persists in a behavior that is annoying to others at the table, send her away temporarily to remain by herself until she chooses to return and behave acceptably.

A MATCHBOOK is one book your kids
should never open!

**Contrary to popular belief,
thumbsucking is harmless, so long as
a child stops before her permanent
teeth erupt
(around age 5 or 6)**

Sign up TODAY for the

INFANT CPR course

CHAPTER 6

RESPIRATORY ILLNESSES

EAR INFECTIONS

Simply stated, there are two types: the most common is the "middle ear" infection or OTITIS MEDIA. Pus accumulates inside the middle ear cavity, the eardrum gets red and sometimes bulges and it may even rupture, thus allowing the pus to drain out. The child may have earache (fussiness and pulling of the ears in babies), fever, cold symptoms, etc.

BEWARE! Sometimes babies have no earache or fever and yet they do indeed have an ear infection. It is not unusual to find otitis media in a baby who just came in the doctor's office for a well-baby check-up.

Another type of ear infection is "swimmer's ear" or OTITIS EXTERNA. This happens almost exclusively during the summer. It consists of an inflammation of the external ear canal due to water, which softens the wax and makes it an ideal growth media for germs.

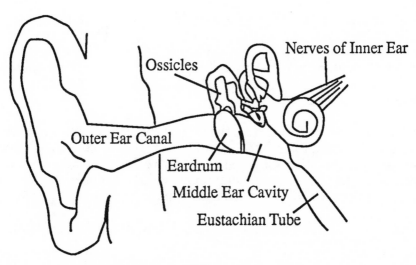

Nerves of Inner Ear

Ossicles

Outer Ear Canal

Eardrum

Middle Ear Cavity

Eustachian Tube

Otitis Media:

Antibiotics: As far as the treatment of otitis media, we usually start children on one antibiotic or another. There are about five antibiotics that are usually effective in the treatment of otitis media. These antibiotics are of about the same efficacy. In other words, there is not one that will be superior to the others all the time. Because of this, doctors prescribe one of them first, and if the child is not better ten days later in follow-up, a second antibiotic is given. If this antibiotic does not clear the infection, a third antibiotic has to be started, and the child is rechecked in another ten days and so on.
If after a month or two the child still has an ear infection, probably the child needs to be referred to an ear specialist.

It is important to give the antibiotic exactly the way it was prescribed. Please be compulsive and make sure that your child takes the medicine every day. Just because the baby gets better after two or three days, it does not mean that you can let up. Keep going for the whole ten days or until you run out of medication. Try not to forget this. Don't save antibiotic for a future time when the child might get sick again. This is a mistake, especially with ear infections, which already are, as I explained before, difficult to cure.

Try to always have some kind of measuring device so that you can measure the exact amount of medication. This is especially important with small babies who require 1/4 of a teaspoonful or 1/2 of a teaspoonful. It is very important that she gets the right amount. Small babies are sometimes hard to give medication. If the baby refuses or spits most of it back, then it is better to give another dose so as to make sure she got the right amount.

Follow-Up Visits: The follow-up of an ear infection ten days after the antibiotic has been started is very important. As I explained above, the treatment might not work. Therefore, one needs to check the child in ten or fifteen days and make sure that the ear infection is completely clear. Parents cannot assume that because the child feels better the ear infection is gone.

If the infection is not cleared, the child either has a relapse, i.e. the child develops an ear infection again or else --and this is even worse-- the infection may continue for weeks or months without symptoms, but one day the mother may notice that either the child is not hearing well or else that he is not acquiring any new language.

EAR INFECTION NOT WELL CURED = DEAFNESS

Surgery: The ear, nose and throat doctor will usually put tubes through the eardrums of both ears and sometimes remove the adenoid glands. These tubes allow the fluid that has built up inside the middle ear cavity to drain and, therefore, to improve hearing or prevent hearing loss if none has occurred by then. Future ear infections may or may not be prevented. In other words, children who have tubes put in their ears still might continue to have ear infections. Which children will and which children will not, one cannot foretell.

In my experience, about 50 percent, or one out of two children who have tubes put in, will continue to have ear infections. When they have an ear infection, usually the pus which forms in the middle ear will come out and will not accumulate in the middle ear. That is good. The children who usually do not respond well to tubes are those who have a history of allergies, sinusitis, asthma, etc.

One question parents may ask is, "Well, why don't we put tubes in more often?" Or, "Why do we wait so long until we finally send the child to an ear specialist?" The answer is that the insertion of tubes in the ears is an operation. The child has to have general anesthesia and there is a certain risk, although minimal.

Cost is another factor, and as I mentioned before, one out of two or maybe one out of three children, will continue to have ear infections in spite of the tubes. One can not generalize or say that every child should have tubes put in his ears after one or two ear infections. The doctor who takes care of the child has to make the decision based on different factors, the number of infections, the persistence of the fluid accumulated in the middle ear, etc.

One question I am often asked is, "Why is it that nowadays so many children get ear infections?" Today's grandmothers especially wonder about this because, when they were raising their kids 15 or 20 years ago, there were not so many ear infections. I think one very logical explanation is the fact that in those days not too many mothers worked outside the home. They usually stayed with their children, and these children were not in contact with other children early in their lives as it happens today. Young children catch colds and ear infections, etc easily in day care centers.

Infants usually get ear infections more easily because of the anatomical configuration of their ear canals. They have short ear canals, short Eustachian tubes. So when they get a cold, the secretions get into the middle ear more easily than when they are older.

Other Causes Are: Allergies and propping the bottle when feeding the baby.

Not much can be done for allergies as they are inherited. Parents who are allergy sufferers themselves must expect their children also to develop allergies. The allergic child has constant congestion of the nose and sinuses. This congestion in turn brings about ear infections.

Propping the bottle is a bad idea because milk gets into the Eustachian tubes (see figure of the ear on page 79) and from there goes into the middle ear cavity which brings about infection.

Often Asked Questions:

Can ear infections (otitis media) be due to:

- water getting into the ears?
- earwax?
- wind?
- teething?

The answer to all of them is NO!

The water in a swimming pool or lake may cause an infection of the outer ear (external canal). This is called "swimmer's ear" or "otitis externa." This is different from otitis media. In the latter, the infection is in the middle ear (behind the eardrum).

Wax: There is nothing unusual about the build-up of earwax, especially in children. Our ears need it, because it lubricates, among other things. We would be very uncomfortable without it. Thus, if your child always has a lot of wax in his ears, do not worry. Just clean it from the outer part of the ear. Never insert pins or cotton applicators inside. It is dangerous and unnecessary. Wax is harmless and no, your child's ears aren't "dirty"!

Wind: Unless your child is in a blizzard, wind will not harm his ears!

Teething: I know that some of you think at times that your baby gets an ear infection every time he cuts a tooth. Infants do get ear infections very often, but remember that teething also is occurring normally at the same time. Thus, one event is not due to the other. They just happen to coincide.

Flying And Ear Infections: People with active ear infections should not fly.

If your child has recently had an ear infection or fluid in his/her ears (called "serous otitis media") and you must fly, follow these instructions:

Soon after boarding the plane, give her a dose of Tylenol or Tempra, and place two drops of Neosynephrine (infant or child depending on his age) nose drops in each nostril.

Have with you a formula or juice bottle (if less than one year of age) or a cup with a spout, etc. If she begins to cry then:

1. Have her drink the juice or formula from a bottle or cup.
2. Put AURALGAN ear drops in her ears.
3. Hold her in your arms and try to console her.

ALLERGIES

Allergies are a frequent, widespread problem. Almost every family has one or two persons who suffer from chronic nasal stuffiness or nasal discharge, sneezing, watery eyes, etc. People who have this symptomatology have what is called "hay fever" or more scientifically it is called *allergic rhinitis*. Allergic rhinitis is a frustrating, difficult-to-control problem.

Allergies comprise a wide range of medical problems. On the mild end of this spectrum there is allergic rhinitis or hay fever. On the other end, there are severe cases of asthma, patients who are sick all the time. They must be hospitalized frequently, and they take powerful and dangerous medications. These patients have such severe cases of asthma that some of them die due to complications.

If somebody is allergic in your family, don't keep pets in your home. Allergy to cats, dogs and other animals may be the cause of a child's wheezing, hay fever, etc. Feather pillows are also to be avoided. Cigarette smoking around any child, but especially an allergic child, should be restricted.

BRONCHIOLITIS

This is a common respiratory *viral* infection which occurs in small infants during the winter months. The baby coughs, has respiratory difficulty (labored breathing) and wheezing, which you can hear from a distance or with a stethoscope applied to her chest. Usually the baby needs to be seen by her doctor as soon as possible. This can be a very serious illness, even fatal, if not caught early.

The RSV virus (Respiratory Syncitial Virus) is the most common agent.

Treatment: Most babies, especially younger ones, have to be hospitalized. Not much can be done at home, other than watching the respiratory pattern (rate, depth of respirations, etc.).

BRONCHITIS

It is an inflammation of the bronchial tubes. Cough is the main symptom, and oftentimes the only one. In general it is a mild, self-limited condition, but complications are possible: pneumonia, otitis media, etc. It is usually due to a virus and therefore antibiotics are of no help. All we can do is treat symptoms. We prescribe a cough medicine (any you can get over the counter is OK as long as you give the proper dose), a decongestant, etc. The vaporizer may help, too, especially if the cough is croupy.

Bronchitis is not contagious. A child with recurrent bronchitis should be worked-up for asthma, cystic fibrosis, etc.

Can a bronchitis turn into a pneumonia? Yes, it can. Can it be prevented with an antibiotic? Maybe, but this is not considered good medical treatment, because only a minority of cases of bronchitis will turn into pneumonia. Why give a medication unless it is strictly necessary?

Your child appears to have bronchitis. When should you call and get an appointment in your doctor's office?

1. When the child is very young (under six months of age) or she has some other debilitating condition, i.e.: cystic fibrosis, heart conditions, etc.

2. The child's chest sounds "very congested, rattly to touch."

3. Her breathing is labored: rapid, deep, the ribs show in every inhalation, etc. "She is gasping for air".

4. You can hear her wheezing (do not confuse wheezing with a "snoring sound" or with "croup").

5. You are just too worried and feel you better call up and check with her doctor. Fine, do so! I always say: In case of doubt, call and ask.

6. The child is prone to otitis media (ear infections). Many times babies have no fever, no obvious earache, and yet when they are examined, the ears are infected. Thus, if a "cold" is persistent, get an office appointment.

CROUP

Croup, or laryngitis, is a respiratory ailment, usually of rapid onset (typically in the middle of the night), called *spasmodic croup."* It can be progressive, over hours or days, is frequently preceded by the symptoms of a "cold" *(viral croup)* and characterized by a typical, loud, croupy sound due to a narrowing of the inside of the voicebox or larynx. This narrowing is caused by swelling of the vocal cords and the immediate area.

Symptoms:

• STRIDOR: inspiratory (when child inhales) coarse, croupy sound due to air passing forcefully through a narrower space between the vocal cords.
• BARKING, DRY COUGH: same cause.
• LABORED BREATHING: can be severe.
• FEVER, HOARSENESS, ETC.

Home treatment:

A vaporizer at the child's bedside is usually helpful. The humid air helps decrease the inflammation of the larynx. If your child is having labored breathing in spite of the use of the vaporizer, convert your bathroom into a "steam room" by opening all the hot water faucets and sit inside with her for 20 to 30 minutes or until you run out of hot water. At this point, if she is better, return her to her bed. If she is not, get in your car with her, roll the windows down and drive to the nearest emergency room.

Most cases of croup are not serious. Croup may recur in some kids. Most children outgrow it by age seven or eight.

Symptoms similar to croup may be due to the ingestion and aspiration of a foreign body, such as a piece of candy, peanuts, etc. These "go the wrong way" into the larynx or trachea (the area below the windpipe) and obstruct the airway.

77

If your child is two or three years of age, has croup with high fever, drools a lot, prefers to sit up rather than lie down, and talks with a "hot potato voice," CALL YOUR DOCTOR RIGHT AWAY: she could have a type of croup called *Epiglotitis,* a very serious illness.

TORTICOLLIS

Some babies tilt their heads to one side. If you notice this, call your doctor's office right away. Your child's doctor will examine her and he'll discuss the problem and its treatment with you. Oftentimes he will obtain X-rays of his neck and if OK, he probably will recommend stretching exercises to correct the problem.

STREP INFECTIONS

Sore throat, fever, white patches (pus) on tonsils are usually suggestive of strep infection.

About 25 percent of those persons exposed to another who is suffering from a strep throat, scarlet fever or scarlatina (same thing) will acquire the disease. Most will develop the same symptoms, like fever, sore throat, etc. Some however, will not, but they should call the doctor's office and come in for a throat culture. Those who are already having some symptoms will be examined as well.

The use of prophylactic treatment -- given an antibiotic to prevent the onset of the infection, is not to be recommended. Only if the throat culture is positive for strep should an antibiotic be given. **Antibiotics are drugs, and as such they may cause certain reactions, some of them serious.** As with all drugs, they should be used only when necessary.

The danger of strep infections lies in their potential harmful effects on the heart (rheumatic fever) and kidneys (nephritis). These are late effects. They do not develop until at least two or three weeks after the onset of the strep throat symptoms or after the exposure to a sick person occurs. Because of this, there is usually no rush in starting antibiotics. One can wait for the result of the throat culture which usually is available in 24 hours.

A person with strep throat is contagious for approximately two to three days after the antibiotic was begun. By that time the fever is gone and the patient is feeling much better. At this time the child may go back to school but should continue taking the antibiotic.

TONSILLECTOMY & ADENOIDECTOMY (T & A)

Tonsils need to be taken out surgically only if the child has severe, repeated tonsillitis, like one or more per month. Reasons to be cautious with surgery are:

1. Child has to be put under anesthesia. Although the risk is low, it is a risk.

2. Throat infections may persist in spite of operations.

3. Tonsils may be useful organs for our health. Once they are removed, we might suffer bad effects in ways that we do not know yet.

PLASTIC BAGS ARE DEADLY!

Garbage, dry-cleaners, and other plastic bags are common death traps for small children. Between 1980 and 1987, 112 children died in U.S.A. suffocated by them according to the CPSC.

Parents! Please keep all plastic bags away from children and infants.

When you're pregnant, if you smoke, your unborn baby smokes too.
CIGARETTE SMOKING
IS
CHILD ABUSE!!

WARNING: IF YOU DON'T OWN AN INFANT WALKER, DON'T BUY ONE. IF YOU OWN ONE, USE IT ONLY SPARINGLY

SHOPPING CARTS MAY BE DANGEROUS

Grocery store shopping carts are responsible for thousands of injuries per year in children. The CPSC reported that during 1990, about 19,000 children under the age of four required emergency room treatment for injuries related to the use of these carts, the majority due to falls from such carts. About one-third of the children suffered head concussions, fractures or internal injuries.

To prevent injuries to your child while you carry her in a shopping cart, either use the restraining belt that many stores provide with these carts or do not place her in one of them.

WATER BEDS

Adult, free-floating water beds are hazardous for young infants. The face of a sleeping infant can become trapped in the depression formed by his head's weight, especially if the water bed is not totally full.

The CPSC reported 6,000 injuries or deaths involving water beds in 1988, 36% of them in children less than five years of age.

ADULT WATER BEDS ARE UNSAFE FOR INFANTS

CHAPTER 7

INFECTIONS AND
OTHER PROBLEMS

CHICKEN POX

Chicken pox is a viral disease. There is no antibiotic or medication which will cure it. All one can do is to treat the symptoms. If your child is really itching you may buy over-the-counter calamine lotion and cover the lesions with this lotion several times a day as needed. For fever you may use Tylenol or Tempra. For relief of itching, you may also give your child Chlor-Trimeton or Benadryl. The syrups and the dosage varies with age. Follow the instructions in the package insert.

Try to keep your child as clean as possible. He or she should take at least one good bath every day and you should use lots of soap in order to keep all the sores and blisters as clean as possible. Phisoderm is a liquid soap which can be squirted in the bathtub water or poured on a towelette which you can use to gently and thoroughly cleanse your child's skin.

Acyclouir, an anti-viral oral medication can be given now. It seems to decrease the pain, itching, etc., and is very safe. However, it is expensive and the benefit is minimal.

A.I.D.S.

The first cases of AIDS in this country were reported in homosexual men. The first cases in children were reported in 1982 from New York and New Jersey.

In the following years, the number of affected children has climbed dramatically. By December 1989, 1995 AIDS patients under the age of 13 years had been reported, representing 1.7 percent of the total AIDS cases in the U.S.A. However, it is estimated that for each reported case of pediatric AIDS, there are between 2 and 10 children with HIV infection who either have no symptoms, or who do not meet the CDC's definition for AIDS. By the end of (1991), there were an estimated 20,000 children infected with the HIV virus in this country alone. AIDS has become one of the five leading causes of death in children.

Initially, children acquired this dreadful disease through blood transfusions. Since 1985, with better methods to detect contaminated blood, the number of pediatric AIDS cases has declined. Currently over 80 percent of the children with AIDS get it from their infected mothers. These women are drug users themselves or the sexual partners of male drug users.

The symptoms of this disease are many. Some children have symptoms that are not specific; i.e.: fever, failure to thrive, weight loss, enlarged liver and spleen, enlarged lymph glands, diarrhea, etc. Other children may show neuro-developmental problems: delay in their development, seizures, microcephaly, etc. Others may have a special type of pneumonia; and still others may develop different serious infections, such as cancer of some organs, anemia, or heart disease.

The diagnosis is made with blood tests that detect the anti-HIV antibodies, or a viral protein (Western blot test), or through viral cultures.

The treatment of AIDS is at the present time not very effective. The drug AZT seems to help, but it has not been yet used in children.

CONVULSIONS

This can be a very scary situation. When it is just due to high fever (febrile convulsions), it is usually very short-lived and not dangerous at all. By the time you realize your child is having one, it is over. Most seizures, febrile or not, are self-limited. If you witness your child having a seizure, try not to panic. Place him on a bed or sofa, on his side, remove any hard or sharp objects close to him so he doesn't hit them. After the seizure stops, he most likely will fall asleep. Call his doctor at this time for further advice. If the seizure doesn't stop after five or 10 minutes, call 911 or an ambulance. If he is not breathing well or has stopped breathing, start CPR. Parents of children with convulsions should know CPR.

Of course, to avoid or virtually eliminate these seizures, you should follow up with your child's doctor. Many seizures occur because the child does not take the medicine properly. Do not miss office visits and have her take medicine as ordered. This is a serious condition and requires proper follow up. If it has been a long time since your child has had a convulsion, you tend to become overconfident and therefore careless. Don't!

HEART MURMURS

A heart murmur is a sound that a physician will hear as he listens to a person's heart (heart auscultation). It is a sound that may or may not be normal. What causes this sound? In general it is due to change in the blood flow inside the chambers of the heart.

Some heart murmurs are due to an inborn or acquired defect inside the heart or the large blood vessels, i.e. a hole through the wall that separates the right and left ventricles, or a narrowing of one of the large vessels,etc.

MOST OF THE TIME, IN CHILDREN, heart murmurs are NOT due to a structural defect of the heart. We do not know for sure why they have a murmur. One explanation is the fact that children's chest walls are thin, and the heart is closer to the skin, allowing us to pick up the murmur. The fact is, that as many as one out of two healthy children may have a normal, so-called "innocent" or "functional" murmur. *Therefore, if your child's doctor is confident that he has a "functional" murmur, and tells you to relax and treat him as the normal child that he is, do indeed relax.*

What treatment or precautions are necessary? None.

Do children outgrow innocent murmurs? The majority of them do.

If your child's doctor is not quite sure whether the heart murmur is innocent or not, then he probably will order a chest X-ray and probably also an electrocardiogram (EKG), or he might refer her to a pediatric cardiologist for consultation.

PROBLEMS WITH FEET AND LEGS

Most apparent foot or leg abnormalities correct themselves or are not abnormal at all.

What is NORMAL in infants:

• Toeing out: between about 6 months and 12 or 18 months, many children's feet point outwards. They have a "Charlie Chaplin" walk. Gradually, feet turn in to adopt the final, normal position,which consists of a slight toeing out.

83

• Toeing in: very common. It is usually outgrown when mild. You know that your infant has a mild toeing in when a) you can bend the foot to the normal position easily, and b) his feet look OK while he is moving and kicking.

• Flat feet: Most infants have or appear to have flat feet. This is due to two factors. First, normal children under the age of six years have weak or flexible bone and joints in their feet. Thus, when they stand, the arches flatten. Second, infants have a "fat padding" on the bottom of their feet which "fills" the space between the soles and the ground. The arch of the foot can be seen clearly when the foot is hanging free or when the child stands on his toes.

• Bowlegs: Very few babies have straight legs. Most have an outward curvature at the level of the knees. This corrects by itself, so that by two or three years legs look straight in most kids.

What Is ABNORMAL?

• **Toeing in:** There are two abnormal situations in children below the age of three years:

A) **Hooked foot:** These are feet in which, the forefoot angles markedly inwards. This can be seen well when you look at his feet from the foot of the bed as he lies on his back. This deformity is due to unusual pressure on the baby's feet inside the uterus during pregnancy. Hooked feet may get better with time, but often a corrective cast must be applied.

B) **Tibial Torsion:** the tibia or shinbone, is twisted inward because of the infant's sleeping posture. (on his stomach, legs twisted inwardly). Most children with tibial torsion get better without treatment by around the age of one year. Occasionally, a splint or metal bar between special shoes may help.

C) **Bowlegs:** severe cases of bowlegs, or those which seem to get worse with time, may be abnormal, but this must be determined by your child's doctor or a bone specialist (orthopedist). If only one leg is affected, consult your child's doctor also..

The ideal characteristics of a child's shoe are:

• The upper should be soft and porous.
• Soles should be flat, flexible and of non-skid material to prevent falls.

• Canvas shoes are OK, because they are soft, more elastic than leather and give feet more room to develop.
• A good shoe does not need to be expensive.
• High top shoes are not necessary. They may hinder a child's walking and cause him to slip or fall.
• Under the age of one year, children could be barefooted or wear thin soles, especially indoors. The more contact his soles have with the floor, the better his foot muscles will develop and grow strong.
• After one year, soles should be just thick enough to protect his feet from rough surfaces, rocks, etc., but should not be stiff.

Minor foot problems: overlapping toes, curly or rotated toes, webbed toes. These minor abnormalities of the feet rarely need any treatment.

LIMPING

A child limps when he does not apply the full weight of his body on one leg as he walks. Young toddlers and preschoolers often limp. There may be many causes of a limp. At home you should check your child for an obvious cause such as a cut, a blister, a red, swollen or tender area, i.e. a joint. A broken bone may not always be obvious. If there is no apparent reason for the limp, and he is otherwise healthy, active and happy, wait a day or two. Oftentimes the limp disappears as mysteriously as it came. However after that time, set up an appointment with his doctor. He might order X-rays, or blood tests or refer him to an orthopedic doctor.

OBESITY

Please forget the popular notion that "the more a child eats the better it is." Let children eat at their own pace. If your child seems to be getting obese, seek medical help. An obese teenager becomes the target for classmates' jokes. This in turn is responsible for shyness, social isolation, etc. Get him enrolled in a fitness program, the YMCA, YWCA, etc. Obesity is linked to many diseases like diabetes, arteriosclerosis and high blood pressure.

CONJUNCTIVITIS

Q. What Is Conjunctivitis?

A. Conjunctivitis, commonly called "pinkeye," is an inflammation of the thin membrane, or conjunctiva, covering both the outer surface of the eye and the inner surface of the eyelids. As a result, **the eye appears pink and irritated.** Other findings may consist of **swollen eyelids,** and a **thick,** sometimes sticky **eye discharge** (mattering). Although conjunctivitis is usually caused by infection, it also may be associated with allergies, air pollution, etc.

When your child's eyes seem to have "pinkeye," you may do either of two things: 1) Call his doctor and make an appointment for him, or -- especially if it is after hours, 2) Get OTC drops like Murine or Visine and use overnight until your doctor's office opens in the morning. If he is better, then just observe him. Otherwise, set an appointment.

Conjunctivitis is quite contagious. Follow these guidelines:

• Give your child his own towels. Make them strictly off-limits to other family members.
• Set aside certain toys that others should not touch.
• Wipe carefully your child's mattering with a soft facial tissue. Discard it immediately.
• Do not send him to school or day care until his eyes are clear.

How to apply eye drops correctly:

If the child is a toddler or older, I would follow this procedure:
• Tilt his head back. Ask him to look upward and gently pull the lower eyelid toward you to form a pocket.
• Place the drops, or ointment, into the pocket.
• Ask him to look down, then slowly to move the lower lid upward until the eye is closed.
• Ask the child to keep the eye closed for one or two minutes.

If the child is an infant, he cannot be given directions; thus, I would hold him probably against his will - if necessary - lying down, and I would place the drops on the inner corner of his eyes. Even if his eyes are closed, when he opens them, the drops will penetrate on the conjunctiva.

PINWORMS

These are small (1 cm. in length) white, wiggly parasites, which infect many families --usually unbeknownst to them-- and which almost NEVER are dangerous! If you see one or more of these creatures either: a) on your child's stool or, b) crawling on or around her anus (or vagina) there is NO NEED TO CALL YOUR DOCTOR RIGHT AWAY, especially if it is after hours! Your child (and maybe you, too) has probably had these pinworms for a long time! Call the next morning and medicine will be prescribed for all your family.

Symptoms: 90 percent of the time there are no symptoms at all. The rest of the time, only rectal or vaginal itching. Pinworms usually do not cause any other problems.

Pinworms are passed from human to human, usually via hands and fingers. The tiny eggs are passed with your stools and are picked up by your fingers which then can touch the food that is eaten by the rest of the family.

In addition to the "worm medicine" (tablets or liquid) you must follow these suggestions:

• All members of the family should be very clean: fingernails frequently trimmed and hands should ALWAYS be washed thoroughly (a brush may be used for fingernails) before EVERY meal.

• Ideally, the underwear and bed sheets of every member of the family should be soaked for 24 hours INDIVIDUALLY in separate buckets (with Kerosene, Clorox, etc.) and only after this should they be tossed into the washer together with the rest of the family members' clothes.

LICE

The head louse is a small (1/6 inch long) insect which infests the hair of humans. They lay eggs (nits) on the hair shaft. These nits are firmly attached and cannot be removed easily as dandruff can. Eggs hatch in about one week. The young lice then suck the blood of the scalp, grow and lay more eggs. People catch lice from using a comb or a hat from some other person who was infested.
Lice causes itching of the scalp, but otherwise it is not a serious illness. The nits are easy to see close to the root of the hairs.(white). Treatment consists of shampooing the hair with one of several OTC remedies. A fine-toothed comb is used to remove any dead eggs still attached to the hair. Use the same shampoo to clean your child's hat, comb or brush, or throw them away. Consult his doctor if the nits persist.

UMBILICAL HERNIAS

It is relatively frequent for babies to develop a bulge on the navel. This type of hernia is harmless. It will never rupture or complicate in any way. If a baby cries, it is not due to the hernia. Most of these hernias slowly shrink and disappear in a few weeks or months. Those which do not and get larger usually require an operation. The surgery is not done until the baby is at least one year old.

DO NOT PUT any bandages or adhesive tape or quarters on it. The hernia cannot rupture, no matter how much the baby cries or strains.

URINARY TRACT INFECTIONS (UTI)

These are infections of any or all parts of the urinary tract, comprising the kidneys, the ureters --the tubes that transfer the urine from kidneys to the bladder-- and the urethra --the tunnel that goes from bladder to the outside of the body.

UTI's are more common in girls than in boys, due to the ease with which stools may contaminate the opening of the urethra.

Common symptoms are: pain or burning sensation during urination, fever, frequent urination, bedwetting --in a previously dry-at-night child, back or belly pain, etc. If you suspect your child may have a UTI, call his doctor.

**A Child A Day
Is Killed
With A Handgun**

**If You Own A Gun,
Keep It Locked Away
From Children**

The Reading Mother

"You may have tangible wealth untold;
"Caskets of jewels and coffers of gold.
"Richer than I you can never be...
"I had a mother who read to me"
by Strickland Gililan

88

CHAPTER 8

YOUR MEDICINE CABINET, ETC

Cough: If your child has a barky, croupy cough, or a nighttime cough which may or may not awaken her and she also has allergies (hay fever, etc.), a cough suppressant would be useful, i.e., Delsym, Tussionex (needs prescription). They last 8 to 12 hours and will allow children to sleep through the night.

Coughs due to bronchitis or pneumonia, shouldn't be suppressed completely. I would recommend Robitussin DM (DM = dextrometorphan, a cough suppressant) or Triaminicol, Dorcol, Triaminic DM, Rondec DM, Tussi-Organidin, Hycomine Pediatric Drops, etc. which contain an expectorant (Expectorant: helps "bring up" bronchial secretions) and also a decongestant to clear up his nose.

Fever: Acetaminophen (Tylenol/Tempra/Panadol). See Fever in Chapter 4.

Poisoning: Syrup of Ipecac. Have two ounces (you may get it over the counter). If your child has swallowed medicine in excess (pills, liquids, etc.), call your doctor or Poison Control Center IMMEDIATELY and give the Syrup of Ipecac only if they say it's okay to give. Syrup of Ipecac will induce vomiting in your child but some ingested substances SHOULDN'T BE VOMITED

Nasal Congestion, Colds: To dry up a runny, stuffy nose, there are many good oral over-the-counter decongestants (Actifed, Dimetapp, Sudafed, Triaminic, etc.)

Prescription-only decongestants: Rynatan, Tavist. Convenient because you give them only twice a day.

Nasal Decongestants: They should be avoided in infants because the rebound mucosal swelling that they usually produce will block their nasal passage. Since babies normally cannot breathe well through their mouth, they will not be able to breathe. For infants stuffy

89

noses (not runny), use Salinex, AYR, or Ocean Spray (they are salt solutions). Place two to three drops in each nostril, wait two to three minutes and then suction with a rubber ear syringe.

For Nasal Discharge: Use the rubber bulb syringe they give you in the hospital after delivery to suck nasal secretions. Pharmacies sell them. They are called ear syringes.

Colic: Mylicon drops (.6 ml x 3/day) may or may not help. Safe. Paregoric (opium tincture): occasionally, a parent will be at his/her wits' end with a 24 hours-a-day screaming infant. Some doctors will prescribe this medication, albeit reluctantly, because it may help. It may cause constipation, though.

Itching: Calamine, Caladryl lotions. Benadryl Elixir by mouth, hydrocortisone cream (.5 percent) (Cortaid, Lanacort). Burrow's solution: cool compresses wet with this solution are excellent for poison ivy, heat rash, insect bites, etc.

Cuts, Minor Burns, Stings: Solarcaine, Dermoplast, povidone iodine for disinfection of wounds, etc., and also Neosporin, Bacitracin ointments.

Sunscreens: Choose one with SPF (sun protection factor) of 15 or more.

Diarrhea: If mild, no drugs are indicated. (see Chapter on Diarrhea.) If your child has frequent watery stools, some doctors recommend Imodium A-D (over the counter) or Pepto Bismol, but contact your doctor's office for advice also.

Earaches: Auralgan, Lidosporin, Americaine. They help by numbing the ear canal and ear drum. Don't use if child has ventilating tubes.

EQUIPMENT/SUPPLIES
FOR THE COMPLETE MEDICINE CABINET:

Every family should have a well-stocked medicine cabinet at home. Items which should be included:

- adhesive strip bandages
- adhesive tape
- rolled sterile gauze (2"x 4")
- elastic bandages
- sterile absorbent cotton
- cotton swabs

- eye dropper
- burn ointment/spray
- nasal syringe .
- sterile eye pads
- antiseptic solution/lotion/spray
- Syrup of Ipecac
- Burrow's solution
- toothache/sore gum product
- antacid
- acetaminophen
- antidiarrheal product
- flashlight
- diaper rash ointment
- cold medications
- antifungal agent
- antipruritic product (itch reliever)
- antitussic (cough) products, including syrups and lozenges
- oral medication syringe
- medicine spoon
- medicine dropper
- rubbing alcohol
- thermometer (oral or axillary, rectal for an infant)
- disposable cups and dispenser
- laxative or suppositories
- petroleum jelly
- icebag
- fountain syringe
- scissors
- tongue depressor
- tweezers

DO NOT "SAVE" AN ANTIBIOTIC SO THAT YOU CAN GIVE
IT TO YOUR CHILD THE NEXT TIME HE GETS SICK!

Giving the right amount of medication to your child

Some people get confused when measuring the medication to give to their children. This is of course dangerous, because if you give too much, it may be harmful. If you give too little, then the illness will not improve.

The relationship between spoons and droppers is illustrated below. Teaspoons usually measure 5 ml. of liquid (never use a teaspoon if you do not know its volume because regular teaspoons come in many sizes).

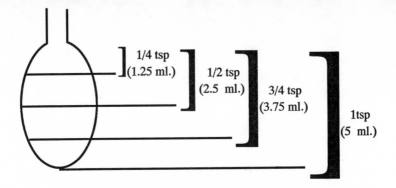

Droppers come in several sizes. Except for the dropper for Tylenol, Tempra, or Panadol, most droppers contain 1 ml. (look carefully if it is so marked on the sides).

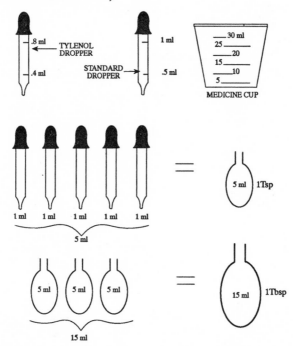

If a medication has to be given "four times a day" it means it may be given during waking hours only. Do not set the alarm clock during the night. Only if the bottle's label says: every 6 hours or every 8 hours, then yes, you must, if necessary, awake at night and give it to your child!

Usually antibiotics are given during daytime only. Anti-asthma medications are given usually at exact times, by the clock: every 12, 8 or 6 hours.

- 1 oz. = 30 ml.
- 1 pt. (pint) =16 oz. = 450 ml. approximately
- 1 qt. (quart) =32 oz. = 950 ml. approximately

Vaporizers: Cold mist or steam. The first is safer, but both are effective. Use them when your child has a cold, croup, bronchitis, etc. Make sure to clean and disinfect the vaporizer frequently. I have recently seen several children burned with hot vaporizers. DO NOT USE THESE ANYMORE:

WHAT NOT TO HAVE IN YOUR MEDICINE CABINET:

(Medicines should not be stored in a bathroom. They should preferably be in a dry place like a closet and locked up).

Boric Acid: We have better antiseptics. It is poisonous. Get rid of it!

Mineral Oil: This medication is good for constipation, but it blocks the absorption and utilization of vitamins A, D, and others like vitamin K. Severe pneumonia may occur if it is aspirated into the lungs.

Camphor: poisonous, useless.

Pills that are outdated or have changed color, etc.

Grandmothers/Grandfathers: When your grandchildren are coming for a visit, do a thorough inspection of your bathroom, kitchen, bedroom, etc., for pill bottles that you normally leave unattended around the house. Many children get poisoned in the home of their grandparents.

BEFORE GIVING YOUR CHILD ANY MEDICATION, MAKE SURE YOU CAN ANSWER THE FOLLOWING QUESTIONS:

1. What is the medicine's name?
2. What does it do?
3. How much do I give?
4. How often must I give it?
5. How long do I need to continue giving the medicine?
6. Are there any special instructions, such as shaking vigorously?
7. Are there special times to give the medicine?
8. Must I refrigerate the medicine?
9. Are there common side effects I can expect?. Rare adverse risks?
10. If my child has a known allergy, might he also be allergic to this drug?
11. How much does this medicine cost?
12. Is there a generic form of comparable quality available?
13. Finally, is this medicine really needed? Do the benefits outweigh the risks and costs?

RULES ON MEDICATIONS

1. LET YOUR DOCTOR -- AND ONLY YOUR DOCTOR -- PRESCRIBE MEDICATION AND DOSAGE. Do not follow a relative or friend's advise without first checking with your doctor or pharmacist.

2. IF YOU HAVE ANY DOUBTS ABOUT YOUR DOCTOR'S INSTRUCTIONS, ASK FOR AN ADDITIONAL EXPLANATION.

3. BE SURE TO FOLLOW YOUR DOCTOR'S INSTRUCTIONS. APPLY THE RIGHT MEDICATION IN THE RIGHT PLACE. For instance, drops may be used inside ears, eyes or may be for oral use. Read label carefully.

4. NEVER STOP ANTIBIOTICS BEFORE CONSULTING YOUR DOCTOR. CONTINUE GIVING THEM UNTIL THEY ARE ALL GONE.
Most antibiotics must be taken for at least ten days. Your child may seem all better after two or three days, but that doesn't mean he is totally cured. After ten days of treatment, all germs will be killed. Doctors usually prescribe enough antibiotic to last ten days.

5. DON'T GIVE MEDICATION TO ANY CHILD OTHER THAN THE ONE FOR WHOM IT WAS PRESCRIBED.

6. DON'T GIVE OLD MEDICINE TO YOUR CHILD WITHOUT FIRST CONSULTING YOUR DOCTOR, OR YOUR PHARMACIST.

MINOR PROBLEMS AND ACCIDENTS

Blisters (Localized)
A blister is a collection of fluid inside the outer layer of the skin (the epidermis). Most common causes of blisters are: Friction (a shoe that doesn't fit well), fire ant bites, chicken pox, etc.

Boils
These are pus formations (infection due to germs, usually staphylococcus) deep in the skin close to the hair follicle. They usually start as red, hard, and tender bumps. They grow until a "head" forms and the pus escapes. The cause or causes of boils are not always clear: Friction, playing in the dirt, scratching, etc., are probable causes.

94

Before consulting your doctor, you could apply hot wet compresses three or four times a day. When the boil comes to a head, you should call your doctor. Do not lance or squeeze it on your own! Sometimes boils will drain on their own. In this case, you should cover them with a clean gauze (the pus that oozes out is very contagious) change this dressing daily and wash thoroughly with soap and water.

Cuts and Scrapes
Blood is the best disinfectant. Let the cut bleed for a minute or two. Run cold water from the faucet over it. No disinfectant is generally needed. You may or may not apply a dressing on the wound. Cuts on the face or those that seem deep or long or jagged will need to be taken care of by a doctor.
To stop the bleeding, apply direct pressure with a gauze or a clean cloth over the wound. It may help to elevate the arm or leg where the bleeding is. Caution: do not move the extremities if there is the possibility of it being fractured. Cuts and scrapes on dirty, gritty surfaces must be cleansed thoroughly with soap and water.

Penis caught in a zipper: Unless only the skin part of the penis was caught, it is best to take him to the Emergency Room without trying to unzipp it. Avoid pulling motions of his pants. Another suggestion: cut with scissors the material around the zipper before leaving to go to the E.R.

Dry Skin
Skin's natural oils prevent dryness, itching, etc. Skin dryness is made worse by: too frequent bathing and soap use, winter weather (cold, windy). Certain soaps are good to prevent skin dryness: Neutrogena, Alpha Keri, Lowila cake, etc.

Bath Oils
Rather than pouring them in the bath water, as most of it will go down the drain, dilute them with water and apply them directly on your baby's skin and right after the bath. Baby oil is cheap and prevents the skin moisture from evaporating.

Puncture Wounds
Deep wounds are dangerous, because germs may be carried into the tissues. Because there is little or no bleeding, infection is more likely. Rusty, dirty nails may cause tetanus. You must seek medical help. Deep cuts with glass, tin cans, etc., also should be cared for by a doctor. Simple scrapes may be just washed well with soap and water and watched. Dirty scrapes (embedded grit, etc.) should be cleaned thoroughly.

Splinters
A pair of tweezers can remove a splinter that is sticking out. If you cannot remove it this way and the splinter is clearly visible under the skin, either try to squeeze it out or use a needle sterilized with a flame to try to pull it out. If you are still unable to remove the splinter, you might leave it alone hoping it will come out on it's own or consult your doctor.

WHEN TO CALL YOUR DOCTOR

Call your child's doctor (day or night) **at once** if there is:

• Fever (see chapter 4).
• Persistent vomiting: three or more times in a row (forceful vomiting).
• Diarrhea: (See chapter 5).
• Crying: If it is persistent (more than four or six hours), unless you already know that the baby is colicky. Also, call if it seems a different kind of crying.
• A severe fall (especially on the head), accidents, burns, poisoning, etc.
• Bleeding that cannot be stopped by direct pressure on the wound.
• Unconsciousness.
• Severe difficulty in breathing: "Gasping for air," labored breathing, or cyanosis (dusky or blue skin color).
• Convulsions.
• Severe acute abdominal pain which lasts for one or two hours.
• Black, bloody or tarry bowel movement in an infant, unless it seems to be a scant amount, or a few streaks.

CALL "911" (Super-emergencies)

• Severe fall/head injury (i.e. child is unconscious, fell from more that 6 feet, bleeding, etc.
• Severe, persistent convulsion.
• Poisoning/overdose.
• Severe allergic reaction (generalized hives, swelling around the eyes, becomes "croupy", i.e. difficulty breathing, etc.
• Severe burn(s)
• Respiratory arrest
• Extreme respiratory difficulty.
• Drowning.
• Choking with food: do the Heimlich maneuver.

LEARN CPR!!!

Call your child's doctor **without rush** (get an appointment) in these situations:

• Black or red stools (unless the baby ate beets or is on iron treatment for anemia).

• Poor feeding.

• Persistent bleeding from the nose.

• Weight loss or lack of weight gain.

• No wet diapers for the whole day (for a period of about 15 to 20 hours).

• A diaper rash which is fiery red and does not improve with the usual ointments. It could be a yeast infection.

• For fever, diarrhea, etc. See information under those subtitles.

• Also: Persistent headaches, unusual fatigue, sore or swollen joints, frequent or painful urination, earache, rashes, etc.

"The best way to inspire self-esteem
in children is to have self-esteem yourself"
(Nathaniel Branden, Ph D.)

Weight and Height Gains by Age

Q. My baby lost weight just after she was born. Will this affect her growth later?

A. Not at all, at least not in any way that should cause you undue concern. It is perfectly normal for a newborn to lose anywhere from four to nine ounces in the first five days.

By the time you read this, she may have had a small growth spurt to make up for lost time!

Q. How fast can I expect her to grow when she does begin to gain weight?

A. You should be aware that your baby will grow and develop faster during the first year than at any other time in her life. For instance, during the first year, a baby's brain weight doubles, his or her height increases by 50 percent and body weight triples.

On the average, your little girl will grow about an inch a month for the first six months.

A baby who is 20 inches at birth will be about 30 inches long at one year. The height and weight growth of an average baby will follow the patterns shown below:

Age	Weight	Height
Birth-5 days	4-9 oz (loss)	—
6-10 days	1 oz per day (gain)	—
10 days-3 months	1 oz per day	3/4 inch per month
3-6 months	5-6 oz / week	Gain of 2-2 1/2 inches
6-12 months	2-3 oz/week	Gain of 3-4 inches
12-24 months	1-2 oz/week	Gain of 6 inches
24-36 months	Gain of 5 lbs	Gain of 3 1/2 inches

As a new parent, please note that these are only averages. All children grow at different rates, and your child may not follow the exact patterns I've described. For example: A small baby at birth will grow faster and a large baby will grow less. Don't worry if your baby is different. However, if you feel there is cause for concern, ask your baby's doctor.

CHAPTER 9

TOILET TRAINING, BEDWETTING, DISCIPLINE, ETC.

THE DEFECATION REFLEX IN INFANTS

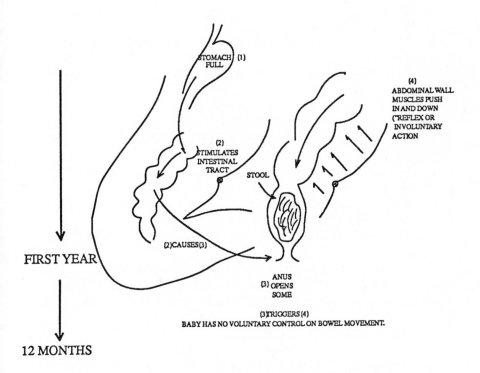

STOMACH (1)
FULL

(4)
ABDOMINAL WALL
MUSCLES PUSH
IN AND DOWN
("REFLEX OR
INVOLUNTARY
ACTION

(2)
STIMULATES
INTESTINAL
TRACT

STOOL

(2)CAUSES(3)

FIRST YEAR

ANUS
(3) OPENS
SOME

(3)TRIGGERS (4)
BABY HAS NO VOLUNTARY CONTROL ON BOWEL MOVEMENT.

12 MONTHS

If a parent seats a baby on the potty chair five to ten minutes after a meal, she can "catch" the bowel movement. If she repeats this for several days, the baby's nervous system becomes "conditioned," so that she will automatically begin to push as soon as she feels the toilet seat under her. (This is called "partial training": baby is not cooperating knowingly.)

Do not engage in "partial training." Baby might "rebel" later on. "Fecal soiling" or bed-wetting may be the result.

Signs of Readiness

Your child is probably ready to begin toilet training if she can do the following:

• Walk alone
• She stays dry for at least 2 hours at a time during the day or is dry after naps.
  • Her bowel movements become regular and predictable.
  • She can follow simple, verbal instructions.
  • She can walk to and from the bathroom, pull down pants, and pull them up again.
  • She becomes uncomfortable with soiled diapers and wants

2nd. to be changed.
YEAR • Remember, though, she need not show all of these signs in order to be ready. No two children are ready to begin toilet training at exactly the same age. A child should be physically, mentally, and emotionally ready.
  • Physically: she can walk, she can control her bladder and rectum to some extent.
  • Mentally: she's not preoccupied with other problems (see below: "When it is better to wait?").
  • Emotionally: she is willing, cooperative, not fighting or showing signs of fear.
Readiness does not just happen. Parents must help her get ready. Read to her one of the special books designed to teach toilet training. (See bibliography at the end of this chapter.)

When It Is Better To Wait

Sometimes it is better to wait, even though she shows signs of being ready. Outside stresses may overwhelm efforts to learn this new skill. It may be a good idea to delay toilet training in the following situations:

• The family has just moved or will do so in the near future.
• A brother or sister has just been born or is expected in the next few months.

100

• There is a major illness in the family.

GRADUALLY SHE BECOMES MORE CONSCIOUS OF WHEN A BOWEL MOVEMENT OCCURS.

(The child "pauses" or changes her facial expression momentarily.)

CAUTION!! If your child alerts you that she is wet or soiled, this may mean only that she is uncomfortable, but not that she KNEW the bowel movement was coming!

To be ready for toilet training, your child must be able to recognize the sensations that precede defecation or urination. In other words, she must know BEFORE the bowel movement and not just AFTER.

INDIRECT SIGNS OF READINESS

• Impulse to give presents.
• Putting things in containers.
• She wants to imitate more and more what parents and siblings do.
• Shows great pride in learning new skills.
• Enjoys being praised.

The following two things must be happening before you actually start the toilet training process:

A)
GREATER AWARENESS OF WHEN A BOWEL MOVEMENT IS COMING OR PASSED.

(She not only pauses or grunts, but she may give out a signal to the parent: may jump, pull at her pants, squat down, etc. You should tell her: "Your body wants to make some poop (or pee)."

B)
DEVELOPMENT OF PREFERENCE FOR CLEANLINESS

(She wants to be cleaned, prefers clean diapers. She understands that the potty means a dry diaper.)

Teach her the meaning of: pee, poop, dry, clean, wet, messy, potty, etc. Let her watch older siblings and parents, etc. teach her how to use the toilet carefully.

18 MOS.
TO
24-30 MOS.

Child Who Should Not Be Toilet Trained Yet:

- close to the time when she begins to walk.
- when in a violently negativistic phase.
- during a stressful phase.

Urine doesn't seem to give children as much pride as bowel movements.

WHEN THE ABOVE ARE PRESENT
(18 months to 30 months of age):

START

T O I L E T   T R A I N I N G

How To Toilet Train:

Doctor Brazelton's method is considered the best. I summarize it below:

Basis: NO COERCION
       TACTFUL SUGGESTIONS
       FLATTERY
       NO PRESSURE TO SIT DOWN ON THE SEAT
       NO DETENTION

This allows the child to decide to gain control, of her own free will. Why? She wants to be GROWN UP!

Parents must: 1) Trust their children's desire to mature.
             2) Have patience.

First Phase:

The "potty chair" (explain to her that it is her very own!) "Try it and sit on it, won't you?" In a suggestive (not coercive) voice, say: "Now or later, okay?"

This is better done with clothes on. You may demonstrate, also with clothes on. No mention of bowel movement (or urine) is made . Goal: sit once/day.

Do this for a few days. If she doesn't sit at all, keep trying for one to two weeks. Quit for a while after that time if she still refuses. Parents should try to be casual, relaxed, very patient, and adopt a good-humored attitude through all these phases of toilet training. Showing impatience or anger is a NO-NO!!

Second Phase:

Now she is used to her seat. Introduce the idea of depositing/doing a bowel movement/urine in there. Say for instance:

"Mommy and Daddy, and Jimmy (a friend or sibling), etc., use their toilet that way . . ." Do this two or three times.

After a while, and preferably after a meal, take her diaper off and suggest she try to "put the poo-poo" in the toilet . . . Don't push her, just suggest. A parent might demonstrate, but better without the child seeing his/her genitals. Continue this ritual once a day for about a week.

When she has a bowel movement in her diapers, lead her to her toilet, sit her on it and opening the diaper that she just soiled, explain again how Mommy and Daddy sit on their seat to have their bowel movements, that now she has her own seat and how someday she will do her bowel movement in it, too. (Yes, this is monotonous for an adult.)

Never scold her for failures: clean her genitals and say: "It's okay. You wanted to poo-poo in the potty, but couldn't. Don't worry, you'll do it very soon . . ."PRAISE! . . . PRAISE! "YOU'RE SO GROWN UP NOW." (Don't over do it though.) Some children need rewards, such as stickers, stars, food: raisins, crackers, etc.

Later on, try to let her play for one to two hours without clothes. Place the potty chair near her "so that you can go all by yourself." Remind her every hour or so. If she resists, put the diapers back on her and wait.

103

Urine Control usually occurs simultaneously with bowel movement control (or soon thereafter). Bladder function matures by itself regardless of training efforts by parents. Having her observe a same-gender family member (older sister, etc.) using the toilet may be very helpful. Boys usually like to imitate other males by urinating while standing up. You can also "toilet train" a doll with the help of your child. You give water to the doll, it is carried to the toilet, lying flat. When the doll is set upright over the potty chair, it will "pee" in it. Show her then how to praise the doll for being successful. "Accidents" (day-time wetting) are common. Nighttime dryness is not achieved in many children until they are four or five years of age.

Third Phase:

When she is controlling her bowel movement's and urine okay, put her in training pants that she can pull down herself. This will be another step in achieving independence and will reinforce her staying trained.

Nighttime dryness: usually comes later (about age three or later) and naturally. Usually, the more "high-strung" or "active" a child is, the later it happens. Parents can do very little to bring on nighttime dryness. Use pride and never scold or show displeasure at having to change wet sheets (Moms especially!). The process of toilet training takes a total of two weeks to two months, depending upon the child.

Fourth Phase:

Eventually, she will use the potty chair without help. Success at toilet training is a sign that she has taken one or more steps in acquiring important life skills and values.

Achieving bowel and bladder control adds to a child's sense of security and independence. The accomplishment will give her confidence that will help her achieve success in other aspects of the growing up process. The friendly teamwork between you and your child that goes into the development of toilet habits will be a model for other experiences on your child's road to maturity.

If Your Child Refuses To Toilet Train, Try To Avoid These Common Pitfalls:

- Don't start toilet training too early.

• Trying "too hard" leads to struggles which may lead to constipation later on. Remember the "terrible twos"? She is not resisting toilet training to spite parents. Lay off the toilet training!!

• She is in bad mood.

• She is in a stressful situation.

• Don't use laxatives, enemas or suppositories during toilet training.

• If child was previously moving her bowels every two to three days, you can't expect her to move daily.

• Rushing to toilet train. Your child can't learn in 24 hours! It takes weeks to a few months). Remember: patience, patience, patience.

• Don't scold or punish. You will delay toilet training.

• Be **consistent**. Make sure, before you start toilet training, you and your spouse agree that it's the right time to start and you both share the same philosophy.

• Don't let your child feel or know that you are anxious or nervous during toilet training.

"Regression"

• Illness   )   Wait and start
• Trip, etc.   )   again later

What To Do When Your Child Refuses To Toilet Train:

If she is less than two and a half years old, review the above "pitfalls" and discontinue toilet training for the time being. Resume in two or three weeks. If your child is older than two and a half, and you have been trying to toilet train for several months, she can be considered "Toilet Training Resistant."

You must shift gears: whereas, before you probably reminded her or lectured her "too often," now you must stop completely. Do, however, give her a final talk: "Your body makes "poop" and "pee" every day. It is your "pee" and "poop." Your poop wants to go in the potty." "From now on, you don't need my help anymore." (The responsibility for toilet training is transferred to the child.) Remember to be consistent.

- NO MORE TALK ABOUT THIS SUBJECT.
- NO MORE REMINDERS (don't even ask her if she has to go!)
- POSITIVE REINFORCEMENT (whenever she uses the toilet, successfully, reward her.)
- RECORD HER PROGRESS IN A CALENDAR.

If she wets/soils herself, have her clean herself and change clothes as soon as possible. You could help her, especially with fecal soiling, but she should also participate. Let her appreciate the "yuckiness" of the act so she has an incentive to do it in the toilet.

Tips On Changing Her Negative Attitude:

Let her watch TV while sitting on the potty chair, or read her a story. Use "stars" as reward for just sitting on the potty. Friendly reminder: if you see her clearly holding a bowel movement, say something like: "You know, your tummy will feel better if you let the poop out. And I'll give you some candy, also." Other inducements: extra TV watching time, tricycle time. Allow her to wear specially designed underpants each day, as long as she keeps them clean.

Washing Up:

She should begin to learn good bathroom habits from the start. Proper wiping after a bowel movement is particularly important for females. Wiping should be done from front to back to keep bacteria from the bowel movement away from the genitals.

Show your child how to throw away the toilet paper and how to wash her hands after wiping. You may want to provide a small, sturdy step stool, so that your child can reach the sink without your help.

Accidents:

They can happen. Do not get upset. CAUSES: Too busy, too tired, ill, under emotional stress.

- Some children want to check out every restroom they encounter even if they do not want to use it. If she wants you to go with her, go! Don't ignore or refuse, otherwise you will be undermining your own procedure.

• Dress for success. If you have ever watched a youngster run to the bathroom, you know that when nature calls on toddlers, every second counts. Choosing the right clothing for a child in toilet training can make all the difference.

• Avoid snaps, zippers, belts, buttons, and unwieldy overall straps that can cause disastrous delays.

• Outfit your child with pants that have an elastic waist or Velcro closures so they will come right off with a good tug.

• Be sure to take a change of clothes (or two) on long outings, just in case.

Final Pointers:

Remember that there are three things you can never make your child do: eat, sleep, or go to the bathroom.

Try not to overuse words that will make your child think of her bodily functions as being dirty (such as "sticky," "yucky").

BEDWETTING OR NOCTURNAL ENURESIS

Up until the age of five in girls, and six years in boys, it is considered normal for children to wet the bed at night. It is clear that daytime dryness is achieved much earlier, around the age of three years. As a practical definition then, it can be said that a child has enuresis if a girl is older than five years of age, or if a boy is older than six.

Eighty percent of enuretic children have **primary enuresis.** These are kids who were never dry at night, or who have not been dry for six months or longer.
Primary enuresis is a result of the immaturity of the child's bladder control.

Secondary enuresis is when a child was dry for a period of six months or more and then begins to wet again. Secondary enuresis is usually due to some emotional upheaval in the life of the youngster: an impending move to another city or state, divorce of her parents, etc.

Enuresis is considered more a social behavior problem than a disease. Parents don't like it when their child is a bedwetter since they have to change wet, smelly sheets, etc., but children don't like it either. Their self-esteem may suffer.

Treatment is important to prevent serious emotional problems. The child should be seen first by her physician to rule out any other urinary problems. If there are no other causes for this problem, then the patient and her family must be reassured that there are no physical abnormalities. The family needs to understand that the condition is self-limited, that it is not the child's fault. She is not wetting the bed to "get back at" the parent; the condition is strictly involuntary.

The most successful treatment at present is the bedwetting alarm. This alarm has a "buzzer" that is connected by wires to the child's underwear. When the child starts to urinate, the alarm sounds a loud noise. The noise wakes the child who then stops urinating, gets up and evacuates in the restroom. With time, the alarm may be discontinued with no bedwetting recurrences. Treatment consists of drugs, which seems to be effective in certain children.

Recently, a new drug, similar to the anti-diuretic hormone which inhibits the loss of water through the kidneys, was introduced. It is a liquid medicine which is deposited inside the patient's nostrils. This treatment is very expensive and should probably be reserved for those children who have not responded to the previous therapies.

THE FIRST ADOLESCENCE

The "Terrible Two's":

When your toddler starts shouting "No! No!" at you, even though you asked her a simple question or gave her a mild command, when she throws herself on the floor, and cries or screams . . . she has entered the "terrible two's" or the "First Adolescence." She might not be 2 years old yet; she may be 15, 18 or 20 months. Some children start earlier than others, and some don't ever enter this phase or show a very mild change.

This is an emotional, transitional stage between babyhood and the more mature child of three, similar to the adolescence of the teenage years, which is a transition between childhood and adulthood.

The Main Goal Of Two-Year-Olds And Adolescents: Autonomy Both stages are full of turmoil and emotional disequilibrium.

During toddlerhood, your child is usually calm, well behaved, "a pleasure to have around" (stage of equilibrium). During the terrible two's she is a "little monster," usually NOT a pleasure to have around (stage of disequilibrium). In spite of your child's rebellion and negativism, this is a POSITIVE STAGE for her. Without it, she would remain a baby forever.

Two year olds are rigid, inflexible and demanding. A two-year-old wants something and she wants it now! She wants things done HER way! She is very contrary. She loves to give orders. She enjoys her roles as "Queen of the house." She frustrates easily. Her mood will go from one extreme to the other. Decisions are hard to make. She is persistent. She will go on and on, pestering Mom if she wants something, like a "broken record."

Why does she rebel against her parents? During this phase she is learning to achieve a real sense of her own unique selfhood. Unless she challenges or negates her parents' authority, she won't develop her own identity.

Also, like teenagers do, she will be, at times, determined to do something for herself (i.e. try to dress herself) and at other times she will proclaim herself "a baby," and Mom will have to dress her. She is struggling between her desire to be independent and her desire to hold on to her babyish dependence from Mother.

Before going any further, I would like to tell you, how NOT to handle your two-year-old.

Parents should avoid OVER-CONTROLING her. If you are constantly frustrating her by saying, "No, don't touch that!", "No, don't go there!" you are thwarting her desires to explore the world, to feel things, to throw them, squeeze them, etc. In general, if you are consistent in this kind of technique, you will raise a child who will be a very timid, unaggressive adult or one who will learn to be "sneaky," or hostile. She will learn to keep her hostility inwards, but she will release it whenever "nobody is watching." She might become a self-righteous, narrow-minded moralist, full of hostility inside.

"The Brat Syndrome" is the result of the other extreme. Parents who are OVER-PERMISSIVE, always giving in to the child's demands, often produce "brats."

Feelings And Actions:

109

These terms are self-explanatory. It is very important for a parent to realize that children can learn to control their actions, but they cannot (and should not be made to) control their feelings. A young child's feelings should be allowed to COME OUT. Even negative feeling (anger and hostility). Repressed feelings may be conducive to mental illness.

Reasonable limits should be set to help guide children's actions.

Where Do You Draw The Limits?

In part it depends on how important you feel the action is. If a child wants to touch a hot stove, run across a busy street, etc., obviously the limits must be very narrow.

A general rule is that the limits be reasonable and consistent:

Not setting any limits or setting too many of them is probably wrong. A happy medium should be found, based on circumstances, temperament of parent, child, etc. During her first adolescence, a toddler should have very few limits, because her nature is to explore her environment. To avoid too many "Nos" from her parents, the house should be child-proofed, adapted to the child.

The Feedback Technique (Active Listening- A.L.):

When your child refuses to do something or refuses to stop something that you want her to stop doing, you listen and carefully try to "decide" or understand her words; then, you send back your interpretation of her feelings. For instance, if Lisa refuses to return Scott's teddy bear to him, you tell her something like: "You're upset because you'd like to continue playing with the teddy bear." You are "mirroring" or "feeding your child back" her feelings. Notice that the parent doesn't repeat the child's words, you try to guess what feeling the child is conveying: anger, frustration, etc.

Children sometimes will be angry with you. Your gut reaction may be to tell her: "Shut up! You don't say that to your Dad!" Of course, that's how many of today's parents have been brought up. However, it is much healthier to allow your child to get her feelings out, then you can deal with them in a positive way. Remember that we separate feelings from actions. If, following a few defiant or offensive words against you, the child starts kicking you, that is where you restrain her. You control her ACTIONS.

Expressing angry feelings is like letting out steam. This will allow her to control her behavior better.

In the example above, Lisa refuses to give up Scott's teddy bear. You may give her five or ten more minutes to play with it. After that, you tell her again to give it back. You reflect her feelings: "I know you don't want to give up the teddy bear; you'd like to keep playing with it. You're having so much fun you don't want to give it up!" At that point, you take the teddy bear from her and give it to Scott. Lisa screams, hits. You pick her up, still reflecting her feelings: "You're mad with Mommy because you want to keep playing with teddy bear."

By taking the teddy bear away from Lisa, this mother didn't allow her to get away with her wish and become a TYRANT. On the other hand, if Mother had not allowed Lisa to ventilate her feelings, and realize that Mommy DID UNDERSTAND THEM, her self-esteem would have suffered.

One caveat for parents to avoid, is the two-year-old who shows verbal negativism but who actually will say yes with his actions. A typical example is when Mom tells her daughter to wear a coat to go outside; she says "NO, I don't want to!" but at the same time stretches forward her arm for you to put on the coat's sleeve!

Foster Cline divides parents in two categories: 1) Those who assume that things are going fine, unless they hear differently, and 2) Those who assume that things are terrible unless they know differently.

The first type of parents will raise children who will talk to them, because growing children naturally learn to use their mouths; they cry, become upset, etc. The second group will raise children who won't talk to them during adolescence. These parents assume that things aren't OK, and so the children develop a response pattern that says: "I'm not going to tell you anything that is going on in my life. If you want to know, try to find out!"

This reciprocal relationship, according to Cline, develops, or "locks in," between the ages of 5 to 28 months. Worried parents raise worrisome children. Anxious parents raise anxiety-ridden children, etc.

Modeling:

111

Modeling is when parents put themselves first. The child then learns to do the same.

Controlling:

Controlling parents say NO seldom, only if the problem is life-threatening or if it affects the parent directly. Controlling parents say NO only once. The parent thinks: "I'll take care of myself first."

Confrontations:

AVOID them. If you can't, WIN. Pick the right issue.
For instance: Parents usually lose when they try to make their children eat or become toilet trained.

How To Make An Obnoxious Child:

Take a typical two-year-old during the terrible two's, throwing temper tantrums, being demanding. Add a weak, anxious parent (a parent who puts herself last). The result is worse, recurrent bad behavior, an obnoxious kid who feels GUILTY and has a POOR SELF-IMAGE. The child has learned to put herself last.

If a child behaves in a persistently antagonistic way, (i.e. she continues to play with the TV knobs, or worse yet, she keeps banging the TV tube with an object, or she kicks you or another child, or she places herself in a dangerous situation) then you must discipline her. Don't let your child harass you!

One basically follows the advice given below "Managing Temper Tantrums": use Time out, or Spanking, etc. If she is in danger, of course, you first remove her from it.

Temper Tantrums:

They represent the maximum degree of negative behavior. The child is so mad that all she can do is cry, scream, kick, throw herself on the floor, etc. The two- year-old has trouble with controls. She can only think and act in terms of ME. She focuses on what SHE wants: to run, feed, say a word, etc. She doesn't care much about the world she lives in. But, she cannot do all the things she wants to do. That frustrates her. She can't wait. She is indecisive, she'd like to run on her own, but she'd also like to stay around Mom. She can't decide and, frustrated, she goes to pieces: She has a temper tantrum.

You, the parents, might feel frustrated, angry or scared. You may start to wonder whether it's your fault. Don't feel bad; it's not your doing. Almost all youngsters have temper tantrums between the ages of one and four and then they stop. These temper tantrums are normal. When children older than four have temper tantrums, this is not normal. The child is a "brat," "spoiled."

Temper tantrums seem to happen only when parents are around. That's because they don't like to "act out" their feelings in front of strangers.

Temper tantrums may be triggered by different causes: she may become frustrated with some manual task she is trying to master. She might not be able to climb a stair, or get down from a chair, or put two things back together. This frustration builds up and finally she explodes in a temper tantrum.

The "attention-getting" temper tantrum is self-explanatory. First adolescents many times throw a temper tantrum to get their way: they want to play with a breakable or dangerous object, they want to eat before dinner is ready, or want candy, or want to go outside when it is raining. At other times, they may be hungry, overtired, or ill. Sometimes nobody knows why a child throws a temper tantrum; she probably wants to test her parents' rules and limits. She is not trying to make your life miserable. A child's outburst can be interpreted as a sign that she trusts her parents and feels safer in trying to assert herself.

A child throwing a temper tantrum may be trying to express her feelings. She is acting out her fear, distress or pain. Remember that first adolescents have had to learn many things in a few months: how to make their wishes known, whom they can trust, when to sleep, when to be awake, how to make their wishes known. Each new day is a new lesson they have to learn. Trying to control temper is a social lesson that is hard to learn.

General Guidelines To Manage The First Adolescents:
(or: How to Handle Her Normal "Negativism", Stubbornness, and Defiance.)

If your two year old answers your request with "No!", do not take it very seriously or personally. She probably means: "Do I have to ?" She is not being disrespectful. She's trying to assert her self-determination and identity. Don't respond to this "no" with punishment. Remember, we do not want to suppress her feelings, only her negative actions. Therefore, ignore her, unless she is about to do something dangerous.

Whenever possible, give her CHOICES. For example, let's say she wants to eat a fruit which you don't have in the house. Say: "We don't have bananas. Do you want an apple or a plum?" Or say: "We don't have any books about dragons. Do you want the one about Mickey Mouse, or the Dumbo book?" If she refuses to take a bath, say: "Do you want me to bathe you, or do you want to bathe yourself?" In this fashion, your first adolescent gets the feeling that she is a decision-maker. If there are no choices, don't give her any! Some things are NOT NEGOTIABLE: dangerous things, taking a bath, going to nursery school, to bed, etc. Instead of saying "Lets go to bed, OR ELSE!!", say: "Let's go to bed," and take her by her hands, or help her to get up, or start yourself walking in the direction of her room.

Always forewarn her that "time to eat," or "time to go to bed" is coming. If she is playing, she will resent being pulled suddenly from her pleasurable activity. "In five minutes, it will be time to stop playing and come sit down for dinner."

Keep your "Nos" to a minimum. Don't over control: avoid too many rules.

Remember also to use "environmental control." In other words, child-proof your home. Avoid long trips, or else prepare yourself before.

Don't try to be perfect. No matter how hard you try, your child will have temper tantrums, either minor or major ones.

Help your youngster put away her toys. Employ fun "clean-up" games. Show her where she CAN throw the ball, instead of against the WINDOW.

Remove your child from dangerous, "tempting" places, like the kitchen, the living-room (where expensive knick-knacks are), or else stay there with her to make sure she won't get into trouble.

Preventing Impending Temper Tantrums:

Watch out for certain times of the day, when your child may be more prone to having a temper tantrum, like when she is tired, or if she is hungry.

If she seems to be getting frustrated with something or someone, intervene by redirecting her attention to something else, or offer her some other object or toy.

Managing Temper Tantrums:

First of all, try to remain calm. If you shout at her, she will scream louder in response. Do not get angry at her, and NEVER SPANK.

With a small child, the parent could initially try to embrace her (especially if the temper tantrum is due to frustration). Hold her as tightly as possible, while saying soothing, comforting words, feedback words. However, if this doesn't work, or if the temper tantrum is directed against the parent, then the child must be left alone. In other words: IGNORE HER, WALK AWAY OUT OF HER SIGHT. You remove the "audience" from the "actor." Do not try to stop the temper tantrum or talk to her. Once a temper tantrum starts, it can't be stopped.

Giving in to the child at this point would reinforce her behavior so that she will continue to do this in the future. Don't try to reason with her, and don't spank her. Walk away out of her sight, and stay away. Do this even if she tends to have "breath-holding spells." Some children stop breathing during a temper tantrum; they may even turn blue. She will resume breathing after a while. I've never heard of any toddler who died asphyxiated due to a breath-holding spell. Do not offer any bribes for stopping this behavior: you will only reinforce this negative behavior.

Do not do anything differently if the child throws a temper tantrum in front of neighbors or relatives. Never mind what they think. If you're at a neighbor's house or in a public place, pick her up and leave. If you can't leave, ANTICIPATE the tantrum by going to the supermarket with your husband, for instance, who can then help so you can finish the shopping. Or, shop at a time when you know your child is less prone to a temper tantrum.

If possible, try to find out the "why" of the temper tantrum. Sometimes, by knowing why your child is throwing a tantrum, you could also anticipate, and prevent it. *Do* reward your child when she seems to be controlling her outbursts. A kiss, a hug, a few words of praise for her actions.

The First Adolescence is the ideal time to teach a child about dangerous things: running in the street, hot things, electric outlets,

115

etc. Also, it's time to control her dangerous behavior: hitting, biting, temper tantrums, before they become a habit.

During toddlerhood-first adolescence, children learn about the "established order of the physical world": a place for things, a time to come and go, concepts of how things "work."

Her desire for independence should be encouraged. The release of her feelings should be fostered. Every time she tries to do or say something new, let her try.

Give her love and respect. Start teaching her what is right, but only things she can comprehend. For instance, she won't understand about being polite, but she will understand gradually that biting or hitting hurts people. At this age, parental approval is very important to her. You can always bring her back to the right track because she wants your approval .

Minor Temper Tantrums:

These are best IGNORED:

• Crying and screaming for attention.
• Whining to get attention.
• Slamming doors, pounding or kicking the floor, wall, or door (unless damage results).
• Sticking her tongue out at you, making faces.

The "Cannot Be Ignored Tantrum":

• Hitting, kicking parent or others.
• Throwing things.
• Prolonged screaming or yelling.
• Temper tantrum in a public place.
• Clinging, or otherwise "hassling" you.

To treat any of the above tantrums: physically restrain her, and use TIME OUT. Remove her from the situation. For head-banging, some doctors recommend throwing a glass of water in the child's face at the beginning of the temper tantrum and then the parent should leave the room.

Some Comments On Discipline :

First of all, it is hard to be a (reasonably) GOOD PARENT! You can read books about discipline until you go blind and still be

116

confused as to how you could be a good parent. Parents are human; they are not God. Parents will make mistakes and lose control at times. But if a parent genuinely loves his child, works at trying to be a good parent, and sets a good example to his child (i.e., she is honest, caring, etc.), then, most likely, the child will turn out O.K.

Remember that no discipline method works all the time. In some situations, you might have to use a combination of methods. Children are different: some are "easier" than others. DO NOT HAVE TOO HIGH EXPECTATIONS, either for yourself, or for your child. Otherwise, guilt may be the end result. Guilt is useless, and it doesn't help. It may in fact, be counterproductive. Just realize that you, as a parent, are human and you are going to make mistakes.

TO HELP YOU DEVELOP GOOD PARENTING SKILLS:

1. Attend Parenting Classes. Both parents need to be informed, and it is much better if you both share the same parenting goals and methods. By reading books on discipline and attending parent classes together, you're using wisdom. It's much easier to prevent undesirable behavior patterns than to correct them after they have developed.

2. Do Not Be Afraid Of Conflicts. Conflicts may be educating. They are part of any healthy relationship. Conflicts are likely to appear when you start a new discipline technique. It will take time for your child to adjust to it.

3. When Trying To Discipline Your Child, Attack Only One Issue At A Time. It's much easier.

4. Try To Avoid Indifference toward your child. Both mothers and fathers must be involved, loving, and nurturing to their children. It takes time and energy to raise a healthy child. Overindulgence also must be avoided; this shows that the parent is too preoccupied to prove to his child that he loves her. Therefore, he buys her things, often, too many of them.

5. Spend Quality Time With Your Child. This is very important and worth remembering. The child will feel loved and appreciated. Whenever we spend time with our children, we are telling them, "You are enjoyable. You are an important person." You don't have to be doing anything special with your child — just sitting together, listening to her, looking through a window, or reading a book together. It may not come spontaneously, especially if you are a very busy person. Do try, though. Make an extra effort. You'll be repaid a thousand times!

6. If We Respect Other People, our children will learn this behavior; such training is called "modeling." Our respect becomes the child's respect. If the child receives no respect from us, she cannot respect herself or others. No child can give back what she hasn't received.

7. Do Not Push Your Child. Pressuring children into acting, dressing, or achieving a skill before they are ready can be too stressful for them. A fruit that is not ripe doesn't taste good. Let her be a child while she can.

8. Try To Be Friendly Toward Your Child, even if her behavior is not right at the moment. If you tell her, "You're a pest. You're acting just like a little baby" you are calling her names and labeling your child. This is very bad for a child's self-esteem. You become her judge. Instead, say, "I am very busy right now. I cannot be interrupted until I finish this work." This limits the behavior without labeling the child. The child thinks, "Daddy is busy now," instead of, "I'm a baby. I'm bad."

9. It Is Very Important To Teach Our Children To Be Ethical, to know the difference between right and wrong. Parents have the major responsibility in this. Church and school play a role, but parents should be the main source of teaching these values. We teach them mostly by our example —by being ethical and doing the right things ourselves.

Thumbsucking: If your thumbsucking child is less than five years, you should not try to make him discontinue this most -- at this age -- helpful, harmless habit. For those children older than five, there is a new book out called *David Decides About Thumbsucking* ($7.95, in many bookstores or contact "Reading Matters," P.O. Box 300309, Denver, CO 80203), written by Dr. Susan M. Heitler, a psychotherapist. This is an upbeat and brightly illustrated story about how five-year-old David decided to stop sucking his thumb.

Heitler says the story should be read to children five and older and is aimed at creating a cooperative climate for helping a child decide to stop. Heitler puts the emphasis on cooperative. "The child must understand why it is best for him or her to stop sucking, and the desire to stop must be a part of the child's thinking," she says.

"The sucking impulse is essential to life," Heitler says in the parents' part of her book. It is a newborn's reflexive response to suck any nipple-shaped object that brushes her cheek or lips, and without it he or she would starve.

Sucking comforts an irritable infant, helps a hungry one wait to be fed and cuts down on fussing when the tot is tired, Heitler says. "SUCKING ON FINGERS, THUMBS, TOES AND TOYS IS HEALTHY AND NORMAL IN INFANCY AND SHOULD NOT BE A CAUSE FOR ALARM," Heitler concludes.

In toddlers ages one to three, sucking can help the child adjust to a rapidly expanding world, Heitler says, and tends not to cause dental or social harm. It is in the preschooler stage, three to five-years-old, that sucking *could* start to cause problems. "Occasional sucking is unlikely to harm teeth or mouth shape if the child does not suck strongly," Heitler says "But vigorous, frequent sucking on thumbs or fingers *could* profoundly alter the growth of the face, the shape of the mouth and the angles of teeth." *However, some dental experts do not believe thumbsucking is able to cause permanent deformities except in extreme conditions.*

Potential problems include overbite, cross bite (in which the roof of the mouth gets pushed upward and the sides narrow or "tongue thrust" (sealing the mouth for swallowing by thrusting the tongue forward against the lips, thereby putting pressure on the front teeth). Speech problems also can be caused by sucking at this age, she says.

If a child continues to suck on into school age, there is also the danger of more infectious diseases caused by germs the child transmits into the mouth.

Sucking usually is not a sign of emotional disturbance, unless the child sucks in isolation for long periods.

As permanent teeth arrive, habitual sucking inevitably causes serious dental consequences. "Unattractive teeth and bite positions will no longer improve spontaneously once permanent teeth have erupted," Heitler warns.

By age five, a child can understand the consequences of sucking and can make the decision to stop. The parents, in addition to giving support and showing appreciation, will find that concrete rewards tend to be a more powerful incentive, Heitler says.

She recommends keeping a chart that will show the child his or her progress. The younger a child is, the more frequent the rewards should be, and Heitler cautions that a reward program should not be launched until the child is sufficiently motivated.

A bandage can be placed on a child's thumb to make him or her more conscious of sucking and a mitten or sock over the child's hand can prevent sucking while the child sleeps.

Solid Foods for babies: Which ones to avoid.

Because of their tendency to trigger allergies, it is best to avoid until one year of age the following foods: **egg whites, fish, corn, pork, berries, etc.**   Hard to digest foods: **bacon, sausage, fried foods, gravy, highly spicy foods, whole kernel corn.**

Do not start, until age nine or ten months: **citrus fruits (tomatoes, oranges, grapefruit).**

Honey should not be given to infants *at all.* A condition called infant botulism may be caused by honey contaminated with a bacteria called C.Botulinum.

Home-prepared spinach, beets, turnips, carrots, or collard greens should be avoided because they may contain sufficient *nitrate* to cause methemoglobinemia (a type of anemia).

Other foods not recommended before one year of age:

- **uncooked apples or pears** (controversial). The peel should be removed, because its fibrous content is hard to digest by infants.
- **"cured" meats (wieners, bacon)** because they have high amounts of nitrites.
- **whole grapes, nuts, hard candy, etc** (danger of choking).
- **Canned adult foods:** best avoided because lead is used to solder these cans. Foods made especially for infants contain no lead and are therefore safer. Adult canned foods also contain too much salt and preservatives.

The following foods should not be started until age two: **nuts, popcorn, peanut butter.** Reasons: the possibility of choking.

Cardinal Rules: **Always start one new food at a time, and give it for four to five days.** If the baby is allergic to that particular food, he will develop a rash, or vomit or he may have diarrhea. Then it is easy to identify the offender which should, therefore, be withheld. Cereals are usually mixed with formula or breast milk. Juices also may be used. Mix well and avoid giving a mixture that is too thick, especially at the beginning.

Should the second or third food be of the same kind as the first? Not necessarily. You may go from cereal to a fruit, then to a vegetable, then to juice (although juices are obviously not solid foods, they are included here because this is a good time to get started with them), then a meat, then back to another cereal, etc.

120

CHAPTER 10

GROWTH AND DEVELOPMENT, HEARING, VISION, SPEECH

It is not possible to set up rigid standards for your baby's growth; since he grows at his own individual pace, he may reach the stages outlined below earlier or later than the suggested ages, so do not be surprised or disturbed at variations in either direction.

First Month

Hearing is fully developed, but eyes do not focus and may appear crossed. Yawns often; hiccups, sneezes. Hands are tightly curled; head needs support. Sleeps most of the time when not being fed. Smiles at mother.

Second Month

Turns head in direction of voices. Cries vary for food, discomfort and excitement. May begin to sleep through the night. Settles into regular routine.

Third Month

Smiles, babbles; learns that crying gets results. Holds up head when one lifts him up by pulling from hands, and can turn from side to back. Enjoys bright colors and can hold toy if placed in hand.

Fourth Month

Holds up head without support. Coos and smiles in response when addressed. Reaches for toes. Plays with hands and can grasp toys.

Fifth Month

Birth weight usually doubled by now. Reaches for object; carries everything to mouth. More selective in taste. Can turn from back to side; raises hands to show desire to be lifted.

Sixth Month

Eyes and hands work together. Sits with some propping. Definite emotions. Makes sounds like "Ma-ma," Da-da.". First teeth may appear, usually the lower ones.

Seven To Eight Months

Sits without support. May start crawling. Transfers toys from hand to hand. Associates ideas with words. Probably can start drinking from cup.

Nine To Twelve Months

Crawls, stands without support, may take first steps. Can say a word or two; understands many. Probably has six to eight teeth. Triples birth weight.

Twelve To Fifteen Months

Uses spoon, spills little. May remove clothes. "Da-da", "Ma-ma" (knows meaning). May point to one named part of her body. May walk up steps. May stack two blocks.

Fifteen To Eighteen Months

Says three words, other than "Ma-ma, Da-da." Throws ball overhand. May stack four blocks. Kicks ball forward. Walks up steps.

Eighteen To Twenty-Four Months

Puts on clothing. Washes and dries hands. Plays "hide-and-seek." Says two word sentences. May say 50 words. May build a tower of eight blocks. May pedal tricycle.

Twenty-Four To Thirty-Six Months

May recognize three out of four colors. May give first and last names. Copies a circle, vertical line. Eight block tower. Pedals tricycle.

SIMPLIFIED DEVELOPMENTAL CHART *
(Or "Must-Pass" Milestones)

By 2 Months:
• Must smile to you in response to your smiling, talking or waving to him.
• Equal movements of all extremities (no jerks, etc.)
• Responds to bell (startles).
• Cooing.

By 4 Months:
• Smiles spontaneously (not just in response to you).
• Follows past midline: When he is shown an object or a light, with baby lying down, he focuses on it and follows it from one side to the other. The midline is an imaginary line that divides his right from his left side.
• On stomach, holds head up at 90 degrees from horizontal.

By 6 Months:
• Sitting: head should be steady.
• While child lies on his stomach, he is able to support chest off table with arms.
• Rolls over both ways.
• One is able to pull infant to a sitting position without infant's head lagging.
• Coos, laughs, squeals, grunts for different needs and to show feelings.
• Notices pellet or raisin.

By 9 Months:
• Sits without any support steadily.
• Bears some weight on his legs (hold him with your hands under his arms).
• Turns his head towards your voice (soft, not loud).
• Must "babble."
• Transfer cube, toy, from one hand to the other.
• Feeds self crackers.

By 12 Months:
• Able to sit up from a lying down position.
• Says "Ma-ma," "Da-da" (doesn't know the meaning).
• Able to grab pellet or raisin with any part of thumb and index finger.

By 15 Months:
• Walks well. (Absolute maximum age: 18 months)
• Stands alone well.
• Says "Ma-ma," "Da-da" (knows meaning)
• Plays "pat-a-cake."
• Says one word (other than "Ma-ma," "Da-da"). (Absolute max: 18 months).
• Bangs two cubes held in hand.
• Pincer grasp (perfect). (Grasps object with tip of index and big fingers.)

By 18 Months:
• Plays ball with Mom or Dad.

By 24 Months:
• Can walk up steps.
• Says three words other than "Mama," "Dada."
• Uses spoon, spills only very little.

* NOTICE: Parents, please report to your doctor if your child fails two or more items in the above list.

HEARING

Parents of an infant or young child want to know if she is hearing well.

Some medical information and risk factors, when present, are important in determining this. If the history is positive, parents should watch their child carefully or consult their child's doctor:

• A family history of hearing loss.
• A history of illness or use of drugs in the mother during pregnancy, prolonged labor or premature birth.
• The presence of other birth defects in the child.
• The child had meningitis or recurrent ear infections, allergies, scarlet fever.

The following observations by parents are important:

1. By about **four months of age** she should be able to respond to the sound of a bell rung behind her by either stopping her movements, especially of the face (called "alerting") or crying

("startle"). She should also be able to laugh aloud, "coo", squeal, and say "Ah-goo."

2. Between **four and six months of age**, she should turn her head towards the direction of a voice, or towards the side where a bell is rung behind her and on either side. She might babble and say "Da-da, "Ma-ma", although at this age she still does not know the meaning.

3. Between **six months and one year,** she waves bye-bye, understands the word "no," imitates noises.

4. Between **one and two years,** she says anywhere from one word to fifty, she follows commands, points to several body parts, counts numbers from one to five by age 2. Also by age 2 she should also be able to combine two different words, (i.e. "baby sick").

Can my baby SEE?

A **four month-old** infant should
  —Regard your face when you are close to her
  —Smile in response to your smile and also spontaneously
  —Follow visually an object past the midline
  —Follow visually an object about 180°

An **eight month old** fails if she:
  —Does not smile spontaneously
  —Does not turn to the side of a loud noise.
  —Doesn't make raspberries with her mouth
  —No squeals, no laughing aloud, and no cooing
  —Does not play "Ah-goo"
Do not panic or draw final conclusion on your own! Ask for an appointment at your child's doctor's office

Is my child's SPEECH developing well?

Your child's doctor, of course, will tell you whether or not speech is developing well.

A **six month old** who:
  —Doesn't "Coo" or "Laugh aloud" or "Squeal" could have a delayed speech

A **ten month old** fails if she does not do the above plus does not say "da-da" or "ma-ma" (nonspecific) does not "turn to a voice" or

125

"turn to the side where a loud noise is coming from. (Her speech may be delayed secondary to an impaired hearing or other causes, see below.)

A **fifteen month old** toddler should (besides the above milestones)
>—Say at least one word other than "Ma-ma/Da-da" (nonspecific)
>—"Ma-ma/Da-da" (specific)
>—Follow one-step commands, accompanied with gestures.
>—Understands the word "No" (without gestures)
>—Wave "bye-bye"

If you think you child's speech is delayed, you should consult your pediatrician. Your child will probably need a medical/speech workup (see below).
Your baby's doctor will have to decide first if her speech is indeed delayed. It could be that you expect too much of her. For instance, if your baby has not yet said one word (other than ma-ma/da-da) at age one year, this is normal.
If your baby's **expressive language**[1] is indeed delayed, but her **receptive language**[2] is not, your baby could be
>a) a late bloomer, or
>b) have a real speech delay. In either case a speech specialist should be consulted.
If both her receptive and expressive language are delayed, then her hearing should be tested. If hearing is O.K., then her problem may be due to:
>1) *An environmental problem:* understimulation, child neglect, maternal depression, deaf parent, etc.
>2) *A problem in the "brain":* cerebral palsy, autism, mental retardation, severe trauma or asphyxia, or severe infection, etc.
>3) *Speech disorders:* a complex group of speech problems. The main problem is poor intelligibility of the speech.

"The Rule of Fours": By one year, 1/4 (25%) of the child's speech should be intelligible (understood) by main caretaker. By two years, 1/2 (50%) of speech should be understood by main caretaker. By three years, 3/4 or 75% of speech should be understandable and by age four, 100% of the child's speech should be understandable.

1 **Expressive language:** When the child speaks, makes sounds, or points.
2 **Receptive language:** The child's response to a sound, voice, etc.

126

CHAPTER 11

ACCIDENTS, POISONS, SAFETY, ETC.

ACCIDENT PREVENTION

Accidents are the number one killer of children, and most happen in your own home.

Please try to prevent FALLS, BURNS, AND POISONINGS.

Medicines:
Don't just put your medicines "on a high shelf." Children can reach anywhere! Lock your medications. This is the only way to prevent kids from reaching them.

Cuts: Put all sharp objects away.

Car Accidents:
Use the proper restraints and above all, set an example by strapping yourself in the car. For more information regarding the proper restraint for your child, ask your doctor, or write: "Physician's for Automotive Safety," 50 Union Ave., Irvington, New Jersey 07111.

Be Always Safety Conscious.
The emphasis is on PREVENTION. Teach your children to do things safely. Show them how sharp a knife can be. Show them what fire and heat are like.

Get the superb book: *A Sigh of Relief.* It includes all major emergencies and is very easy to read.

POISONS IN THE HOME

Remember that preschool children like to put things in their mouths. Store all potential poisons out of their reach, all the time. Cabinets and drawers with locks are a necessity.

Check your kitchen shelves and under the sink for any of the following cleaning supplies and polishing agents. They could be dangerous to your child, so lock these items up:

127

Lye	Rug cleaner	Metal polish
Ammonia	Wallpaper cleaner	Dry cleaning fluid
Disinfectant	Laundry ink	Oven cleaner
Detergent	Furniture polish	Toilet bowl cleaner
Drain cleaner	Furniture wax	Grease remover
Bleach	Fire extinguishing fluid	

Check your bathroom for the following items and make sure they are locked away from your child:

Shampoo	After-shave lotion	Hair spray & lotions
Deodorant	Nail polish	Hair dye and tints
Perfume	Nail polish remover	Wave solution or hair
Sun tan lotion	Skin preparations	Depilatory

Lock up all medicines, including those for:

Fever	Weight reduction	Antiseptics
Colds	Arthritis	Vitamins
Cough	Eye disorders	Iron
Sleep	Heart disorders	Paregoric
Nervousness	"Pep" drugs	Rubbing alcohol
Seizures	Constipation	Many creams & ointments

Are the following on your table top or within easy reach:

Medicine	Many house plants	Wax crayons
Lighter fluid	Shoe polish	Ink

Check your storeroom, garage and basement for these items, all of which should be locked up:

Painting supplies:

Paint	Paint thinner	Turpentine
Varnish	Paint remover	Putty

Pesticides:

Insecticide	Insect repellant	Roach & rodent poison
Moth balls	Weed killer	Plant spray or powder

Others:

Gasoline	Glue	Charcoal lighting fluid

Antifreeze   Auto polish   Kerosene

Keep your child away from these yard plants:

Cherry	Castor bean	Lily of the Valley
Oleander	Jimson weed	Mushroom
Foxglove	Privet	Rhododendron
Laurel	Poppy	Hydrangea

Many other substances are also poisonous. Call your doctor or the Poison Control Center immediately if you do not know whether a material your child has swallowed is harmful. Always keep Ipecac syrup in your home to give if so advised by a physician.

FREQUENTLY INGESTED PRODUCTS THAT ARE USUALLY NONTOXIC:
(unless ingested in large amounts)

Abrasives
Adhesives
Antacids
Antibiotics
Baby-product cosmetics
Ballpoint pen ink
Bathtub floating toy
Bath oil (castor oil and
   perfume
Bleach (less than five percent
   sodium hypochlorite)
Body conditioners
Bubble-bath soaps
   (detergents)
Calamine lotion
Candles (beeswax or
   paraffin)
Caps (toy pistols)
   (potassium chlorate)
Chalk (calcium carbon-
   ate)
Cigarettes or cigars
   (nicotine)
Clay (modeling)
Colognes
Contraceptive pills
Corticosteroids
Cosmetics
Crayons (marked AP,

Laxatives
Lipstick
Lubricant
Lubricating oils
Lysol brand
   disinfectant
   (not toilet-bowl
   cleaner)
Magic markers
Makeup (eye, liquid
   facial)
Matches
Mineral Oil
Newspaper
Paint (indoor, latex)
Pencil (lead-graphite,
   coloring)
Perfumes
Petroleum jelly
   (vaseline)
Phenolphtalein
   laxatives (Ex-Lax)
Play-Doh
Polaroid picture
   coating fluid
Porus-tip ink marking
   pens)
Prussian blue
   (feri-cyanide)

CP)
Dehumidifying packets
  (silica or charcoal)
Detergents (Phosphate)
Deodorants
Deodorizers (spray and
  refrigerator)
Elmer's glue
Etch-A-Sketch ingredients
Eye makeup
Fabric softeners
Fertilizer (if no insec-
  ticides or herbicides
  added)
Fish-bowl additives
Glues and pastes
Golf ball (core may
  cause mechanical
  injury)
Grease
Hair products (dyes,
  sprays, tonics)
Hand lotions and
  creams
Hydrogen peroxide
  (medicinal three percent)
Incense
Indelible markers
Ink (black, blue)
Iodophil disinfectant

Putty (less than two
  oz.)
Rouge
Rubber cement
Sachets (essential
  oils, (powders)
Shampoos (liquid)
Shaving creams and
  lotions
Soap and soap
  products
Spackles
Suntan preparation
Sweetening agents
  (saccharin,
  cyclamates)
Teething rings (water
  sterility)
Thermometers
  (mercury)
Thyroid tablet
Toilet water
Toothpaste (with or
  without fluoride)
Vaseline
Vitamins
Warfarin
Watercolors
Zinc Oxide
Zirconium oxide

HEAD INJURIES

Most head injuries (HI) are mild, inconsequential and thus require no treatment.   However, *how does a parent know when a HI is a serious one? When is a parent supposed to panic and call 911 or rush her child to the ER?*

To help you answer these questions, I will classify below the different types of HI based on their severity. Note that these are guidelines only. You should use your own judgment and, if in doubt, call your child's doctor.

A. CALL 911 IMMEDIATELY!.... if your child is or shows:
(Severe Head Injury)
- Unconscious for more than five seconds. †
- Breathing with difficulty (panting, labored breathing).
- Vomiting in quick succession for more than three times
- Clear fluid or blood from ears, nose or mouth.

- Can't move arms/legs (paralysis).†
- Loss of bladder/bowel control.
- Unequal pupils (the dark circle in the center of each eye, one larger than the other.) †
- His scalp --the surface of his head-- appears deformed (especially watch for a depressed, sunken area. A "goose egg" swelling is not usually a sign of trouble.)
- Severe and persistent bleeding from scalp or any other area.

† Signifies that brain injury is occurring.

While You Wait For The Ambulance:

- If breathing has stopped, give mouth-to-mouth resuscitation.
- If there is a loss of consciousness, assume it is a neck injury. DO NOT MOVE THE CHILD!
- If there is an impaled object, i.e. a metal wire, knife, etc in the skull: DO NOT REMOVE! If in the face, remove, watch for bleeding, and stop it by applying pressure.
- If bleeding, apply pressure with a gauze or some other clean cloth.

B. Call Or Go To A Doctor's Office Or ER ... if your child has or shows: *(Moderate Head Injury)*

- An injury due to a motor vehicle accident (MVA), or due to a baseball bat, a fall from a high place such as a tree, roof or ladder.
- A young age: six months or less.
- Loss of consciousness even if it lasted only a few seconds (it indicates *concussion*).
- A headache that is getting worse with time.
- A swelling above or in front of an ear.
- Pupils are unequal in size and/or are unresponsive to a light shone in front of his eyes (pupils normally are reduced in size by a strong light). †
- Mental confusion: he is disoriented, forgetful, etc. †
- That he is acting "sick", "not OK."
- That he can't be aroused from sleep. †
- Speech difficulty.
- Blurred or double vision. †
- Can't move arms or walk. †
- Neck pain.
- Vomiting three or more times. †
- Moderate to severe bleeding from face, scalp, etc.

- Laceration of scalp that needs suturing (apply pressure on the bleeding site).
- Possible child abuse.
- Persistent crying (more than 10 continuous minutes).

C. Wait And Watch...if he: *(Mild Head Injury)*

- Fell from a low height, i.e.from a couch or bed onto a carpeted or wooden floor. A toddler stumbles and falls while not running, etc.
- Is acting O.K.; has no complaints.
- Cried briefly right after fall (less than ten minutes).
- Has a small/moderate size "goose-egg" swelling of the scalp.
- Has no lacerations of the scalp that seem to require stitches.
- Is bleeding only slightly or the bleeding has stopped.

The third situation (C), or *mild head injury* is by far the most common type of HI. As long as your child has no signs of "brain injury" (marked by †), you can continue to watch and wait, UNLESS you are very worried and you would rather his doctor see him. A "goose egg" is a common finding in HI. By itself, it does not have any ominous meaning. Its size is also of limited or no meaning. It does not indicate that there is a skull fracture, for instance.

Q. How do you watch a child who seemingly only has suffered a mild HI?

• Care of the wound if any: soap and water are best. Use an ice pack to decrease the swelling of the scalp. Whether a tetanus shot will be needed is up to his doctor.

• Diet: Start with clear liquids only . If there is no vomiting after a few hours, increase his diet gradually or check with his doctor.

• Pain killers: acetaminophen is OK, but if possible, avoid or check with the doctor's office, because drugs may alter his mental status and therefore hide or somehow alter symptoms.

• Awaken him every two to four hours and check the following:

-- His arousability, i.e. is he easy to wake up? (Note: contrary to popular belief, you don't have to keep awake a child who just had a HI). However, watch him often during sleep. Bad signs: difficult

132

respirations, pale skin. Wake him up: If he arouses easily, OK. If not, call his doctor right away.

    -- The size of his pupils: equal or not? Check during the daytime also. Do they respond to light?

    -- After 24 to 36 hours, you may discontinue the vigil, or follow his doctor's directions.

    -- Call the doctor if: he develops a headache, a fever, vomits more than three times, has unequal pupils, his behavior becomes abnormal or any signs of "brain injury" appear.

Q. When Should A Child With A HI Have A Skull X-ray?

A. Only 1 to 2 percent of HI's result in a broken skull. Most X-rays taken because of a HI are not necessary, except for medico-legal reasons or so called "defensive medicine." However, the decision whether or not to get an X-ray is up to the treating physician. The problem with X-rays is that they show only bones, not the brain. EVEN IF THERE IS NO FRACTURE, SEVERE BRAIN INJURY MAY EXIST, AND VICE VERSA.

Q. My Child Has A Skull Fracture. Is This Serious?

A. Not necessarily. As explained above, the seriousness of a HI does not depend on whether or not there is a skull fracture. For instance, a simple "crack" of the skull heals without treatment. If the child has no symptoms, or minor ones and no "brain injury" signs, then he is most likely alright.

Q. What Is A Depressed Fracture?

A. In this case, a piece of the broken skull is pushing inwards pressing and possibly injuring the brain matter. This is a *complicated* skull fracture and requires immediate care.

Q. What Is A *Concussion*?

A. In a more-than-mild HI, the brain is knocked against the inside of the skull. No bleeding occurs inside the head. The child usually has only a brief loss of consciousness or acts "like in a daze" and may or may not have some vomiting.

PREVENTING HEAD INJURIES

Teach your children safety tips. Think of ways to make the lessons fun. Following a few precautions can help prevent a HI.

At home:
- Never leave an infant alone on a high place such as a table, counter, etc.
- Follow crib safety rules (i.e. side rails always up).
- Do not use bunk beds for children less than five years of age.
- Be careful with walkers: buy only the best quality and watch for stairs, or better yet, install a strong gate at the top of the stairway.
- Prevent falls from windows: Install locks or guards.
- All doors leading to a basement or outdoors should always be securely locked, or an extra latch should be installed away from your children's reach.
- Never let a child less than five or six cross a street by himself (some say even less than nine).
- Do not leave a younger child in the house alone with an older, aggressive sibling.
- Do not have a trampoline in your house regardless of your child's age: They are deadly!

On the playground:

- Play on soft surfaces, such as sand, grass or cedar chips.
- Slide down slides feet-first, never head-first.
- Use both hands when climbing jungle-gyms; never climb when it is wet.
- Teach your child never to jump off the seesaw and never to stand on the board.

Around town:

- Always place your child in a car safety seat and use it properly.
- Wear reflective clothing when riding at night with your child and use reflectors on your bike. Follow bicycle safety rules. Never wear headphones when driving a car or riding a bicycle in traffic: you won't be able to hear other cars or people.
- Look both ways before crossing the street with your child.
- Have your children equipped with quality helmets when riding a bike.
  Look for certifying stickers from the ANSI (American National Standards Institute) or Snell Memorial Foundation. The sticker means the helmet has been properly safety-tested and approved. Make sure the helmet fits well and is properly worn.

Wearing a bicycle helmet can reduce your child's risk of serious injury by 85 percent.

BABY SITTING TIPS

Parents should:
- Check the sitter's references, training and general health in advance.
- Allow the sitter to become acquainted with the child and his routine (feeding, bedtime, etc.) before actually sitting.
- Tell the sitter of any special allergies, medicines or special needs of your child.
- Familiarize the sitter with the house and fire escape routes. Show her where a flashlight is kept in an emergency.
- Provide a number where you can be reached in case of an emergency.

Sitters should:
- Phone for help whenever in doubt.
- Never open the door to anyone not cleared by the parents.
- Never leave a child alone in the house—not even for a minute. Keep your eye on the child at all times.
- Never give food or medicine unless instructed to do so.
- Ask the parents what kind of discipline they prefer you to use, should discipline become necessary.
- Remember that your primary job is to care for the child in a tender, loving way. Older children will probably appreciate some interactive play.

CHILD SAFETY

Reprinted here with permission of Metropolitan Life Insurance Company. Copyright 1990

Child safety—always a concern of parents—should be everybody's business. Accidents claim the lives of more children ages 1 to 14 than the leading diseases combined. Each year millions of children are either hurt or killed by falls, traffic accidents, drowning, burns, firearms, poisoning, choking and suffocation. Prevention requires adult awareness of hazardous conditions and, then, knowing what to do to reduce the dangers. Environment, supervision and teaching are keys to child safety.

Basic to protecting infants and young children is an understanding of their early need to touch, taste, feel and investigate --all necessary for learning. Adult patience and practically constant supervision help babies and young children to learn within the limits of safety. As they grow, youngsters learn not only from what we show and tell them, but also from what we do. So it's up to all of us who care for them to set safe examples.

Naturally curious young children want to explore and try new things. The very qualities that motivate them to learn and master skills can also get them into trouble. It's up to all of us --parents, grandparents, teachers, baby-sitters-- to encourage adventure while helping children to stay out of harm. Start early --even before the baby comes-- to train your powers of observation to become alert to dangers in and around the home.

PROTECTING THE VERY YOUNG

From Birth To 6 Months:

From that very first car ride home from the hospital, safety begins with the use of a good infant car carrier. A parent's arms cannot prevent the baby from being thrown helplessly in a sudden stop. Excellent crash-tested infant carriers are now available to hold baby securely.

As the newborn is lovingly cared for, you need to watch-out for choking on milk or food and for suffocation. Make sure baby's face is free of covers, clothing or anything that might interfere with breathing. The crib mattress should be firm. Don't use pillows. Don't prop the bottle; hold the baby during feeding. After feeding, place the baby on his stomach. In this position, if the baby should vomit, he will be less likely to choke.

Babies soon learn to reach and grab and put things into their mouths. So clear away any sharp objects and things that are easily swallowed -- buttons, pins, beads, coins, small detachable parts on toys. Avoid hanging toys on long cords that could get tangled around the baby's neck. Toys should be too large to swallow, too tough to break and should have no sharp points or edges. Keep the crib or playpen away from tables or dressers that hold perfumes, powder, cosmetics, pills, cigarettes, handbags --anything harmful that the baby might reach out and grab.

To prevent falls, remember that even a new baby can move considerably by kicking and wriggling. In a split second, when your back is turned, a baby can tumble off a bed, sofa or dressing table. So never leave the baby alone on anything from which he could fall. Make sure crib sides are up when not tending the baby.

136

To prevent burns, check baby's bath water with your elbow to make sure it's comfortable, not hot. Never drink hot liquids with baby in your lap. If possible, keep baby out of the kitchen and certainly away from the stove. (When cooking, make it a habit to turn pot handles inward so that hot food cannot easily be spilled.) Put screens in front of fireplaces and heaters.

6 to 12 Months -- Age Of The Crawlers:

Between 6 and 12 months --even sooner-- babies roll over and push backwards and forwards. They learn to sit, creep, crawl, and then pull up to standing. Everything in low places is within reach. It's a good idea to get down on your hands and knees to see the world as your inquisitive, crawling baby explores it. Those low shelves and storage areas frequently hold poisonous substances such as pesticides, weed killers, furniture polish, drain cleaners, bleach, lye, kerosene. Scan tables and shelves in the bedroom and bathroom. All medicines, cosmetics, lotions, razor blades, sewing kits and the like should be well out of reach.

Check for other dangers, too --open stairways, sharp objects, matches and lighters, electrical outlets, stoves, hot pots and pans, heaters, lamps and lamp cords, breakable things. Child-proof your home by removing all these or guarding against those that cannot be removed. If a baby does grab a forbidden object, take it away matter-of-factly, say "no" and, perhaps, divert attention to something else that's safe to play with. Large-size blocks, rubber and plastic rings, large bells and ball, pots and pans, soft plastic measuring cups and spoons, washable cuddle toys (without pin or button eyes) -- all are fine.

Never leave the baby alone in the bath. It takes only seconds to risk drowning.

Age One -- Toddlers And Climbers:

Even before learning to walk, babies can climb. With boundless energy, virtually no fear and a flair for adventure, they easily get into trouble. No high places are safe. Even cabinets above floor level may be within reach. Be sure to use window guards and secure window screens. Keep safety gates latched at the top and bottom of stairs.

Again, water presents a danger. Even shallow water in a bathtub or wading pool can be a hazard if a child slips under.

137

Avoid highly waxed floors and stairways, loose throw rugs and stray toys underfoot. Continue to keep all possible poisons out of reach and locked away. Each year, new drugs and chemicals come on the market. Be sure to read the labels and use child-safe packages and containers. Some household plants, too, are poisonous if eaten. You can check with your library and Poison Control Center.

If, despite precautions, your child does swallow a poisonous substance, call the nearest Poison Control Center, physician, hospital or rescue unit without delay, and follow their instructions. Keep the telephone numbers of these facilities near your phone. If at all possible, have the label or container when you phone (or if you go to the the hospital emergency room), so that the proper treatment for that particular substance can be given quickly.

PROTECTING PRE-SCHOOLERS

Two To Four Years:

Around age two, children know how to do many more things, and seldom sit still for a moment. Turning a doorknob becomes a new skill that may mean trouble unless you lock or latch doors leading to the street or other dangerous places.

Young children enjoy taking things apart and putting them together again. Safe, pull-apart and put-together toys and puzzles are designed for fun and learning, but remember, everything else also fascinates children. So don't let inquisitive fingers touch electrical equipment, mixers and slicers. Watch out for matches and lighters. Since opening and closing drawers and cabinets is great fun, make sure that the contents are harmless.

Continue to be vigilant around water. Never leave a child alone in the bathtub. If out on a boat, be sure the child wears a floatation device.

Two-year olds can follow simple directions, but it's natural for them to resist a steady stream of "don'ts," When there's plenty of absorbing and safe activity indoors and out, the likelihood of getting into trouble is lessened.

Around age three, children have greater understanding and self-control and are usually cooperative. A three-year old is nimble and quick. Teach the child to use handrails. Hold the child's hand

138

when near or crossing the street. Otherwise, he may dart away from you without thinking. Begin to explain the meaning of traffic lights.

Around age 4, children are very active --probably able to ride a tricycle or pedal-car. Teach them to ride only on the sidewalk and away from driveways. When playing ball, throwing and catching, caution the child to "let the ball roll." That is, never run after it when it goes into the street.

Since four-year-olds are great climbers, it's best if they can enjoy doing this in a play area equipped with a sturdy apparatus. When sharing the swings, see-saws and jungle gyms with others, the older ones sometimes get too rough for the little ones. Supervision is necessary.

Five to Seven Years:

Children of five to seven certainly are not babies and don't like to be treated so. Still, you have to be there to help and watch --to offer reminders and suggestions-- then step aside when the child seems to be doing all right.

By age five, a child can hop, skip, and turn somersaults. Outdoors (and sometimes, indoors) he or she enjoys running games such as tag and hide-and-seek. Do not permit play with sharp objects --dart games, knives, pointed scissors or sticks.

If the child has a tricycle or a bike, allow riding only in a safe place away from traffic, out of the street and driveways. Don't allow any play in streets, driveways, garages or tool sheds. Before they go to kindergarten or first grade, children should be taught how to cross the streets. They need to learn to cross on the green light only, and wait at the curb on the red light; to cross only at the corner and to look both ways before crossing. Explain these things when out walking with the child.

When children take the school bus, caution them always to stop and look both ways before crossing the road or highway to and from the bus. They should learn to stand in a safe place while waiting for the bus.

Where there's a pool or wading pool, make sure it's fenced in. Keep a close watch every moment when children are in or around the water. Of course, this is a must at the beach. Children should be taught to swim at an early age, always under adult supervision.

139

In the car: Each year nearly 1,000 children under five years are killed in car crashes. And many thousands are injured. Crash protection begins with use of the infant carrier. For children from one to four years, special car seats that face forward are required. Make sure these have been crash tested. A list of acceptable car seats is available on request with a self-addressed stamped envelope, from the American Academy of Pediatrics, P.O.Box 927, Elk Grove Village, IL 60009-0927.

Children who have outgrown their car seats always should be buckled comfortably into standard lap seatbelts. Make seatbelt use a habit for the entire family. Keep car doors locked. Explain to your child the importance of not distracting the driver. On long trips, take along interesting toys, tapes, books and games to occupy a child.

Reducing the risks to child safety at home, at play, in the car is a very real and effective way to demonstrate love and concern for children.

LEARN CPR

SIGN UP FOR A COURSE AT A LOCAL HOSPITAL

SUNBATHING: Precautions

Small children, especially white, fair-skinned ones, should not be exposed to direct sunlight because they tend to burn easily. Keep your child in the shade or cover his skin. Use long sleeves and hat. Sunscreens only offer relative, not absolute protection from the sun rays. Beware of reflected light. Water, cement and other surfaces may reflect sun rays and burn even if your child is in the shade.

Prevention Of Aging And Skin Cancer:
1. Know your risk factors.
2. USE SUNSCREENS—sunscreens also allow repair of damaged skin.
3. Cover up.
4. Avoid sun between 10 a.m. and 2 p.m.
5. Monthly self-exam for suspicious moles.
6. Yearly exam by physician -- be sure to mention any area you are concerned about.

Recommended Sunscreen SPF: SP 15 or Greater no matter what skin type.

Sunscreen Formulas:
1. Cream or lotion preferred -- they tend to remain on skin better; they are especially good if swimming or sweating.
2. Water-resistant/water proof.
3. Most effective sunscreen -- PABA/benzophenone combination. (Note: It is very rare for children to be allergic to PABA.)
4. Most sunscreens are not tested on children less than six months of age, which is why the labels say "for use in children over six months of age."

Non-Stinging Sunscreens:
1. Ti Screen.
2. Supershade (specifically the non-stinging formula).
3. Sundown (not the ultra protection formula).

CHOKING/SUFFOCATION

By Bandages:

Physicians have been alerted that a bandage placed on an infant's finger after drawing a blood sample can be dangerous. There is at least one report of a baby who, while sucking on his fingers, sucked the bandage off his finger and aspirated it. The infant managed to cough it up, but it could have been dangerous. Parents at home also may be tempted to use bandages for small cuts.

By Labels:

Warning labels placed on the myriad of children's products and toys may be hazardous! The warnings are usually decorative and brightly colored and may or may not be conspicuously displayed. Several infants have been reported to peel these labels off and ingest them or choke on them. Check for and remove all labels on all children's products.

By Balloons:

Young children under the age of three should not be allowed to play with balloons. Young children may chew on the balloon and when it pops, have pieces of the rubber fly down their throat, cutting off their air. Balloons are one of the most dangerous items because the rubber is flexible. Also be careful of other rubber items, such as pacifiers, Saran Wrap, and plastic bags.

By Bean Bag Cushions:

As of early 1991, 31 infants under the age of six months died asphyxiated by lying on soft cushions filled with polystyrene beads. Death occurs because the baby's face is down against the cushion. He breathes through it but the air he exhales becomes trapped in the beads. This same air, now poor in oxygen is inhaled again by the infant which causes asphyxia. In one study, it was thought that up to 25 to 50 percent of SIDS deaths might be due to these cushions. For information, call 800-638-2772.

Automatic Garage Doors:

The Consumer Product Safety Commission reports that 45 children between the ages of 2 and 14 years were trapped and killed under automatic garage doors from March 1982 to June 1990. Others suffered brain damage or serious injuries. The CPSC recommends that automatic doors that do not reverse upon touching an obstacle be replaced by those that do. It is also recommended that this reversing capability be tested often by placing a two inch wooden block on the floor of the garage in the door's path. All A.G.D.'s should meet ANS/UL standard 325-1982. Additional safety may be achieved by installing an automatic "electric eye" near floor level to reverse a closing door automatically when an object, body crosses the door's path.

Also, children should never play with remote garage door openers!

The CPSC warns that artificial fingernail glue remover is poisonous if swallowed. One death has been reported so far. Use press-on artificial nails instead.

Other Accidents:

The latest statistics about accidents (1990), based on visits to 65 hospital emergency rooms in the U.S.A. show that 19,000 children under age 4 years were treated for shopping cart injuries. Baby walkers or jumpers caused injuries in 23,000 children under the same age. Bicycles continue to cause many injuries in children between the ages 5 and 14: almost 330,000 were so injured.

Skateboards caused 54,000 children ages 5 to 14 to be injured, and 60,000 children in the same range were injured while roller skating.

Monkey bars and other playground equipment caused 69,000 children up to the age of 14 to get hurt.

Basketball caused more visits to emergency rooms than football: in the age range from 5 to 24 years, 345,000 people were injured playing basketball and 202,000 playing football.

INFANT WALKERS ARE NOT OKAY!

It is estimated that walkers are found in more than 75 percent of homes with children in this country. Most parents believe that walkers help their infants in two major ways: 1) They help children's motor development; 2) They provide a safe place for babies to play.

In fact, research performed in the last decade shows the opposite. (Note: the statements below apply to "baby bouncers," also).

By making infants push mostly with their extensor leg muscles, instead of their using flexor and extensor muscles equally, walkers make them walk "stiff-legged" and on tiptoes. Walkers also modify babies' center of gravity (they lean forward for support), therefore interfering with their development of normal balance. Walkers prevent babies from developing protective and balancing reflexes, too.

Although crawling is not considered a "must" for proper motor development, experts believe that crawling allows infants to learn to walk. Since crawling is prevented by walkers, then walking may be delayed. Walkers also prevent babies from exploring under and around things, because the walker's frame is in the way.

As for safety, the Consumer Product Safety Commission (CPSC) estimates that every year 16,000 children receive emergency room care for injuries related to walker use.

The most common accidents are falls and tip-overs. The extent of the injuries vary from pinched or burned fingers (i.e. falling against a fireplace), to severe head injuries. Babies in walkers have more access to hazards, such as dangling electrical cords, pot handles, and table-cloth edges.

Falls down a staircase may not be prevented by safety gates. Because walkers allow babies to move at high speeds they can force the gate to open or break.

If you feel that your child "hates to be lying on the floor," or "loves to stand," use an infant swing, or a seat with a safety belt. To enhance floor play, give her a nonbreakable flat mirror, a pat-mat, or a play quilt, push toys, riding toys, etc.

PLEASE, HELP SPREAD THE WORD:
WALKERS ARE NOT OK!

Use of Industrial (5 Ga) Buckets
in Homes is Hazardous
to Infants and Toddlers: Drowning
may occur

Between 1980 and 1987, 112 children died when their faces were covered by plastic bags according to the CPSC. Garbage and dry cleaner's bags are the most common offenders.
MAKE SURE TO KEEP PLASTIC
BAGS AWAY FROM SMALL CHILDREN!

CHAPTER 12

CHILDREN AND TELEVISION, TOYS, DON'TS, ETC.

By the time an average child graduates from high school, she may witness 13,000 murders, plus countless other crimes such as robberies, muggings and tortures.

TV does influence children's attitudes and actions. Some children have imitated behavior they have seen on TV. It also affects attitudes about race, sex roles, etc. Physical health may be affected because of the advertisements for food, which may have little or no nutritional value.

What Should You Do Regarding Your Child's Television Viewing Habits?

Parents must supervise what their children watch. Choose programs which:

- Encourage good behavior.
- Encourage worthwhile ideas, values, and beliefs.
- Present problems a child can understand and show positive ways of resolving them.
- Present sex and adult roles positively.
- Present racial groups positively.
- Eliminate violent programs.

Finally, ask yourself: "Has my child seen enough television for the day?" If the answer is yes, turn the set off and help your child find activities other than TV.

TOYS

Toys are important tools in children's development. They stimulate them to develop new skills, such as grasping, shaking, pulling, squeezing, throwing, etc. in their early years. Through the use of toys small children improve their social skills while they play with other children. Babies coo and babble at toys, thereby practising language and communication.

145

Children under one year of age are becoming aware of sound, motion, touch, and color, and develop hand-to-mouth curiosity. For this age group, toys should be simple, washable, large, lightweight and brightly colored.

Some examples: Squeak toys, rattles, mobiles, washable dolls and stuffed animals with embroidered features. Brightly colored balls with textured surfaces (large enough not to be swallowed). Unbreakable teethers that can be sterilized, activity centers Other excellent toys: blocks, cars, crayons, paints, playdough, rocking horses, small trikes, pots, pans, building toys, wading pools, sandboxes, floating toys for the bathtub, mirrors,

Children from 1 to 2 years of age are learning mobility and continue in hand-to-mouth exploration. Curiosity should be encouraged.

Some appropriate toys: cloth blocks, pull toys, take-apart toys with large pieces, non-glass mirrors, cloth and stiff pasteboard books, nesting toys (sets of blocks, etc.), snap-lock beads, stacking toys, vinyl books, shape sorters, wagons, cars, etc.

Children between 2 to 3 years of age are developing language skills. Curiosity should still be encouraged.

Chalkboards, a low rocking horse or wheeled scoot toy (no pedals), simple musical instruments, play telephone, play kitchen, toy cars and trucks, tricycle, simple jigsaw puzzles with large pieces, wooden animals, matching games, blocks with letters and numbers, sandboxes, sand toys, baby dolls, large interlocking blocks, pounding bench, large peg board, pull-toy xylophone, etc.

Children between 3 and 4 years of age: At this age, children display vigorous physical activity, imagination and imitation.

Excellent toys for this age: Dolls with simple wrap around clothing, doll buggies and furniture, broom and carpet sweeper (small size), miniature garden tools, non-electrical trains, clothes, building blocks, drum, toy telephone, metal tea set, construction sets with easy-to-connect large pieces, counting frame with large beads, pegboard, blunt scissors, jigsaw puzzles with large pieces.

Children between 4 and 6 years: Social, cooperative play, and physical coordination are important at this age.

Good toys are: Picture books, magnetic numbers and letters, activity books, paints and paint books, board and card games, modeling clay, skipping rope, washtub and board, flame-retardant costumes, hand and finger puppets, kites, pail and shovel.

Children between 6 and 8 years: At this age they display independent play, and improve their physical dexterity.

Appropriate toys: Dolls and accessories, kites, puppets and puppet theater, magnets, magnifiers and other toys that demonstrate simple scientific facts, lightweight tool sets, jigsaw puzzles (more difficult ones), musical instruments, games requiring some reading, roller skates, approved electrical toys, sled, playground equipment.

Toys catalogs: (full of ingenious, wonderful toys).

• **Toys to grow on,** P.O.Box 17, Long Beach, CA 90801, or call 1-800-874-4242.

• **Discovery Toys, Inc.** Martinez, CA 94553, or call 1-800-4264777.

Toy-related accidents

According to the Consumer Product Safety Commission (CPSC), about 150,000 children visit hospital emergency rooms with toy-related injuries every year. This figure does not include visits to doctors' offices.

Some toys are dangerous because of an actual defect or because they can be dangerous for children of a different age. When purchasing a toy, try to see it from a child's-eye view. Ask yourself: What will she do with it? How is she likely to use it wrongly? How could the toy be dangerous? For instance, a toy may be dangerous if it has sharp edges or corners, small parts that can be swallowed by a young child. A flammable toy, a toy that shoots something-popguns, darts, etc--, toys painted with toxic products-lead, mercury- should be avoided.

For more information on toy safety, see the *Hotlines and Resources* section in the Appendix.

YOUR BABY'S NAME

Choosing that *perfect* name for your unborn, unseen child is a monumental task! It must be a name that both parents agree upon, that looks right and sounds right, that is not too common or too old-fashioned, that conveys the ideal characteristics for your child. The problem is compounded by the fact that, unless you know the sex of your child before birth, you have to choose *the* perfect girl's name and *the* perfect boy's name.

Whatever name you choose, remember that your child will live with that name throughout her life and see the world through associations attached to that name. The following guidelines will help you choose a name for which your child can be proud.

1. You may want to look up the meaning of certain names (i.e., Amy or Aimee means *beloved*, Belinda means *beautiful, wise, shrewd*, and Bethany means *house of poverty*).

2. Generally it is best to choose a name that goes well with your last name. If your last name is two or three syllables long, a short one-syllable first name would sound better, and vice versa.

3. Avoid choosing names that rhyme or create "cute" phrases (i.e., Cory Story, Candy Caine, Johnny B. Good, Hazel Mae Call, Wood Burns, or Seldom Worthit, Blue Denim, Ima Hog, etc.). These names do not generate a sense of self-esteem.

4. Select a first and a middle name to aid in identification, but be sure the initials do not spell a word that could be embarrassing (i.e., Felicia Ann Tucker: FAT).

5. Say the names aloud with the last name to see if the tongue trips or flows over the names. Avoid consonance, such as repetition of *s* sounds (i.e., Susan Cecile Strauss). Also, try saying the first and last name together, omitting the middle name.

6. Write the names down on paper to see how they look. Unusual spellings generally cause confusion and annoyance for the child both in spelling and pronunciation. Also, some letters have a soft and a hard sound, such as *c* and *g,* and a name like Genna would cause both spelling and pronunciation problems.

7. Choose names for which the gender is apparent (i.e., William: boy; Melissa: girl). Names with unclear gender distinctions can cause problems in this computer-oriented world (i.e., Jean or Gene; Billie or Billy; Leslie or Lesley). *Girls have been known to get draft notices or be excluded from all-girl parties because of a male-sounding name.*

8. Don't choose a name if you don't like the nickname. (i.e., Margaret -- Meg; Richard -- Dick, William -- Will, Bill, Willy or Billy). Invariably, someone will use it. Also, beware of names

such as Samantha for which a nickname, Sam or Sammy, confuses the child's gender.

9. Don't forget the possibility of using names from your ethnic heritage or of using the first or last name of a deceased relative as a middle name. If the name is outdated, try adapting it to a more popular version (i.e., Liz can become Lisa or Liza).

> *"In America, the freedom to be stupid, insensitive, or star-struck when naming children is a national right"--Jon Stewart.*

Names such as Moonunit (Frank Zappa's daughter --she later changed her name) may be cute and show your disregard for structure or society, but they may place the child at a disadvantage within society as she grows up. In France, magistrates can declare illegal any name which they consider out of bounds for the protection of the child. There are no such restraints in the United States, so CHOOSE A NAME CAREFULLY FOR WHICH THE CHILD CAN BE PROUD, OR WHICH LINKS HER TO HER HERITAGE.

SOME GENERAL DON'TS FOR PARENTS:

1. Do not threaten your children with taking them to the doctor "if they don't behave!"

2. Do not use bubble soap for baths. It is known to cause irritation of the vagina and urinary meatus.

3. Do not try to clean your child's ears by inserting a Q-tip or any other object inside the ear canal. All you will get is to push the wax (which, incidentally, is a normal substance) further into the ear. Just clean the outside of the ear canal entrance.

4. Do not wipe off the anus from back to front; rather, wipe front to back. Otherwise, fecal material will deposit on or in the vagina and produce an infection.

5. Never leave your infant or toddler alone in the house, not even "for a few minutes." Even if you really intend to return right away, you may be detained by a neighbor, etc. A lot can happen in a few minutes if young children are left unsupervised.

6. Do not use baking soda powder for diaper rash.

7. Do not let your toddler wander in the night and go to sleep in your bed. There are two reasons why you shouldn't: 1) It is a bad

149

sleeping habit; 2) He may wander around the house (or even outside) and get hurt. (There was a recent news report of a toddler who froze to death outside his house during the night.) Use a gate in his room's door. It should be two inches taller than he is and have no footholds.

8. Don't constantly check on your small baby at night. You would be transmitting your own insecurity to your child. I feel that parents who sleep the soundest and make the fewest trips into their infant's room will have the securest and emotionally healthiest children.

9. Don't smoke during pregnancy. There is an increased incidence of prematurity because of smoking. This decreases the chances of survival for your baby.

10. Do not drink alcohol, except in minimal amounts, during pregnancy. Birth defects are associated with drinking and, although the more you drink the worse the effect on the baby, even moderate drinking may affect him.

11. Guns and children. This is an emotional issue, but it shouldn't be. *Guns are six times more likely to kill or injure a member of the owner's household than an intruding criminal.* And the victim is usually a child!

CHILDREN AND PETS

According to a veterinarian, Prof. Dr. Mueller, children are quite safe with a pet. "A visiting aunt can give them a cold more easily than a puppy who kisses them." He says it is OK for children to hug pets and carry them in their arms, as long as some precautions are taken:

1. Pets should be bought only from a reputable dealer who has good sanitation practices.

2. Every new pet should be taken to a vet for a checkup and immunization.

3. Check the animal yourself for observable skin diseases.

SOME MYTHS OR "OLD WIVES" TALES:

1. Serious consequences may derive from not moving one's bowels "regularly." "Irregularity" is a myth. A person can have one

150

stool every three to four days, and as long as the consistency is not hard, then there is no problem.

2. "Baby's legs will bow if he is standing too long." This is just not true. Leg bowing is mostly a genetic condition. Actually, when babies start to walk, the legs straighten up.

3. "Adding cereal to formula at night will make the baby sleep through the night." If the reasoning is that a baby will sleep longer if her stomach is completely full, the same may be accomplished with just milk alone.

4. Thinking that time of teething and healthy, robust teeth have any connection with the amount of milk the child drinks. Milk, and the calcium it contains are needed by our bodies; however, many babies who drink a lot of milk do not get their teeth until quite late, and vice versa.

5. "A child who wets the bed does it on purpose to upset her parents." WRONG! This problem is completely involuntary, and, therefore, the child shouldn't be punished or scolded. She should be helped. Consult your doctor.

6. Thinking that it can be in some way harmful "if measles or chicken-pox do not break out real well: "*If they do not come out.*". The severity of either disease has, of course, nothing to do with the amount or severity of the skin rash.

7. It is wrong to cover a baby a lot, trying to keep her warm when she has fever. Actually, the opposite is true. You should try to keep her as cool as possible. Also, she will not get pneumonia if you sponge-bathe her.

8. Some people think that if water is given to a child with diarrhea, the condition will worsen. This is not true at all.

```
NEVER LEAVE A SMALL CHILD
UNATTENDED IN A BATHTUB.
A CHILD CAN DROWN IN 2 "
          OF WATER!
```

GLOSSARY

(Note: Only those items or conditions considered most relevant, and those that are not in the Index are included here)

Acyclovir (Zovirax) anti-viral drug. Effective against Herpes simplex.

Adenoids: lymphatic glands situated in the back of the nasal passages.

Adenoiditis: inflammation or infection of the adenoids.

Aganglionic megacolon (Hirschprung's Disease). A rather serious condition of the rectum and lower large bowels, due to maldevelopment of the tissues. Severe constipation ensues.

Albinism: Total or partial absence of pigment in the skin, hair and eyes. (recessive inheritance, see below).

Albumin: a protein found in animals, plants and egg whites.

Allergen: substances that trigger allergies: i.e. pollen, foods, etc.

Alopecia: loss of hair, usually meaning from the scalp.

Alpha-fetoprotein: when this substance is found to be in the blood of a pregnant woman in high amounts, it may indicate that the fetus is affected with a neural tube defect (i.e. spina bifida) (see below).

Amblyopia: ("Lazy eye") An eye that does not see clearly, usually because both eyes in that child have different degrees of nearsightedness or farsightedness, or because of squinting.

Amnion: the "bag of waters" covering fetus and the amniotic fluid.

Amniotic fluid: see above.

Anal fissure: a small, usually painful tear of the skin of the anus, secondary to constipation. Blood streaking commonly seen in toilet or toilet paper.

Analgesic: pain killer drug. (i.e. aspirin, acetaminophen, morphine, etc.).

Anaphylaxis/Anaphylactic shock: sudden, severe allergic reaction characterized mainly by wheezing, labored breathing and circulatory collapse (shock). Death may occur.

Anencephaly: congenital absence of parts of the brain and spinal cord. The infant is stillborn or dies soon after birth.

Antibody: blood proteins which the body produces to fight infections.

Antigen: a substance, usually a protein, found in bacteria, viruses and foreign tissues that stimulates the production of antibodies.

Antihistaminics: drugs that fight allergic reactions by reducing mucus secretions. During an allergic reaction, tissues release histamine, a chemical that dilates blood vessels and swelling.

Antipyretics: anti-fever drugs (acetaminophen, aspirin).

Apgar score: to see how well a newborn is adjusting to life outside the womb, he is given a score at one and five minutes after birth, based on signs that indicate whether enough oxygen is reaching his brain. Each of the five signs is scored as O, 1 and 2. Scores above 6 or 7 at one minute, and 8 or 9 at five minutes are good.

Apnea: lack of breathing.

Arrhythmia: abnormal pacing of the heart (too fast, too slow, etc.).

Asphyxia: suffocation due either to lack of oxygen or excessive amount of carbon dioxide.

Asthma: chronic respiratory ailment characterized by spasm of the bronchioles (bronchoconstriction or bronchospasm), the smallest bronchial tubes. The patient "wheezes" and may also have "labored breathing.". Triggers of asthma include allergies, infections, exertion, and tobacco smoke.

Atelectasis: a collapsed lung or portion of same.

Atopic dermatitis: see Eczema.

Atrial Septal Defect: a congenital heart defect consisting of an abnormal opening in the wall that separates the right from the left atrium. Blood pools in the right atrium.

Attention Deficit Disorder (A.D.D.): For unknown reasons, some children cannot "concentrate" or pay attention for a time long enough to acquire knowledge. They may also be "hyperactive," impulsive, etc., or not.

Audiometry: test designed to measure hearing

Auscultation: listening to sounds in some organs of the body (heart, lungs, etc.) with an instrument called a stethoscope.

Autism: complex disorder characterized by solitary behavior, poor development of speech, and an inability to relate.

Autoimmune disease: several diseases are due to this mechanism. The body's immune system produces antibodies against some of its own tissues because it considers them "foreign."

Bacteria: microscopic organism (microbe) capable of causing infections. Unlike viruses, they may be killed with antibiotics.

Barium: a chalky contrast material used to enhance X-rays of stomach, bowels, etc.

BCG vaccine: a vaccine against tuberculosis, used in countries where this disease is more common.

Biliary atresia: congenital obstruction or absence of the ducts or tubes between the liver and the gallbladder.

Birthmarks: an inaccurate name, but unfortunately another name is hard to come by. Includes many skin "bumps" or spots, i.e. salmon patch, strawberry hemangioma, port wine stain, and mongolian spots, which are noticed in a newborn either at birth, OR THEY MAY APPEAR AFTER BIRTH!

Blepharitis: infection of the edges of the eyelids.

Blood groups: grouping of the hereditary factors in the blood. There are major and minor groups. The major groupings are O, A, B and AB.

Boil: (furuncle) painful, pus-filled bacterial infection of a hair follicle. Usually due to Staphylococcus Aureus.

Bone age: by taking X-rays of the left hand (and sometimes other bones), the maturity of the bone, or the "age" can be measured.

Bone marrow: a soft substance inside most bones where the cells of the blood are formed.

Botulism: a severe infection (food poisoning) due to the toxin of a bacteria called Clostridium Botulinum. Paralysis or respiratory arrest may occur.

Bradychardia: slow heartbeat.

Breath-holding spells (BHS): Some infants, toddlers, two or three year olds will stop breathing for a few seconds, with or without loss of consciousness, during a fit, or extreme crying, usually triggered by anger or frustration. Children may turn blue or not, but they always start breathing again.

Bronchioles: (see Asthma)

Bronchoconstriction: (see Asthma)

Bronchopneumonia: a pneumonia due to a virus, with patchy inflammation of the lower part of the lungs.

Broncho-pulmonary dysplasia (BPD): lung damage due to the use of ventilators and oxygen to save the life of premature infants affected with severe respiratory syndromes.

Bronchoscopy: procedure that allows a doctor to visualize the inside of the bronchial tubes.

Bronchospasm: (see Asthma)

Candida, candidiasis = Monilia, moniliasis: A yeast microorganism, and the infection it causes. In children it usually affects the mouth (thrush), or the diaper area.

Canker sore: ulcer or sore of the inside of the mouth, lip.

Caries: cavities.

Cartilage: a special tissue that can be found in ear lobes, the sternum or "chicken breast," ribs, etc.

Cataracts: clouding of the lens of the eye, due to deposits of calcium usually. Babies may be born with this, i.e. the *Congenital Rubella Syndrome,* or it may happen later due to *galactosemia, hypervitaminosis D, hyperparathyroidism,* etc.

Cecum: the first part of the large intestine, where the appendix is located.

Celiac Disease: uncommon intestinal disease manifested by persistent diarrhea, malabsorption of nutrients, failure to gain weight and height due to injury to the lining of the small bowels by a chemical in gluten, a protein found in cereals. Starts between the ages of eight months and two years. A gluten-free diet improves the condition.

Cellulitis: infection of the skin down into deeper tissues. Similar to an abscess.

Cerebral Palsy: a name that includes different injuries to the brain, and manifested by abnormal movements, spastic or tight muscles, etc. Intelligence is usually intact.

Cervical adenitis: infection of lymph nodes of the neck, due to bacteria and other infectious organisms. Glands become swollen, tender, etc.

Cervix: the entrance to the uterus, located at the end of the vagina.

Chalazion: A localized lump in the middle of the underside of the eyelid, due to swelling of an oil gland.

Cheesing: Said of the spitting up of milk by infants because of its appearance.

Chlamydia: virus that may infect eyes, cervix, urethra, etc.

Chromosomes: rod-shaped bodies inside the nucleus of all cells. Carry the genes, the heredity factors.

Clavicle: collarbone.

Cleft lip (harelip): Congenital separation of the upper lip.

Cleft palate: congenital separation of the bones that form the hard palate.

Cochlea: a snail-shaped organ covered with tiny hair-like parts inside the inner ear. These hairs perceive sound vibrations and in turn pass them to the nerves and the brain so we can hear.

Cold sores: fever blisters. (see Herpes simplex).

Colitis: inflammation of the large intestine (colon), manifested by spasms, diarrhea or constipation.

Colostomy: the making of an artificial anus in the abdominal wall. Example: in a child born without anus (imperforate anus).

Complete blood count (CBC): a blood test that determines the number of each type of blood cells, etc.

Computerized tomographic scan (CT scan): an image of a thin cross-section of a part of the body made with an X-ray beam that is converted by a computer into a picture on a screen. Almost any part of the body can be looked at, allowing doctors to find tumors and other abnormal tissues that previously escaped discovery by conventional X-rays.

Concussion: temporary loss of consciousness due to a blow to the head.

Conductive hearing loss: deafness due to faulty transmission of sound waves from the outer ear to the cochlea. (see above)

Congenital: a condition that is present at or before birth. Congenital defects may be due to certain toxic substances, drugs taken during pregnancy, or to unknown factors.

Contact dermatitis: a skin inflammation produced by an allergic reaction with substances that touch the area affected.

Cornea: the transparent part of the globe of the eye that is located in front of the pupil.

Cortisone: hormone used to reduce inflammation in ointments, pills, etc.

Cradle cap: white or yellow, scaly and oily substance produced by an infant's scalp. Not contagious. Usually cured with proper treatment.

Cretinism: severe mental retardation due to a congenital lack of thyroid hormone.

Chron's disease: a rare, chronic inflammatory disease of the small bowel. Diarrhea, weight loss, abdominal pain, etc. occur on and off. May be debilitating and very serious. No specific treatment exists, but it can be controlled.

Crib death: same as SIDS.

Crossed eyes: Strabismus. Due to weakness of muscles, eyes "cross" instead of both looking in the same direction. Many causes.

Cryptorchidism: undescended testicles.

Cyanosis: a dusky to dark-blue color of the skin caused by a lack of proper oxygenation of the body (i.e. "the blue baby," due to a severe congenital heart defect).

Cyst: abnormal sac or cavity. May be filled by fluid, gas, etc.

Cystic fibrosis: recessive disease, involving several organs, but mainly the lungs. The body cannot get rid of mucus and other secretions that build up. Severe complications may ensue, like recurrent pneumonias, chronic diarrhea, failure to growth, malnutrition, etc. Death usually occurs at a young age. No specific cure exists.

Cystitis: bladder infection.

Cytomegalic Virus (CMV): a virus that, if contracted by a pregnant woman, may affect the fetus: brain damage, microcephaly, etc.

Decongestant: a medication that "shrinks" swollen mucus nasal membranes, i.e. useful when a child has a cold.

Dermatitis: inflammation of the skin. Several causes.

Diabetes mellitus: chronic illness due to defective insulin (a hormone), production from the pancreas, manifested by high glucose (sugar) level in blood and other tissues. Diabetes in children requires insulin shots. Diabetes is inherited but not in a predictable fashion.

Dislocation: when one of two bones slips out of alignment in a joint.

Diuretic: A medication that enhances the voiding of urine by the kidneys.

Dominant inheritance, genes: when a person has or inherits a dominant gene, even if the gene he acquires from the other parent is different or opposite, the dominant gene will "show" in that person's body. For example, the dominant gene for "polydactily" (extra fingers) will show, no matter what the other gene is. Dominant hereditary disorders occur in all generations whereas recessive disorders skip generations. Examples: Achondroplasia, Marfan's Syndrome, congenital cataract, and many others.

Down's syndrome: an inherited disease, manifested by mental retardation, a typical "facies" (the appearance of the face), and many other anomalies. Due to a defect in a specific chromosome.

Droopy eyelid (s): Also called *Ptosis*. The eyelid stays "down" in variable degrees. Due to weakness of some eye muscles due to disease of nerves or muscles.

Dyslexia: impaired ability to interpret written language. Can also be defined as a reading learning disability. Some experts consider dyslexia the same as learning disability syndrome (LDS). The cause is not clear.

Dyspnea: difficulty in breathing. Respiratory distress.

Ectopic: An organ that is out of its proper place; i.e. *ectopic kidney* -a kidney that is situated in a place other than where it normally should be. Other examples: *ectopic ureter, ectopic lens,* etc.

Eczema: Also called atopic dermatitis. Skin inflammation and rash of a scaly, itchy nature.

Edema: swelling of parts of the body tissues caused by an accumulation of fluid. May be due to kidney or heart diseases or to inflammation, etc.

Electrolytes: the salts in the body fluids and cells.

Embryo: an earlier stage of development of the fetus.

Emetic: a drug that induces vomiting (i.e., syrup of ipecac is used commonly in children after they ingested certain poisons, to prevent their absorption into the body.)

Encephalitis: inflammation of the brain due to viruses, poisons (i.e., lead), etc.

Encopresis: also called "fecal soiling." The child usually has a long history of constipation. The child either has a few "accidents," or leaks stools continuously. Later on, the child may develop emotional problems secondary to the shame associated with his problem.

Endocarditis: inflammation of the inside lining of the heart.

Endocrine glands: several organs that produce hormones and release them into the bloodstream to control many functions. Examples are the thyroid, adrenal, pituitary, and other glands.

Endotracheal tube: a tube that is inserted into the trachea to provide an airway for the patient.

Enzymes: chemical substances that participate in digestive and many other important functions in the body.

Epiglottis: a membrane made up of cartilage that covers the larynx or windpipe during swallowing and prevents food from entering the latter.

Epilepsy: Seizures or convulsions of unknown cause. Usually controllable with medications. There are several different types.

Epinephrine: a hormone produced in the adrenal gland. Released during "stress" and other situations.

Epistaxis: nosebleed.

Epstein-Barr virus: causes infectious mononucleosis.

Erysipelas: severe skin infection caused streptococcus. Redness and swelling are the main signs.

Erythema: reddening of the skin due to dilatation of the capillary vessels under the skin. Many causes: viruses, sunburn, etc.

Erythema Infectiosum: See Fifth Disease below.

Erythema Multiforme: potentially serious disease. Rash and fever. Several types of rashes may occur: flat or raised red blotches, blisters, etc. May be fatal. May be due to allergic reaction to medications.

Erythrocytes: red blood cells (RBC'S).

Escherichia Coli (E.Coli): bacteria found in normal bowels. Commonly causes urinary tract infections, and diarrhea.

Esophagus: the "food tube" that connects the throat with the stomach.

Esotropia: Crossed eyes. One eye "turns in".

ESR (Erythro-sedimentation rate): test that measures the time it takes in a column of blood, for the RBC's to deposit (to sediment) at the bottom of the test tube. If result is higher than normal, it indicates an inflammatory process is occurring in the body.

Estrogens: the female sex hormones. Responsible for puberty, menstruation, pregnancy, etc. Secreted mainly by the ovaries.

Eustacian or Eustachian tube: see ear infections.

Exanthem Subitum: also called Roseola, a viral illness. Typically manifests itself with high fever for about four days. On the fifth day, the fever disappears and a pink/reddish rash appears on the body. No treatment necessary other than antipyretics, etc. Self-limited.

Exchange transfusion: a procedure that consists of removing in steps the baby's blood with another compatible blood. Typically used to treat babies born of Rh(-) (a blood group) mothers. Because the baby's blood group is different than mother's, she develops antibodies to baby's RBC's. These are then destroyed and severe anemia may ensue.

Exhaling: breathing out.

Exotropia: crossed eyes. One eye turns in.

Expectorant: a medication that loosens mucus inside the bronchial tubes. It helps the patient "expectorate," i.e., to "bring up the mucus and cough it out."

Expiration: breathing out. Exhaling.

Exstrophy: rare congenital defect, in which an organ, such as the urinary bladder, is turned inside out or opens directly on the skin of the abdomen.

"Eyeteeth": canines. Four teeth situated between the incisors and the first molars.

Failure to thrive: not gaining weight and growth properly.

Febrile seizure: a short, generalized (all extremities and body shakes) seizure. Happens during infancy until about age three. No special treatment necessary. It is outgrown.

Fecal incontinence: See *Encopresis* above.

Fecal soiling: See *Encopresis* above.

Femur: the thighbone.

Fibula: one of the two bones of the leg. The thin one. The other is called tibia.

Fifth disease: Also called erythema infectiosum and due to Parvovirus B, this infection occurs in school age children usually, and rarely causes any symptoms other than the rash.

The typical illness starts with red cheeks. One or two days later a lacy flat pink rash develops in forearms, and later on on thighs. The patients do not feel ill at all. No known complications or sequelae occur.

Floppy infant: term used to describe an infant with poor muscle tone. May be due to a serious disease of the nerves or muscles. Many times the condition is self-limited.

Focal seizure: a localized seizure. i.e., only one arm jerks.

Fontanel: the "soft spot" of the head. Also called anterior fontanel. Size is variable. Closes after nine months of age. The posterior fontanel may or may not be open at birth. Smaller and situated more toward the top and back of the skull.

Fracture: broken bone. Several types.

Fungus: yeast.

Furuncle: same as boil.

Galactosemia: inborn metabolic defect. The tissues cannot utilize galactose, a sugar. This accumulates in tissues and causes illness (cataracts, liver disease, etc.)

Gallbladder: a sac situated below the liver. Serves as a storage of bile.

Gamma globulin: a blood protein containing antibodies to fight infection. It is used to booster immunity against several infections.

Gangrene: tissue death, usually due to lack of sufficient blood supply.

Gastritis: inflammation of the lining of the stomach.

Gastroenteritis: as above, but involving also the bowels. Vomiting, diarrhea, etc. are symptoms of this disease.

Gastroesophageal reflux: an abnormal backward flow of the contents of the stomach into the esophagus and mouth. Spitting up, vomiting are symptoms of this condition, common in infants.

Gastroscopy: looking inside the stomach with a special tube.

Gavage feeding: putting food (usually milk) into a baby's stomach through a tube or canula passed through the nostrils.

Gestational age: term used to describe the age of the fetus. It is given in weeks: i.e., a "37 weeks GA newborn" is a baby born 37 weeks after conception.

Gestational diabetes: diabetes that occurs only while a woman is pregnant.

Gingivitis, gingivostomatitis: inflammation of the gums, and the mouth, also.

Glaucoma: A serious disease of the eye manifested by increased pressure inside and leading to damage to the eye and decrease in vision. May occur in infants, due to defects before birth.

Glottis: the space between the vocal cords. Inside the larynx (see under Larynx below). Air, passing up out of the lungs through the glottis, causes a vibration of the vocal folds (sound).

Glucose: the simplest and most common form of sugar. The main source of energy for the human body.

Goiter: enlargement of the thyroid gland. Many causes.

Gonads: testicles and ovaries.

Gonorrhea: sexually transmitted disease due to a germ called gonococcus. Severe inflammation of the genitalia in both males and females may occurs. It can cause blindness in newborn babies if not discovered and treated properly.

Grand mal seizure: generalized jerking and stiffness of the body. Synonymous with epilepsy, but other causes may produce it.

Heat stroke: due to exposure to extreme temperatures, the sweating (cooling) mechanism of the body fails. The child's own temperature rises and death may ensue. One common situation is that of an infant or toddler left inside a parked car in a hot day.

Hematocrit: the percentage of the RBC's volume in the blood compared to the plasma (the liquid part of the blood). A low hematocrit usually indicates anemia.

Hematoma: a blood-filled swelling due to blood vessels ruptured as a consequence of a blow.

Hematuria: blood in the urine.

Hemiparesis: Paralysis of one half of the body.

Hemoglobin: the red pigment contained in RBC's and attached to iron. Hemoglobin is very important because it binds and transports oxygen to all the tissues of the body.

Hemolysis: the breakage of RBC's.

Hemolytic anemia: anemia, or "low blood," due the rupture of too many RBC's. May be due to toxins, infections, antibodies, etc.

Hemophilia: inherited disease. Blood cannot clot. Bleeding results from even minor blows or wounds. It only affects males. Female are carriers (sex-linked recessive). Treatment consists of injecting the blood protein or factor that is missing in these children.

Hemorrhage: bleeding due to the rupture of any vessel.

Hepatitis: viral infection of the liver. Hepatitis A is caught usually by eating contaminated food, typically in restaurants. Hepatitis B is acquired through needles or blood transfusions.

Hepatomegaly: Enlargement of the liver.

Hepatosplenomegaly: Enlargement of liver and spleen

Hernia: part or all of an organ, usually the small bowels, slides out of the abdomen and gets through other tissues. Swelling is the most common sign. Surgery is usually indicated. Most common: inguinal hernia (groin area).

Herpangina: An infectious illness due to Cocksackie viruses. Symptoms are blisters and ulcerations of the throat, hard and soft palate, tonsils, with fever, vomiting, etc. Cures without treatment.

Herpes simplex: virus that causes recurrent infections. Herpes type 1 (HSV-1) produces blisters/sores around the mouth (cold sores or fever blisters), severe pain, fever, drooling, etc. The condition is called **Herpetic Gingivostomatitis.** Herpes type 2 (HSV-2), consists of sores in the genitalia or **Genital Herpes.** Both can affect other parts of the body, (i.e., brain, eyes, etc). Infants born to mothers with active herpes infections at the time of birth may develop herpes encephalitis, a very serious illness.

Herpes Zoster: "shingles." Painful viral infection, manifested by a blistery rash following the path of a nerve, commonly involving the area of the trunk. The virus is the same that causes chicken-pox.

Hirschsprung's disease: see aganglionic megacolon.

Histamine: a chemical found in tissues that stimulates production of mucus, (i.e., in the nasal mucosa, or juices or in the lining of the stomach or gastric mucosa). Histamine is released during allergic reactions and causes inflammation.

Hives: or urticaria. Red, itchy, slightly raised skin patches caused sometimes by a substance that a child eats, or somehow comes in contact with, or a viral infection, but no cause can be uncovered in 90 percent of affected people. Usually self-limited. Treatment is directed to alleviate the symptoms.

Hodgkin's disease: a type of cancer of the lymphatic system.

Hormones: chemical substances produced by endocrine glands. They travel through the blood stream and regulate important functions of the body.

Hyaline Membrane Disease (HMD): also called RDS, or respiratory distress syndrome. Severe respiratory ailment usually associated with premature babies and due to an immaturity of the bronchial tubes.

Hydrocele: accumulation of fluid inside the same sac that envelopes the testicle. Usually causes no problem. Fairly common occurrence in newborns.

Hydrocephalus: "water in the brain." Excessive amount of fluid collects inside the hollow areas of the brain called ventricles. Enlargement of the head follows. May cause brain damage. Treatment is available, but it depends on the type.

Hypercalcemia: high levels of calcium in the blood.

Hyperhidrosis: excessive perspiration.

Hyperlipidemia: high blood levels of "lipids" (fatty substances in).

Hypernatremia: high levels of the electrolyte sodium in the blood.

Hyperopia: Farsightedness. The opposite of myopia.

Hyperparathyroidism: Excessive production of *parathyroid hormone* by tiny glands called *parathyroid glands* situated inside the thyroid gland. The patient develops a serious illness due to excessive release of calcium from his bones, kidney damage, etc.

Hyperthyroidism: disease due to an overactive thyroid gland. Main symptoms consist of excessive sweating, decreased sleep, weight loss, etc.

Hypertrophy: increased size of a tissue or organ.

Hypervitaminosis: Illness due to excessive intake of certain vitamins, i.e. Vitamin A, D, etc.

Hypocalcemia: low blood calcium level.

Hypoglycemia: low blood sugar.

Hyponatremia: low blood levels of sodium.

Hypoplasia: lack of good development of an organ or tissue.

Hypospadias: congenital defect of the penis. The opening of the urethra, called meatus, is placed on the underside of the penis. This may cause urinary difficulties and surgery may be necessary.

Hypothyroidism: an underactive thyroid gland. Failure to grow, sluggishness, constipation, etc. are symptoms.

Hypotonia: decreased muscle tone, with or without weakness. Many causes.

Hypoxia: lack of oxygen.

Idiopathic: said of an illness that has no known cause.

Idiopathic thrombocytopenic purpura (ITP): destruction of platelets due to an autoimmune reaction. Many spots appear on the skin (purpura:large ones; petechiae: small ones). Unknown cause.

Immunoglobulins: name given to the five major types of antibodies: IgE, IgA, IgD, IgG and IgM.

Immunotherapy: desensitization by frequent injection of increasing amounts of allergen.

Imperforate anus: congenital absence, total or partial, of the anal opening.

Impetigo: skin infection. Sores and crusty weepy lesions. Treatment: thorough washings and antibiotic ointments.

Inborn Errors of Metabolism: Said of several hereditary biochemical disorders of the metabolic processes (See Metabolism below) of the body tissues.

More than a hundred defects exist. There are defects of the protein metabolism (PKU, Albinism, Homocystinuria, etc.), carbohydrate metabolism (Galactosemia, , fat metabolism (Tay-Sachs disease, Glycogen Storage diseases, etc.), and many others.

Incarcerated hernia: a hernia that cannot be reduced that is pushed back into its normal place. Usually, if not treated promptly, it may produce gangrene of the tissue, i.e., bowel with serious illness.

Incisors: the four upper and four lower front teeth.

Incontinentia pigmenti (I.P.): Serious congenital (born with) illness. X-linked dominant, lethal in males, consists of skin rashes, alopecia, mental retardation, microcephaly, seizures, eye defects, etc.

Incontinence: See *Fecal, Urinary Incontinence.*

Infantile spasm: a type of seizure occurring mostly in infants.

Influenza: Flu. Contagious viral illness. Occurs in epidemics.

Inguinal: the groin; i.e., inguinal hernia.

Inspiration: inhalation.

Insulin: the hormone missing in diabetes.

Intra-uterine growth retardation (IUGR): due to malfunction of the placenta, fetus does not grow as it should. Newborn is small.

IVP or intravenous pyelogram: special X-Rays of the kidneys.

Intraventricular hemorrhage: bleeding into the brain. In preemies, due to hypoxia.

Intussusception: intestinal obstruction due to telescoping of one part of the small bowel into another. May be a serious problem.

IPV: inactivated polio vaccine (the Salk polio vaccine). Given by shots.

Kawasaki disease: acute disease of unknown origin. Consists of rashes, conjunctivitis, fever, and involvement of the heart. May be fatal. High doses of immunoglobulin intravenously effective in many cases.

Labiae: Lips of the vaginal area: Inner lips or **labiae minorae.** Outer lips or **labiae majorae.**

Labial fusion: Common, usually harmless condition. The inner lips of the vagina stick and grow together. Must consult doctor.

Lactose: a sugar found in milk.

Laryngitis: inflammation of the voicebox.

Laryngomalacia: a larynx that is congenitally soft, and therefore tends to "collapse" during breathing, causing stridor. It usually improves with age, but it may cause respiratory problems for some time.

Larynx: or *voice box;* the passageway between the pharynx or throat and the *trachea* or *windpipe.* The larynx has the shape of a tube. It contains nine cartilages. One of them, the epiglottis is responsible for covering the opening of the larynx when the person is in the process of swallowing. This lid action prevents the entrance of food into the larynx and lungs.

Leukemia: blood cancer of the white cells. Several types.

Leukocytes: the white blood cells.

Luxation: dislocation of a joint.

Lyme disease: infection due to a bacteria carried by ticks. Occurs mostly in northeastern states. Symptoms: rashes, fever, involvement of joints, nervous system, etc. Treatment: antibiotics in the early phase might cure.

Lymph: normal fluid found in lymphatic vessels and lymph glands. Contain white cells called lymphocytes, very important cells designed to fight infections.

Lymph nodes: lymph glands. They fight infection by trapping bacteria, etc.

Lymphoma: cancer of the lymphatic tissues.

Malabsorption: decreased absorption of foodstuffs by the lining of the bowels, leading to loss of important nutrient through the stools, i.e. proteins, fats, vitamins, etc. and leading to decreased growth, etc. See Celiac Disease, and Cystic Fibrosis above.

160

Mastoid bones: the bony parts behind our ears.

Mastoiditis: infection of the cavities inside the mastoid bones.

Meatal stenosis: narrowing of the opening of the urethra (meatus).

Meconium: dark green, thick, sticky discharge found inside the bowels of newborns.

Megaencephaly: "mega" means large; "encephaly" means brain; large brain. Therefore, "large brain,"

Meningitis: severe bacterial infection of the central nervous system (brain, spinal cord, etc.) causing fever, convulsions, and possible death or severe sequelae -- aftereffects-- like paralysis, deafness, brain damage, etc. Viral meningitis is usually benign.

Metabolism: the chemical and physical changes that occur inside the tissue cells of the body, essential to sustain the life processes.

Microcephaly: small brain. May or not be associated with mental retardation.

Milia: tiny bumps on face of newborns. Self-limited.

Molars: the grinding teeth at the back of the mouth.

Mongolian spots: bluish discoloration, usually on the lower back. Disappear later on. Occurs in some races like Asian, Mediterranean, and Hispanic people.

Mononucleosis: see Infectious mono.

MRI or magnetic resonance imaging. A new diagnostic test, better than conventional X-rays. Based on measuring differences in magnetic energy in the body. Produces cross-sections of the body with remarkable details.

Myocarditis: inflammation of the muscle of the heart.

Myopia: nearsightedness. Only very near vision is not blurred.

Myringotomy: surgical opening of the eardrum.

Neonatal herpes: See herpes simplex.

Neonatal Intensive Care Unit (NICU): a special ward equipped to treat premature and sick newborns.

Neonatal sepsis: severe bacterial infection, acquired by the newborn just before birth or at the time of birth.

Neonatologist: a pediatrician who specializes only in treating premature and full term sick newborns. His main working area is the Neonatal Intensive Care Unit or NICU.

Nervous system: it consists of two parts: the central nervous system or CNS (the brain, spinal cord) and the peripheral nervous system, the network of nerves that spread through the body.

Neural tube: an embryonic (fetal) part that later becomes the nervous system. See embryo above.

Neural tube defects: congenital defects affecting the nervous system, i.e. spina bifida, encephalocele, etc. See also alpha-fetoprotein.

Neurogenic bladder: because of poorly developed nerves in the bladder, the patient has constant urine leakage.

Nevus: a congenital pigmented area of the skin. A birth mark.

Nightmares: fearful episodes at night occurring during a dream. They take place later in the night, close to its end. Usually due to watching a scary movie, etc.

Night terrors: during deep sleep, usually early in the night, the child awakes, screams loudly, thrashes about, does not recognize parent and looks as if he is very frightened. He is asleep during the attack. He has no no recollection of this episode upon awakening in the morning. Many causes: overtiredness, emotional upheaval in the household, etc.

Nits: lice eggs. Can be seen stuck to the hair shafts.

Nursing caries or nursing bottle tooth decay: cavities typically occurring in toddlers who are still drinking from the bottle.

Oral Polio vaccine (OPV): the Savin vaccine.

Orbit: the eye socket.

Orbital cellulitis: severe infection of the tissues surrounding the eyeball.

Ossicles: three small bones inside the middle ear cavity. Called: the malleus, incus and stapes. They transmit the sound waves into the inner ear. They act as sound amplifiers.

Osteomyelitis: infection of the bone.

Otoscope: instrument used to examine the ear.

Oxygen: Essential gas needed for survival. Air contains 20% oxygen and about 80% nitrogen.

Oxygen bag: Special bellows to puff oxygen into child's lungs.

Oxyhood: Plastic cylinder where the head of the infant is introduced. Oxygen is piped in for baby to breathe.

Pancreas: a solid organ situated behind the stomach. Produces insulin, other hormones and several substances (enzymes) that, flowing into the bowels, aid in the digestion of food.

Paralysis: Total inability to use muscles.

Paresis: partial muscular weakness.

Paranasal sinuses: or most commonly "sinuses." Air-filled cavities behind the facial bones and to each side of the nose (frontal, maxillary sinuses, etc.).

Pectus carinatum: a congenital protrussion of the breast bone or sternum. No medical problems usually.

Pectus excavatum: a congenital depression of the sternum or breast bone. Usually of no consequence.

Pediculosis: lice infestation.

Periodic breathing: cycles of fast and slow breathing separated by short no-breathing periods. This is a normal pattern in prematures.

Petechiae: tiny red spots due to micro-hemorrhages under the skin.

Petit mal seizures: short episodes of staring. Amenable to drug treatment.

Pharyngitis: infection of the throat (pharynx).

Phenylketonuria (PKU): rare hereditary metabolic disease caused by a defective enzyme. Severe brain damage occurs if not diagnosed and treated early.

Phlegm: mucus.

Pica: some infants crave non-nutritious substances, including dirt. They usually have a deficiency of iron.

Pinworms: small worms, passed from human to human through contaminated food. Treatment is available and all members of the family must be medicated.

PKU test: not a good name, because this test, which is done by law in all newborns, tests not only for PKU but for other rare but serious metabolic diseases, like galactosemia, hypothyroidism, etc.

Plasma: the part of the blood that is fluid (90 percent water). The rest consists of electrolytes, hormones, waste products, clotting agents, antibodies, etc.

Platelets: colorless bodies in the blood that play an important role in the clotting process. If their number is reduced, bleeding in different tissues will ensue, i.e., petechiae, etc.

Pneumothorax: abnormal air between the lung and the thoracic cage, plus collapse of the lung.

Poison Ivy, P. Oak, P. Sumac: Itchy skin rash due to contact with certain plants.

Pollen: microscopic grains of plant protein used for reproduction.

Precocious puberty: puberty that begins before the age of eight in girls and nine in boys.

Prematurity: birth that occurs between the 20th and 38th weeks of gestation.

Prickly heat: "heat rash."

Prophylactic: preventative.

Ptosis: drooping of one or both eyelids.

Pyloric stenosis: disease of unknown cause, consisting of a narrowing and eventually complete closure of the end of the stomach, where it joins the small bowel (the site of the pyloric valve). Occurs between four and eight weeks of age. Main symptom is persistent vomiting and dehydration. Treatment is surgical to relieve the obstruction.

Rabies: or hydrophobia. Deadly disease caused by a virus, and passed on by a rabid animal, like a dog, or other wild animals.

Recessive gene: a gene that when inherited only from one parent, does not produce a trait -a defect or abnormality- but is passed on to the next generation. When these genes are inherited from both parents, then they do produce a trait. The chances of this occurring are one in four or 25 percent of their offspring. Examples of recessive inheritance: Most inborn errors of metabolism (see above), cystic fibrosis, deaf-mutism, total color blindness, etc.

Rectal prolapse: protrusion of rectal mucosa through the anus.

Rectum: the last part of the intestine.

Red blood cells: RBC's.

REM (rapid eye movement): the first, lighter stage of sleep. This is when dreams occur.

Renal: pertaining to the kidneys.

Respiratory distress syndrome (RDS): see Hyaline Membrane disease.

Respiratory syncitial virus (RSV): a common virus; produces bronchiolitis in infants.

Retinoblastoma: Malignant tumor inside the eye. May affect one or both eyes. An infant may be born with it. It usually requires ablation (extraction of) the eye (s) and/or radiotherapy.

Retractile testicles: testicles that go "up and down" from the scrotum to the groin.

Reye Syndrome: a serious, possibly fatal disease of unknown cause, that occurs only in children up to age 19 and affects mainly the liver and brain.

Rh factor: a group of antigens in the RBC's. People without this factor are said to be Rh negative.

Rhinitis: or coryza, or "cold,", inflammation of the nose (runny or stuffy nose).

Rickets: deficiency of vitamin D. Bones suffer, including teeth. Very rare in this country since vitamin D was added to milk.

Ringworm: a skin fungal infection manifested by patches with a ring-like appearance.

Rocky Mountain Spotted fever: disease due to a tiny bacterium transmitted to human by carrier ticks. Without proper early antibiotic treatment may be serious and may cause death.

Roseola: see under Exanthem subitum.

Rubella: German measles. **Congenital Rubella Syndrome:** serious defects in fetus due to passage of the rubella virus from an unprotected -unimmunized- mother. Main defects are: mental retardation, cataracts, and serious heart defects.

Rubeola: measles or hard measles.

Salmon patch: a birthmark very common on the nape of the neck ("the stork's bite").May also show on forehead, eyelids. Disappears with time.

Scabies: contagious skin disease due to a tiny parasite. Intense itching and rash.

Sclera: the "white" of the eye.

Scoliosis: abnormal sideway curvature of the spine.

Scrotum: the sac where testicles rest.

Sequela, Sequelae: residual, remaining lesion or defect leftover from a previous illness. Example: deafness may be a sequela of meningitis, etc.

Serum: the liquid that remains after blood clots.

Sex-linked: a type of inheritance of traits from genes that are situated in the "sex" chromosomes (Males have an X, "female chromosome,"and a Y, or "male chromosome." Females have two X chromosomes, or XX). Hemophilia is a trait that is sex- or X-linked inherited. (See Hemophilia above.)

163

Shigellosis: (dysentery) An intestinal infection. Usually causes bloody diarrhea and severe cramping, dehydration, etc.

Shingles: Herpes Zoster.

Shock: sudden, severe drop in blood pressure. May be the preceding stage to death if not treated promptly. Most important causes are: severe infections, heart failure, dehydration, blood loss, allergic reaction, etc.

Sickle-Cell Anemia: recessive, inherited disease of the RBC's. Mostly in black persons. Anemia, swellings, pain. No cure.

SIDS: sudden infant death syndrome or crib death. Unknown cause or causes. Most common around the age of six months.

Sinusitis: infection of the paranasal sinuses.

Small for date or Small for gestational age (SGA): an infant who is born with a weight below the expected for her GA.

Spastic, Spasticity: Increased muscle tone -stiffness- due to some neuromuscular conditions (See *Cerebral Pasy* above).

Sphincter: a muscle ring or "valve" that opens and closes, controlling what passes through an orifice, i.e., anal sphincter, etc.

Spina bifida: congenital defect, that manifests itself by the absence of the posterior part of some vertebrae. Nervous tissue from the spine protrude, and the skin that covers this area is usually also absent. Patients have urinary incontinence and other associated paralysis.

Spinal fluid: the fluid that circulates through the CNS (the ventricles of the brain and the spinal cord).

Splenomegaly: Enlargement of the spleen.

Spinal tap, or lumbar puncture: procedure in which a needle is introduced through the spinal vertebrae to collect spinal fluid.

Sprain: injury to soft tissues, like ligaments.

Stenosis: a narrowing, i.e., pulmonary stenosis, pyloric stenosis, etc.

Stillbirth: birth of a dead fetus older than 20 weeks gestation.

Strabismus: crossed eyes, squint. Eyes cannot focus simultaneously.

Strain: Minor injury caused by overuse or misuse of a muscle.

Strawberry hemangioma: a birth defect of the skin. Consists of numerous blood vessels bunched together. Unknown cause.

Stridor: a croupy inspiratory sound due to swelling of the vocal cords. This in turn may be due to a virus, etc.

Sty: an infection localized on the edge of the eyelid.

Subconjunctival hemorrhage: tiny red spots in the white of the eye common in newborns. They represent micro-hemorrhages due to the tremendous pressure exerted on the head at the time of birth. Self-limited. No symptoms.

Syndrome: a condition that may be due to more than one cause. Notice the difference between it and a disease which has only one possible cause.

Syrup of ipecac: see Emetics.

Tachycardia: fast heart beat.

Tachypnea: rapid breathing.

Tapeworm: intestinal parasite acquired by eating uncooked pork or beef.

Testis: or testicles. The male reproductive glands.

Testicular torsion: twisting of the cord from which the testicle hangs. Pain, swelling. Medical help must be obtained quickly for best results.

Theeth grinding: This is one of several common *habit disorders*. Others are: head banging, body-rocking, nail biting, hair pulling, etc. They may be normal phases in a child's development or may indicate an internal tension resulting from repressed anger.

Thorax: chest.

Thrombocytopenia: decreased number of thrombocytes or platelets. See under Platelets.

Thrush: oral moniliasis. Yeast infection of the mouth or oral mucosa. Shows as white patches.

Tibia: shinbone.

Torticollis: see Wryneck

Trachea: Or windpipe. The part of the airway just below the larynx. It ends in the two bronchi, the right and the left bronchi. (singular: bronchus).

Trench mouth: Disease of gums, due probably to one or more bacteriae, with rednes, ulcers, bad breath, fever, cervical gland enlargement. Responds to antibiotics usually. Not contagious. Herpetic gingivostomatitis (see above) is very similar, but due to Herpes Simplex type 1 (HSV 1). Does not respond to antibiotics.

Undescended testicles: failure of testicles to descend into the scrotum. Also called cryptorchidism.

Upper respiratory infection: (URI): Infection of the nose, throat, due to viruses. Also known as "the common cold."

Ureters: tubes that connect the kidneys to the bladder.

Uretero-vesical reflux: abnormal backflow of urine from bladder to the ureters.

Urethra: the canal through which the urine flows from the bladder down to the meatus. Short in females, longer in males, as it must travel inside the penis.

Urinary incontinence: Inability to control the release of urine by the bladder. Causes vary. Usually there is a neurological impairment, i.e. spina bifida, or some other less severe dysfuncions.

Ventricles: the two larger chambers of the heart. Also, the cavities inside the brain.

Ventricular septal defect (VSD): a congenital heart defect, consisting of an abnormal hole in the wall that separates the right from the left ventricle. The larger the hole the more severe the disease.

Vernix caseosa: a fatty, white, sticky substance that covers the fetus. Made up of oil and dead skin cells. It is seen in newborns, when they are premature

Vertebra: one of the 33 flat, roundish bones that make up the spinal column.

Wry neck: torticollis. The child keeps his head turned to one side. If not properly treated, the condition may become permanent. The most common cause in infants is an injury to a neck muscle. This may happen inside the utero, or during a breech or a difficult delivery. The injured muscle appears shorter and a lump may or may not be detected by your child's doctor. The treatment consists of muscle stretching exercises.

X-linked inheritance: The defective gene is carried by the X chromosome. Normal females carry two X chromosomes. Normal males carry an X and a Y chromosome. If a male child inherits an X chromosome with a gene defect from his mother, he will develop the disease (example: *Hemophilia*). A female of that same mother, will be a carrier, because the other X chromosome passed on from her father will counteract the X chromosome from her mother. This is the reason why women cannot develop hemophilia. Other X-linked diseases: Color blindness, some types of muscular dystrophy, agammaglobulinemia, hyperparathyroidism, congenital deafness, etc.

APPENDIX

YOUR CHILD'S HEALTH RECORD

It is important that you keep good records of your child's health supervision visits to the doctor, immunizations, illnesses. Use the following pages for this purpose.

BIRTH RECORD

Baby's name
Date of birth   Time
Place of birth
Weight   Height
Blood Group   Apgar Score
Problems during pregnancy
Type of Delivery
Problems with Delivery
Post Partum Problems

TELEPHONE NUMBERS

Child's doctor   Dentist
Family doctor   Police
Hospital   Fire Dept.
Drugstore   Poison Control Center

FAMILY HISTORY

	Mother	Father	Siblings	Other
Allergies				
Asthma				
Blood Diseases				
Cancer				
Congenital defects				
Infectious diseases				
Other				

ALLERGIES TO:

RECORD OF ILLNESSES / ACCIDENTS

Date	Age	Problem

WELL BABY CHECK UPS

Date	Height/ Weight	Problems	Dr's Advice

IMMUNIZATIONS AND TESTS

VACCINE	DATE	Dr.	REACTION
2 mos. DPT POLIO HIB			
4 mos. DPT POLIO HIB			
6 mos. DPT POLIO HIB			
15 mos. HIB MMR			
18 mos. DPT POLIO			
4-6 yrs. DPT POLIO			
11-12 yrs. MMR			
14-16 yrs. DT			

TB Tests
CBC
Cholesterol
Hepatitis B Vaccine
Chicken Pox Vaccine

Question: My 1 year old infant has a yellow discoloration of his skin? Is this jaundice? Is there something wrong with his liver?

Answer: If your child appears healthy, has a yellow tint on his skin, BUT the white part of the eyes --called sclerae-- is white, he most likely has CAROTINEMIA, a normal condition due to the rather large intake of fruits and vegetables in infants and toddlers. These foods have pigments --chemicals-- or *carotenes*. The human body makes retinol --Vitamin A-- from the carotenes. When a large amount of carotenes exists, the excess attaches to the skin and gives it its yellow-orange color.

In rare occasions carotinemia may indicate a serious condition: diabetes, liver disease, hypothyroidism --underactive thyroid gland-- etc.

You should ask your child's doctor if his carotenemia is normal or not. If it is the most common normal type, nothing needs to be done. Do not reduce the vegetable/fruit intake of your child without his doctor approving of it. Usually the yellow skin color will disappear by the child's second birthday or sooner.

•••••••••••••••••••••

Following is a consent form for medical treatment. DO NOT WRITE ON THE FORM. Make copies, fill them out and give one to each person--sitter, day care provider, grandparent, aunt and uncle, neighbor--who takes care of your child. Be sure to update the form regularly.
(NOTE: Not all medical facilities will accept this form; some hospitals/doctors require that their own release be completed. And if a parent or legal guardian cannot be contacted personally, some hospitals will not treat a minor, even with a consent form, unless the problem is considered life-threatening. Check the policy in the area where your child would be treated).

CONSENT FOR EMERGENCY MEDICAL CARE

I, _____

☐ Mother ☐ Father ☐ Legal Guardian

hereby give my consent to _____
(Caregiver/Day Care Center)

who will be caring for my child _____
(Name)

_____ _____
(Birth Date)   (S.S. No.)

for the period _____ to _____

to arrange for emergency medical/surgical/dental care and treatment (including diagnostic procedures) necessary to preserve the health of my child.
I acknowledge that I am responsible for all reasonable charges in connection with any care and treatment rendered.

Print Name: _____

Home Address: _____

_____

Home Telphone No. _____

Business Telphone No. _____

Name & Address of Primary Health Ins. Carrier: _____

_____

Group No. _____

Agreement No. _____

Pediatrician: _____

Address: _____

_____

Telephone No. _____

Child's Allergies, if any: _____

_____

Chronic Illnesses, if any: _____

_____

Date of Last Tetanus Booster: _____

Medicines Child is Taking: _____

_____

Signature _____

(Mother, Father or Legal Guardian)   (Date)

IN CASE OF EMERGENCY I CAN BE REACHED AT:

_____

_____

171

SOME USEFUL, COMMON MEDICAL ABBREVIATIONS

A.D.D.: attention deficit disorder.

A.D.H.D.: attention deficit hyperactivity disorder. (ADD + hyperactive behavior).

AIDS: acquired immunodeficiency syndrome.

AMA: American Medical Association. Also means, "against medical advice"; i.e., a patient leaves the hospital without a doctor's order.

ASAP: as soon as possible.

C.F.: Cystic fibrosis.

CMV: cytomegalo-virus.

C.P.: cerebral palsy.

C.P.R.: cardio-pulmonary resuscitation.

DOA: dead on arrival.

Dx: diagnosis.

E.R.: emergency room.

FTNB: full term newborn.

FTT: failure to thrive.

G.A.: gestational age.

G.E.R.: gastro-esophageal reflux.

HIV virus: human immunodeficiency virus.

IV: intravenous.

IVP: intravenous pyelogram. See glossary.

L & D: Labor and delivery (the area of the hospital where babies are delivered.

LLL: La Leche League.

HOTLINES AND RESOURCES

AIDS
(800)-342-2437/
U.S.Dep. of Public Health Hotline for information, services available, etc.: (800) 458-5231.
For an informative booklet titled AIDS Prevention Guide, call the Center for Disease Control's National AIDS Hotline, at 800--342-AIDS.

ADOLESCENTS
BOOKS:
Between Parent & Teenager, Dr.Haim Ginott, Avon.
The Facts of Love By Alex and Jane Comfort (questions related to sex and relationships).
Stop Struggling with your Teen, by Evonne Weinhaus, M.A. and Karen Friedman, M.S.W.
Teenagers: when to worry and what to do, by Douglas H. Powell, Doubleday.
You and Your Adolescent, by Laurence Steinberg, Ph.D., and Ann Levine. Harper & Row.

ALLERGIES/ASTHMA

American Allergy Association Box 7273 Menlo Park, CA 94025. (415) 322-1663.
Some local chapters will make referrals and give lists of special programs for children with asthma.

The Food Allergy Center: (800)-YES-RELIEF.
It can't diagnose, but it will answer questions about food allergies.

ADOPTION

Adoptive Parents' Education Program. P.O. Box 32114 Phoenix, AZ 85064
(602) 277-3564
The program offers pre-adoption classes and has a bimonthly newsletter with information and referrals. Please include a self-addressed envelope with 45 cents postage.

Council on Adoptable Children 1205 Olivia Avenue Ann Arbor, MI 48104.
Information for parents and prospective parents of adopted children.

National Adoption Information Clearinghouse 14001 I Street NW, Suite 310, Washington, DC 20001.

To adopt a child with special needs, write to:
Aid to Adoption of Special Kids (AASK) America (657 Mission Street, S.601, San Francisco, CA 94105; 800-23A-ASK1, or
Children Awaiting Parents. 700 Exchange Street, Rochester, NY 14608; 716-232-5110. They have national listing, with photos, etc. of hundreds of special-needs children.

ADOPTION - BOOKS ABOUT

Adoption Factbook ($ 39.95, available from the National Committee for Adoption, (202) 328-1200.

The Adoption Resource Book, by Lois Gilman (Harper & Row, 1987. $ 18.95).
Raising Adopted Children, by Lois Melina (Harper & Row, 1986, $ 9.95)

For Children:
The Chosen Baby by Valentina Wasson (lippincott Junior Books, 1977, $ 11.70)
Our Baby: A birth and Adoption Story, by Janiced Koch (Perspectives Press, 1985, $ 9.95)

ATTENTION DEFICIT DISORDERS

Books for Parents:
The Parent's Guide to Attention Deficit Disorders. Hawthorne Educationa Services. (314)-874-1710.

The Difficult Child. Stanley Turecki, M.D.

Support group: Children with Attention Deficit Disorders (CH.A.D.D.), 1859 N.Pine Island Rd., Suite 185, Plantation, FL, 33322, 1-305-587-3700.

AUTISM

National Society for Autistic Children 621 Central Avenue Albany, NY 12206. Central source for information, providing a referral service also.

BABY CARE

A Guide to Feeding Your Baby. Bright Beginnings, an informative pamphlet from Evenflo, offers tips on bottlefeeding and describes Evenflo's Pacer nipple line #733-FREE. Write to Booklets & Samples Editor, American Baby Magazine, P.O. Box 2847, Clinton, IA 52732.

A Mother's Guide to Infant Skin Care. Informative 20-page booklet tells how to keep an infant's skin clean and healthy. Covers diaper rash, cradle cap, and eczema. Includes coupons. From Diaparene/Glenbrook Laboratories, #755-FREE. Write to Booklets & Samples Editor, American Baby Magazine, P.O. Box 2847, Clinton, IA 52732.

Baby Care Basics. This 48-page, illustrated handy reference guide from Johnson & Johnson Baby Products CO. is a combination of four booklets. Baby's Eating and Sleeping Habits, Keeping your Baby Clean, When Baby is Ill, and A Safer World for Babies and Toddlers. #745-FREE. Write to Booklets & Samples Editor, American Baby Magazine, P.O. Box 2847, Clinton, IA 52732.

Baby Ray Teething Booklet. This informative booklet explains the teething process, its symptoms, and possible remedies. Includes a chart on the rate and order of primary teeth development, along with a $.25 coupon toward the purchase of Orajel. From the makers of Orajel products. #863-FREE Write to Booklets & Samples Editor, American Baby Magazine, P.O. Box 2847, Clinton, IA 52732.

The 10 Most Asked Question about Babies' Feet. This informative booklet from Stride Rite by pediatrician William Sears, M.D. answers the questions most frequently asked by parents regarding babies feet, shoes vs. sneakers, and proper fit. #868-FREE. Write to Booklets & Samples Editor, American Baby Magazine, P.O. Box 2847, Clinton, IA 52732.

Your Baby's Oral Development. Reliance Products offers an informative color brochure that helps you understand your baby's natural urge and healthy way to satisfy it. By the makers of the Nuk orthontic nipple. #604-$.25. Write to Booklets & Samples Editor, American Baby Magazine, P.O. Box 2847, Clinton, IA 52732.

BABY PRODUCTS

Guide to Baby Products, 3rd ed. S.Jones, W. Freitag and the Editors of Consumer Reports Books. Up-to-date buying advise on toys, clothing, cradles, strollers, etc.,etc. $ 12.95.
Consumer Reports Books, 1-513-860-1178.

BABYSITTERS

The BabySitters' Checklist is a reusable, laminated wall chart telling sitters what to do in the event of an emergency. Parents can also write down pertinent information. Send $1 to the Council on Family Health, 225 Park Avenue, South, 17th floor, New York, NW, 10003.

BIRTH DEFECTS

March of Dimes/Birth Defects Foundation 1275 Mamarneck Avenue White Plains, NY 10605. (914) 428-7100. The organization can make referrals to local genetics clinics, clinics that handle high-risk pregnancy and those that treat children with birth defects.

The National Center for Education in Maternal & Child Health (NCEMCH), 38th and R Streets, N.W., Washington, D.C. 20057, (202) 625-8400
NCEMCH provides information services, educational materials, and technical assistance to organizations, agencies and individuals with maternal and child-health interests.

BLINDNESS

American Foundation for the Blind 15 West 16th Street New York, NY 10011. Nationwide clearinghouse on information and services for the blind.

National Society to Prevent Blindness.
500 East Remington Road. Schaunburg, Illinois, 60173-4557. (800)-331-2020. Ask for a complete catalog (pamphlets, books, videotapes,etc.)

BOOKS FOR CHILDREN

Cloth books, vinyl books, board books texture books and pop-up books are excellent books to start with infants. These books are generally sturdy, allowing the infant to crumple, gnaw, and manipulate the book without tearing the book up. Yet the book entices the infant with its colors and pictures. Some books encourage interaction with objects to push for sound, textures to feel, tabs to pull, etc.

BREASTFEEDING BOOKS:
Huggins, Kathleen *The Nursing Mother's Companion.* Boston,Harvard Common Press, 1986.
La Leche League International. *The Womanly Art of Breast-feeding.* New York. New American Library, 1987.

Satter, Ellyn, R.D. *Child of Mine: Feeding with Love and Good Sense.* Palo Alto, California: Bull. Publishing Company, 1986.
Grams, Marilyn, M.D. *Breastfeeding Success for Working Mothers.* Carson City, Nev., National Capital Resources, 1985.
Marvin S. Eiger, M.D., and S. Wendkos Olds. *The Complete Book of Breast-feeding,* Workman Publishing.

VIDEOS:
Teitel, Maurice, M.D., Delaney, Sylvia, R.N. B.S : *Breast-feeding. The Art of Mothering.* Alive Productions, Ltd. Port Washington, N.Y. 110501, 1987.

BREASTFEEDING SUPPORT, EDUCATION:
La Leche League International,9616 Minneapolis Ave., Franklin Park, Illinois 60131, (312) 455-7730.
Nursing Mothers Counsel, Inc. P.O.Box 50063, Palo Alto, California 94303, (408) 272-1448
Lactation Consultant Association, P.O.Box 4031, University of Virginia Station, Charlottesville, Virginia 22903

BURNS

Action for Prevention of Burn Injuries to Children
45 School Street
Boston, Mass, 02108.
Information on fire prevention, fire-proof clothing and other products.

CANCER

American Cancer Society 1599 Clifton, Road, NE Atlanta, GA 30329.
(404) 892-0026. Some local chapters will make referrals.

CARDIOPULMONARY RESUSCITATION (CPR), CHOKING.

For courses to learn CPR, contact your local American Red Cross or American Heart Association.

Baby Alive is a useful video ($19.95, plus $5 for postage and handling). Order from Alive Productions, P.O.Box 72, Port Washington, New York, 11050.

CAR SAFETY

For Your Precious Cargo. This colorfully illustrated brochure answers parents questions about car seats--why they are so important and how to choose one for your child. From Trimble. #901-FREE. Write to Booklets and Samples Editor, American Baby Magazine. P.O. Box 2847, Clinton, IA 52732

National Safety Council 444 N. Michigan Avenue Chicago, IL 60611

Safe Ride Program c/o American Academy of Pediatrics, 141 Northwest Point Rd., Elk Grove Village, IL 6007: Ask for these brochures:
1991 Family Shopping Guide to Car Seats: Comprehensive list of approved available infant car seats.
Don't Risk Your Child's Life: important general information on car seats, and car safety in general.

Safe Passage booklet.   This comprehensive booklet provides safety facts, precautions, car-seat information and traveling tips from Evenflo. #858-Free. Write to Booklets and Samples Editor, American Baby Magazine, P.O. Box 2847. Clinton, IA 52832.

CEREBRAL PALSY

United Cerebral Palsy Associations 66 East 34th Street New York, NY 10016
The professional services department will make referrals to centers for diagnosis, treatment, and therapy.

CHILDBIRTH

American Foundation for Maternal and Child Health
30 Beckman Place. New York, N.Y. 10022 Specifically concerned with aspects of the pre-natal period.
ASPO/Lamaze 1101 Connecticut Ave.NW. Suite 300. Washinton, D.C. 20036. (800) 368-4404.
Birth Without Violence, By Frederick Leboyer (Knopf).
Birth Reborn, by Michael Odent (Pantheon).
Caesarean/Support, Education and Concern, Inc. 22 Forest Road Framingham, MA 01701. (508) 877-8266.
Childbirth Preparation Classes. The Bradley Method. P.O. Box 5224
Sherman Oaks, CA 91413 (800) 423-2397, or (800) 422-4784 in California.
Informed Homebirth-Informed Parenting P.O. Box 3675 Ann Arbor, MI 48106 (313)662-6857.

National Institute of Child Health and Human Development NIH Campus Bethesda, MD 20014. Central government clearinghouse for information.

Planned Parenthood Federation of America 810 Seventh Avenue New York, NY 10016. Information about parenthood and birth control.

The Father Book: Pregnancy and Beyond, by Rae Grade (Acropolis). Vaginal Birth After Caesarean (V-BAC) Caesarean Prevention Movement P.O. Box 152, Syracuse, NY 13210 (315) 424-1942.

POSTPARTUM PROBLEMS

The Complete Postpartum Guide: Everything You Need to Know to Take Care of Yourself After You've Had A Baby, by Diane Lynch-Fraser (Harper & Row, 1983, $15.34). Helpful advice from a seasoned exercise and pregnancy consultant on getting back into shape and sorting out conflicting feelings about new motherhood.

The New Mother Syndrome: Coping with Postpartum Stress and Depression (pocket Books) This book discusses puerperal psychosis, a severe form of postpartum depression.

Depression after Delivery (DAD) P.O.Box 1282 Morrisville, PA 19067 (215) 295-3994

CHILD CARE (HOW-TO)
(See Parenting below)

CHILD DAY CARE (See Day Care below)

CHILD DEVELOPMENT BOOKS (for parents)

Birth to One Year, by Marilyn Segal (Mailman Family Press, 1984, $7.95. (A guide to what you can generally expect from your newborn each month.
The First Twelve Months of Life by Frank Caplan, (Bantam, 1978, $4.95) A photo-filled, month-by-month guide to your baby's physical, social, and psychological development by founder of the Princeton Center for Infancy and Early Childhood.
The Second Twelve Months of Life, by Frank Caplan (Bantam Books).
Your Child's First Year by Lee Salk, M.D. (Simon & Schuster, 1983, $8.95) A psychiatrist's advice for giving your baby a secure start in life.
The First Three Years of Life, by Burton White, Prentice Hall Press.
The Developing Person, by Kathleen Berger (Worth Publishers).
The Early Childhood Years: The Two to Six Year Old, Theresa and Frank Caplan (Putnam)

CHILD BEHAVIOR & DISCIPLINE (see under Discipline).

CIRCUMCISION

Free pamphlets:
Circumcision: a Personal Choice. American College of Obstetricians and Gynecologists, Resource Center, 409 12th street SW, Washington, D.C., 20024.

Care of the Uncircumcised Penis. American Academy of Pediatrics, Department C, P.O. Box 927, Elk Grove Village, IL, 60009.

CLEFT LIP/PALATE

American Cleft Palate Education Foundation 331 Salk Hall University of Pittsburg Pittsburg, PA 15261. Booklets and bibliographies available. Referral service through their directory and parent liaison committee.

The Road to Normalcy for the Cleft Lip and Palate Child, by Samuel Berkowitz, D.D.S., M.S. Booklet to answer questions with pictures.

CONSUMER PRODUCTS SAFETY COMMISION

About your Medicines ($ 7.50), from USPC, 12601 Twinbrook Parkway, Rockville, MD 20852, (800) 227-8772.

U.S. Consumer Product Safety Commission Washington, D.C. 20207. (800)-638-CPSC.
By calling the above toll-free number, you can get information on safety standards for cribs, toys and other accessories for children. Or contact the SPCS office in the city nearest you.

CRIB DEATH (See SUDDEN INFANT DEATH SYNDROME)

CYSTIC FIBROSIS

Cystic Fibrosis Foundation 2250 N. Druid Hills Dr. Suite 275, Atlanta, GA 30329 (404) 325-6973 Local chapters make referrals.

DAYCARE

Resources for Child Caring: Catalog involves books, training guides, and AV materials. Write to Toys 'N Things Press. A Division of Resources for Child Caring, Inc. 906 North Pole Street, Box 03, St. Paul, MN 55103 or call (612) 488-7284.

United Way, Inc. 621 Virgil Avenue Los Angeles, CA 90005.
In response to recent cases of sexual abuse in day-care centers, the United Way has prepared a booklet for parents on evaluating day-care. To order a free copy, send a business sized self-addressed stamped envelope to the Communications Division at the above address.

The Complete Guide to Choosing Child Care. Random House, 320 pages, $ 12.95.

DEAFNESS (See Hearing & Speech)

DEATH/ LOSS OF A CHILD

Blood of the Lamb (Little, Brown) by Peter DeVries.
Recovering from the Loss of a Child (MacMillan), by Katherine Fair Donnelly.

Support groups:
1) Candlelighters (for parents of cancer patients), 1312 18th St. NW, Washington, D.C. 20036. (202) 659-5136.
2) The Compassionate Friends, National Headquarters, (312) 323-5010 or try this other address: The Compassionate Friend, Box 3696, Oak Brook, Illinois, 60522-3696.
5) National SIDS Alliance, 10500 Little Patuxent Pkwy. Suite 420. Columbia, Maryland, 21044 (800) 221-SIDS, or in MD, (301) 459-3388.
6) SHARE (miscarriage and neonatal deaths), St. John's Hospital, 800 E. Carpenter, Springfield, ILL 62769. (217) 544-6464

When a Baby Dies: A Handbook for Healing and Helping, by Rana K. Limbo and Sara Rich Wheeler. Published by Resolve Through Sharing, La Crosse, WI.
When Pregnancy Fails (Beacon), by Susan Borg and Judith Lasker.

Books for children:
Everett Anderson's Goodbye, Lucille Clifton (Holt, 1988), Afro-Americans, primary grades $ 3.95.
My Grandpa Died Today, Joan Fassler (Behavioral, 1971), Jewish culture, primary grades $ 16.95.
The Tenth Good Thing about Barney, Judith Viorst (Atheneum, 1971), primary grades, $ 3.95. About the death of pet cat. It helps children accept the death of their pet.

DENTAL CARE

American Society of Dentistry for Children211 E.Chicago Ave,Chicago, IL 60611

DEVELOPMENTAL DISABILITIES

Administration of Developmental Disabilities 330 Independence Avenue SW Washington, D.C. 20201 (202) 245-7719

Association for Children with Learning Disabilities 4156 Library Road
Pittsburg, PA   15234 (412) 341-1515

DIABETES

American Diabetes Association 18 East 48th Street New York, NY 10017.

Juvenile Diabetes Foundation International 432 Park Ave. S. (16th floor)
New York, NY 10016. (212)889-7575
 Hotline: (800) 223-1138, in New York, NY, 889-7575.

DISCIPLINE (See also Parenting below)

Child Behavior, by Frances Ilg, M.D., Luise Bates Ames, Ph.D., Sidney Baker, M.D.
Your Child's Self Esteem, by Dorothy Corkille Briggs.
Shaking, Hitting, Spanking: What to Do Instead. An excellent video that helps you
to " keep your cool ".$ 69,95, call 800-688-5822.

DIVORCE

Where is Daddy? by Goff, B: Beacon Press, 1969. This book reveals anger between
adults and between adults and children, as well as the guilt and loneliness that
youngsters feel when they think they are to blame for the divorce. For children ages
2-6 years.

Quality Time: Easing the Children Through Divorce by Melvin G. Boldzband,
McGraw-Hill.

Growing Up Divorced by Linda Bird Francke, Fawcett Books.

Books for children:
How It Feels When Parents Divorce by Jill Krementz, Knopf.
The Boys' and Girls' Book About One-Parent Families by Richard A., Gardner,
Bantam. (See also under SINGLE PARENTS, below).

DRUGS

National Cocaine Hotline: 1-800-COCAINE
National Institute on Drug Abuse Cocaine Hotline: 1-800-662-4357.
ACTION/PRIDE (Drug Information Hotline); 1-800-677-7433.
Target (Drug and Alcohol Information for kids):L 1-800-366-6667
Narcotics Anonymous: 818-780-3951

EMERGENCIES (See also CPR)

A Sigh of Relief, by Martin I. Green, Bantam Books.
Excellent book for parents. Illustrated, easy to understand instructions on how to
manage childhood emergencies at home. THIS BOOK SHOULD BE IN EVERY HOME
WITH CHILDREN.

Childhood Emergencies-What to Do: A Quick Reference Guide, by Project Care for
Children. The problem with most first aid manuals or chapters is that you can not
imagine taking the time to look up and read the needed information in an emergency.
This wall-mounted flip chart is an ingenious solution. The labeled, color-coded

format invites browsing for brushups and offers first aid basics in seconds. There are blanks for posting emergency phone numbers, and simple explanation on how to handle everything from broken teeth to animal bites. The emergency procedures were written by child health experts. If the guide isn't available in your local bookstore, order it for $12.95 (plus $3.00 shipping) from Bull Publishing Col, P.O. Box 208, Palo Alto, CA, 94302, or call (415) 322-2855.

EPILEPSY

Epilepsy Foundation of America Suite 406 4351 Garden City Drive Landover, MD, 20785. (800) 332-1000.

Book: *Does Your Child Have Epilepsy?* by J.Jan, R.Ziegler & E.Erba/ (Baltimore: University Park Press, 1982).

FOOT

American Association of Foot Specialists, P.O.Box 54, Union, N.J. 07083. (201)688-1616.

Pediatric Orthopedic Society of North America, 222 South Prospect Ave. Suite 127. Park Ridge, IL, 60068 (708) 698-1628.

GAMES, TOYS (See below, TOYS)

GENETIC DISORDERS

March of Dimes/Birth Defects Foundation 1275 Mamaroneck Avenue White Plains, NY 10605 (914) 428-7100

GROWTH DISORDERS

Human Growth Foundation Montgomery Building 4720 Montgomery Lane Bethesda, MD 20814

GROWTH & DEVELOPMENT (See Child Development above)

HANDICAPPED CHILDREN

Action for Brain-Handicapped Children 300 Wilder Building St. Paul, MN 55102. Clearinghouse of information for parents, teachers and professionals on brain handicaps.

Association for Children with Learning Disabilities 5225 Grace Street Pittsburg, PA 15235. Information and referral.

National Easter Seal Society Foundation for Crippled Children & Adults
2303 W. Ogen Avenue
Chicago, IL 60612.
Offers a wide range of programs and information for and about the handicapped.

HEARING AND SPEECH

National Association for Hearing and Speech Action 10801 Rockville Pike Rockville, MD 20852 (800) 638-8255

181

Referrals to speech pathologists and otolaryngologists.

HEART DISEASE/DEFECTS

American Heart Association 7320 Greenville Avenue Dallas, TX 75231 (214) 373-6300 AHA does not make referrals, but local chapters can identify area hospitals that have pediatric cardiology departments.

HEMOPHILIA

National Hemophilia Foundation 110 Greene Street (Suite 303) New York, NY 10012--(212) 219-8180

HYPERACTIVITY (See "Attention Deficit Disorders").

INFECTIOUS DISEASES

Pamphlets for the general public (NIAID Educational Publications) on allergies, and infectious diseases. To order, write to Superintendant of Documents, Government Printing Offices, Washington, D.C. 20402-4325 or call 202-783-3238.

INSECT REPELLENTS (See "Pesticide Network below)

LEAD TESTING

New lead test kits from Verify (415) 578-9401. Signals lead content in paint, pipes, dishes, toys and material painted or soldered with copper. A water testing kit is also available. Call EPA's safe drinking water hotline (800) 426-4791.

LEFT-HANDEDNESS

To make life easier for a left-handed child in this right-handed world, order the "Left-handers International catalog" which lists 130 products made especially for southpaws. Send $ 2 to
Lefthanders International, Box 8249, Topeka, KS, 66608.

LEUKEMIA

Leukemia Society of America, Inc. 733 Third Avenue New York, 10017 (212) 573-8484 Some referrals, as well as lists of comprehensive cancers, major hospitals dealing with cancer.

KIDNEY DISEASE

National Kidney Foundation .116 East 27th Street, New York, NY 10016

MAGAZINES

Highlights for Children: Non-fiction, fiction, and lots of activities have made this magazine a favorite with children 2-12. Features are mixed with such monthly favorites as Headwork, Our Own Pages and Hidden Pictures. ($49.95 for three years, 33 issues). Highlights for Children, P.O. Box 269, Columbus, OH 43272-0002.

Sesame Street Magazine. Muppets teach preschoolers the basics while using various monthly themes such as: You're invited to a Party! Learn About Colors, Let's Make Believe! $1.25 newstand price, $10.95/year (10 issues) Sesame Street Magazine, P.O. Box 52000, Boulder, CO 80321-2000.

The Exceptional Parent - a one-year subscription magazine. The magazine offers practical guidelines and emotional support to parents of children with physical disabilities, mental retardation, learning disabilities, emotional problems, hearing or visual impairments, and chronic illness. The magazine, in its 15th year, publishes with issues annually - February, April, May , July, September, October, November, and December. Write to Waiting Room, The Exceptional Parent, 605 Commonwealth Avenue, Boston, MA 02215.
In magazine stands: American Baby, Parents, Parenting, Child, etc.

MENTAL HEALTH

National Association for Mental Health 1800 North Kent Street Rosslyn Station, Arlington, VA 22209

National Association for Retarded Citizens 2709 Avenue E. East Arlington, TX 76001. Promotes treatment, research and disseminates information, serves as a nationwide clearinghouse of services.

National Down's Syndrome Society (NDSS) 666 Broadway New York, NY 10012
National Down's Syndrome Society Hotline: 800-221-4602. In New York, 212-764, 3070. NDSS can provide information on Down's Syndrome and referrals to local programs.

National Mental Health Association 1021 Prince Street Arlington, VA 22314

One to One (advocacy for the mentally retarded) c/o Cantor, Fitzgerald, Inc. One World Trade Center, 105th floor New York, NY 10048

MUSCULAR DYSTROPHY

Muscular Dystrophy Association of America, Inc. 3561 East Sunrise Dr., Tucson, AZ, 85718. (602) 529-2000. Referrals to a system of local clinics throughout the country that provide diagnosis and treatment

NANNIES

Nanny Times: Magazine published by Ms. Gillian Gordon, President, NANNY Times, P.O. Box 31, Rutherford, NJ, 07070. Annual Subscription $15.95. This publication is devoted to childcare providers and those seeking childcare for their families. Article topics in the bimonthly magazine include: child psychology, first aid, nutrition, and safety.

NUTRITION

American Nutrition Society. P.O. Box 158-C Pasadena, CA 91104.
For lay persons interested in nutrition.
Beech-Nut Nutrition Hotline: 800-523-6633. In PA, 800-492-2384.
Dietary Guidelines for Infants. In formation on sodium intake, fats, cholesterol, fiber and more. Free from Gerber. Call 1-800-4-GERBER, *9-5. M-F, EST.*

PARENTING

Baby and Child Care, by Benjamin McLaine Spock, Simon & Schuster, Inc., New York, NY, 1992. Contains important psychological and developmental concepts in readable and understandable language.

Baby's First Year, book from Beech-Nut. This baby book contains a nutritional reference section, album, recordingkeeping section, developmental guide, and mother's handbook. Also includes charts to record baby's favorite foods, growth, activities, even immunization data. Best of all-you get coupons that can save you more than $1.50 on Beech-Nut Foods. #111-$1.50 Write to Booklets & Samples, American Baby Magazine, P.O. Box 2847, Clinton, IA 52732.

Between Parent and Child, New Solutions to Old Problems, by Haim G. Ginott, MacMillan, New York, NY 1965 (hardcover) Avon, New York, NY 1969 (paperback). Stresses the importance of opening the lines of communications between parent and child and offers an approach to understanding and coping with feelings in the process.

Bright Beginnings Warmline (412) 647-4546, *M-F, 9-9 EST, weekends 1-5*
Non-medical parent support service answers questions on topics ranging from sleep disruption, toilet training, to dealing with temper tantrums.

Doctor and Child, by T. Berry Brazelton, Delacorte Press, New York, NY. Explores the doctor-patient (parent) aspect of parenting in a series of well written essays.

Fatherhood U.S.A., by Debra Klinman, Ph.D., Phiana Kohl, and the Fatherhood Project at Bank St. College of Education (Garland, 1984, $14.95) This national catalog of programs, services, books and resources for and about father is the first of its kind. There are special sections for teen dads, divorced dads, single dads, and fathers of handicapped children.

First Feeling, by Stanley Greenspan, M.D. and Nancy Thorndike Greenspan (Viking Penguin, Inc., 1985, $17.95) A ground-breaking book that explains the milestones of babies' emotional development. The focus is on parent-child interactions and how to provide nurturing encouragement.

How Do Your Children Grow? A Dialog with Parents, by Eda Le Shan, David McKay Company, New York, NY, 1972 (hardcover), Warner Paperback Library, New York, NY 1973 (paperback). Deals with specific questions which worry many parents and suggests for coping with them.

How to Father, by Fitzhugh Dodson, Signet Books, New York, NY 1974 (paperback) Nash Publishing Corporation, Los Angeles, CA 1974 (hardcover). A practical approach to fathering, as well as material on the older child.

How to Parent, by Fitzhugh Dodson. Signet Books, New York, NY 1974 (paperback). Nash Publishing Corporation, Los Angeles, CA 1970 (hardcover). A practical way to parenting.

National Parenting Center Tipline 1-900-246-MOMS. 24 hours Caller hears pre-recorded messages from a variety of specialists. Message changes daily.

P.E.T.: Parent Effectiveness Training, by Thomas Gordon, P.E.T., Plume Books, New American Library, New York, NY 1975 (paperback) Peter H. Wyden, Inc, New

York, NY, 1970 (Hardcover). Author elaborates and explains his three cardinal concepts of child rearing: active listening, sending "I-messages", and resolving conflicts by the "no-lose" method.

Parents Help Line
1-800-421-0353, or in CA, 1-800-352-0386. M-F, 8:30-5 PST
This number connects you to a national office of Parents Anonymous, an international, nonprofit, self-help organization for parents angered and frustrated over child-rearing. (Address: 6733 South Sepulveda Blvd., Suite 270. Los Angeles, CA, 90045.

1-900-321-KIDS (95 cents/call) *Parents Magazine* provides a new idea every day for kids—age specific! New games, fun projects, collages, rhymes, riddles, recipes!

PESTICIDES

Pesticide Network (800)-858-7378. They will answer questions about health dangers of pesticides, insect repellents, etc.

PLANTS

Useful book: *Baby-Safe Houseplants & Cut Flowers: A Guide to Keeping Children & Plants Safely Under the Same Roof.*
John & Delores Alber (Genus $ 12.95).

PLASTIC SURGERY

American Society of Plastic and Reconstructive Surgeons 444 E. Algonquin RD. Arlington Heights, Illinois, 60005. (800) 635-0635 Will send list of 10 plastic surgeons in your geographical area who specialize in the type of plastic surgery you need.

PREMATURES

The Premature Baby Book, A Parent's Guide to Coping and Caring in the First Years.
By Helen Harrison with Ann Kositsky.
The Premie Parents Handbook: A Lifeline for the New Parents of a Premature Baby.
By Adrienne B. Lieberman and Thomas G. Sheagren.
Your Premature Baby, The Complete Guide to Premie Care During That Crucial First Year. By Robin Marantz Henig and Anne B. Fletcher
Born too Soon, Preterm Birth and Early Development. By Susan Goldberg and Barbara DiVitto.

SAFETY

Baby Alive. This program is advertised, not unreasonably, as "the video that could save your child's life." Produced in cooperation with the American Academy of Pediatrics and hosted by The Bill Cosby Show's Phylicia Rashad. The hour-long tape is a crisply paced, step-by-step guide to prevention and treatment of life-threatening situations in children from birth to age 5. Topics include CPR, the Heimlich maneuver, first-aid, home child-proofing, and proper use of infant car seats. There is a companion book, but nothing beats popping the tape in the VCR for a yearly refresher. To order, send $19.95 per copy (plus $4 shipping and handling) to J-2

Communications, Newborn Baby Video, P.O. Box 7169, Burbank, California, 91505. Or call 800-453-7300.

Baby's Home Safety Kit. Kit includes 20 electrical outlet plugs and seven safety latches, plus informative booklet on baby-proofing your home. #047-$5.25. Write to Booklets & Samples Editor, American Baby Magazine, P.O. Box 2847, Clinton, IA 52732.

First-Aid Facts Slide Guide. Easy-to-read emergency information pack provides doctor-approved methods for treating cuts and bruises, burns, fever, croup, poisoning, and more. #026-$1.50. Write to Booklets & Samples Editor, American Baby Magazine, P.O. Box 2847, Clinton, IA 52732.

How to Make Bathtime Safer for Baby & Easier for Parents. This step-by-step guide to bathing your baby contains helpful hints and illustrations to make bathtime safe and easy. Includes information on the slip-resistant "Sponge Bather" and other bath aids from A-Plus Products. #886-FREE. Write to Booklets & Samples Editor, American Baby Magazine, P.O. Box 2847, Clinton, IA 52732.

How to Protect Your Loved Ones in Your Car. This informative, illustrated booklet contains important facts about child car safety plus a $5.00 rebate coupon towards the purchase of certain Century Products car seats. #796-FREE. Write to Booklets & Samples Editor, American Baby Magazine, P.O. Box 2847, Clinton, IA 52732.

Never Talk to Strangers by Irma Joyce: Golden Books/Wester Publishing. 1220 Mound Avenue, Racine, WI 53404 (414-533-2431) 1967, $3.50.

Nursery Equipment Safety Checklist. Baby News Children's Stores produced the checklist, designed by the Consumer Product Safety Commission, to assist you in choosing the safest nursery equipment for your child. #100-$.25. Write to Booklets & Samples Editor, American Baby Magazine, P.O. Box 2847, Clinton, IA 52732.

OUCHY Safety Stickers. Teach your child that these stickers mean "Don't Touch", then place them wherever necessary. Bonus: They are removable. For two free stickers, an order form and more information, send a business-size self-addressed stamped envelope to OUCHY Enterprises, P.O. Box 17249, Department P, Pittsburg, PA 15235. (Note: Child proofing products are available aids; however, they do not eliminate the need for careful adult supervision of children.)

Private Zone by Frances Dayee: Charles Franklin Press, 18409 90th Avenue West, Edmonds, WA 98020 (206-774-6979) 1982,$3 plus 75 cents shipping.

Poison Control Center
U.S. Department of Health, Education & Welfare Public Health Service Food & Drug Administration Bethesda, MD 20016. Information about poisons, prevention of poisoning and remedies.

Safety Phone Card and Baby Sleeping sign. Leave babysitter important numbers on the Safety Phone Card, which comes with a pad of self-stick note paper for messages. Reverse the card to a Baby Sleeping hang-up sign for your front door. Comes with velcro fasteners for easy hanging. #050-$2.00. Write to Booklets & Samples Editor, American Baby Magazine, P.O. Box 2847, Clinton, IA 52732.

The Baby Test. A video which addresses whether parents can increase their children's attention span, whether nursing babies get all the vitamins they need, which plaything is the most common cause of choking and suffocation and whether boys learn motor skills faster than girls. Pediatricians, psychologists and child care experts offer advice on temper tantrums, nutritional needs, discipline and safety measures. 30 minutes. FREE/ VHS. Order from Hoffman-LaRoche, Inc, 340 Kingsland Street, Nutley, NJ 07110 (201) 235-5000.

The video *"A Safe and Comfortable World for Baby"* is produced by Juvenile Products Manufacturer's Association. Order form JPMA Videotape, 2 Greentree Centre, Suite 225, P.O. Box 955, Marlton, NJ 08053 for $15.00.

The Reasons People Drown. A video teaching parents why drowning is the second leading cause of accidental death of children from infancy through adolescence. Shows children drowning and being rescued. 25 minutes. $140/VHS

When Every Second Counts. A video which shows adults how to rescue choking children birth to 8 years. From the American Heart Association, 40 minutes. $19.95/VHS.

The Pool Care Hotline: (800)-222-2348. Expert advice on pool safety and maintenance.

SEX EDUCATION

A Bibliography of Educational Material for Children, Adolescents, and their families, by the American Academy of Pediatrics. For a copy, contact the American Academy of Pediatrics, 141 Northwest Point Boulevard, P.O. Box 927, Elk Grove, IL 60009-0927. Minimum order 100. Price is $15.00/100 (members), $20.00/100 (non-members).

Books:
A Kid's First Book About Sex (Yes Press, $ 5.50), by Joani Blank and Marcia Quackenbush; *Did The Sun Shine Before You Were Born?* A sex education primer (Ed-U Press, $ 7.95), by Sol and Judith Gordon; *Outside-In* (Barron's Educational Series, $ 13.95) by Clare Smallman; *The Bare Naked Book* (Annick Press, $4.95), by Kathy Stinson; and *Where Do Babies Come From?* (Alfred A.Knopf, $16.95), by Margaret Sheffield, for primary grades. To order any of these books call: (800)-677-7760.

SIBLING RIVALRY

Our New Baby, by Pleasant T. Rowland. This hands-on primers aims to make the older toddler feel less threatened and shows how to care for the newborn brother or sister with pull tabs to make the baby's feet kick in the bath.... $19.95. To order, call 800-845-0005
Mom's Home by Jan Ormerod, Lothrop, Lee & Shepard. Nearly wordless book in which a pregnant mother shares a private moment with her toddler.
The Baby, by John Burningham, Crowell. Simple, direct pictures, for toddlers.
It's Not Fair! by Anita Harper. A young kangaroo lists her grievances during baby's first days, then gradually sees that being older has its advantages.

SIBLINGS
Nobody Asked Me if I Wanted A Baby Sister by Martha Alexander (Dial, 1971), preschool, primary grades $ 10.95
Go And Hush The Baby, by Betsey Byars (Penguin, 1971), preschool, $ 3.95.

The New Baby at Your House, by Joanna Cole (Morrow, 1985), preschool $ 11.95
A Baby Sister for Frances, Lillian and Russell Hoban (Harper and Row, 1964), preschool $ 12.95.

SICKLE CELL ANEMIA

National Sickle Cell Disease Program Division of Blood Diseases and Resources National Heart, Lung and Blood Institute Room 504, Federal Building 7550 Wisconsin, MD   20892 (301) 496-6931   Staff referrals will make referrals when possible.

SPEECH (See "Hearing" above).

SPINA BIFIDA

Spina Bifida Association of America Suite 540 1700 Rockville Pike Rockville, MD 20852 (800) 621 3141 Referrals to specialists, where to go for AFP testing

STUTTERING

If Your Child Stutters, a guide written for parents, published by the Speech Foundation of America. Toll free 800-992-9392 or $1 to P.O. Box 11749, Memphis TN 38111.

National Center for Stuttering: 800-221-2483, in New York, 212-532-1460. Will send information to help remedy this problem. The organization also provides listings of upcoming National Workshops.

Stuttering Foundation of America. A Non-Profit Organization, P.O.Box 11749, Memphis, TN 38111-0749. Books about stuttering, any age bracket.

SUDDEN INFANT DEATH SYNDROME (SIDS)

National SIDS Foundation Two Metro Plaza 8240 Professional Place, Suite 205 Landover, MD 20785

TOILET TRAINING --Books for Parents:

The Parent's Book of Toilet Teaching, Joanna Cole,(Ballantine Books, 1983)
Developing Toilet Habits, (Ross Laboratories). Available free from your doctor's office.
Toilet Learning: The Picture Book, by Allison Mack (Little Brown)
One Stage at a Time: A Guide to Toilet Training with Less Stress, by Roger Barkin, M.D.(Available from Gerry Baby Products Company)

Books to read to your child:
Your New Potty, by Joanna Cole (Morrow Junior Books).
Koko Bear's New Potty, by Vicky Lansky (Bantam Books)
The Toddler"s Potty Book, by Alida Allison (Stern/Sloan Publishers)
Going to the Potty, by Fred Rogers (Putnam)
Once Upon a Potty, by Alona Frankel (Barrons)
No More Diapers! by Joae Graham Brooks, M.D. (Dell Publications).

TOYS

"Toys to Grow On" catalog. Write to: Toys to Grow On, P.O. Box 17, Long Beach, CA 90801 or call toll-free, 24 hours, 7 days/week: 1-800-542-8338.

Consumer Product Safety Commission. Free CPSC brochure, "Which Toy for Which Child". Write CPSC, Office of information and Public Affairs, Washington, DC, 20207. Hotline: 800-638-2772

Toy Manufacturers of America. Free booklet, "The TMA Guide to Toys and Play". Write :Toy Booklet, P.O.Box 866, Madison Square Station, New York, NY 19159-0866.

TWINS

Nobel, E: *Having Twins - A Parents' Guide to Pregnancy, Birth and Early Childhood.* Boston, Houghton-Mifflin, 1980.
Therous TR, Tingley, JF: *The Care of Twin Children: A Common Sense Guide for Parents.* Chicago, The Center for Study of Multiple Birth, 1978.
Gromada K: *Mothering Multiples.* Franklin Park, IL, La Leche League International, 1981.
Cassill K: *Twins: Nature's Amazing Mystery.* New York, Atheneum, 1982.
Clegg A, Woollett A: *Twins From Conception to Five Years.* New York, Van Nostrand Reinhold, 1983.
Double Talk (Newsletter). Department T, PO Box 412 Amella, OH 45102.

Twin Services P.O.Box 10066 Berkeley, CA 94709 (415) 524-0863

Twin Magazine P.O.Box 12045 Overland Park, KS 66212 (800) 821-5533

VISION (See also Blindness)

The American Council of the Blind
1010 Vermont Avenue, Suite 1100
Washington, D.C. 20005.
800-424-8666
Will send free literature to the parents of visually impaired children. This group also informs callers of the various educational programs available by personalized letter response (send letter to attention of Mr. Richard Hannigan.)

BOOKS YOU CANNOT BE WITHOUT
(AND SURVIVE IN *CHILDCARELAND*)

THE CHILDWISE CATALOG

This most useful consumer guide has a complete, detailed description of all kinds of products for children: From Auto Safety Seats to Beds, Books, Cribs, Carriages, to Toys, Unsafe Products, Videos and TV, Walkers, etc.
Jack Gillis and Mary Ellen R. Fise
Perennial Library, about $ 12.95

A SIGH OF RELIEF. The first-aid handbook for childhood emergencies.
A remarkable book, written in a simple, straightforward style, with large character letters and excellent drawings. Makes finding a quick solution to many emergency situations very easy.
Waritten by Martin I. Green, Bantam Books, about $ 12.95.

FIREPLACE AND WOOD STOVE WARNINGS

Fires in the fireplace are cozy, attractive. In a wood burning stove, they may also save money. However, they may be quite dangerous!
· Before buying a wood stove, read your building's codes, and look for one that has the sign of approval of a national inspection agency.
· Only a qualified professional installer should set it up. The stove should be placed at least 36" away from the walls.
· When using the stove keep always a window slightly open.
· Don't use flammable liquids to start a fire.
· Keep a fire extinguisher close at hand.
· Have the stove and chimney inspected and cleaned yearly.
· Install a safety screen in front of the fireplace to keep children away.

BABIES' TOOTH CHART

FIRST TEETH		When teeth "come in"	When teeth "fall out"
UPPER	Central incisors Lateral incisors Canines (cuspids) First molars Second molars	7-12 mths 9-13 mths 16-22 mths 13-19 mths 25-33 mths	6-8 yrs. 7-8 yrs. 10-12 yrs. 9-11 yrs. 10-12 yrs.
LOWER	Second molars First molars Canines (cuspids) Lateral incisors Central incisors	20-31 mths 12-18 mths 16-23 mths 7-16 mths 6-10 mths	10-12 yrs. 9-11 yrs. 9-12 yrs. 7-8 yrs. 6-8 yrs.

Don't worry if your infant is late in cutting his teeth: tooth eruption varies a lot in children.

Also, the order in which they appear is inconsistent. Check with your doctor during Well Baby check-up visits.

1992
Family Shopping Guide
to
CAR SEATS

(This section reproduced here with permission of the American Academy of Pediatrics. Copyright 1992)

Buckling your children up shows you care about their safety.

More children in the US are killed and crippled in car crashes than from any other cause of injury. Therefore, it is now the law in every state that infants and children must ride buckled up in car seats or seat belts.

When used correctly, car seats provide excellent protection in most crashes. Car seats keep children from being slammed into the windshield or dashboard, thrown against other people, or flung out of the car in even a low-speed collision. They also keep children in their places, so that you, the driver, can pay attention to the road.

Choosing a Car Seat

- The "best" car seat is one that fits your child's size and weight, fits in your car, and can be used correctly every time.
- Check the label on the seat to make sure it meets current federal safety standards.
- Low- and high-priced models generally provide equally crash protection. Higher prices usually mean convenience features, which make the seat easier to use correctly.
- Tray-shields and T-shields keep harnesses from tangling. They must be low to restrain the hips. For small newborns, they often are too high and too far from the body to fit correctly.
- Find a seat with straps that are simple to adjust while the seat is in the car and one that has a seat belt path through which your car's belt can be fastened easily.
- If you must get a used seat, look at the label on the seat to make sure it was made after January 1, 1981. Those made earlier do not meet the same strict crash standards. Be sure to get instructions and all parts for any used seat.

Basics of Car Seat Use

- Always use a car seat, starting with your baby's first ride home from the hospital. Help your child form a lifelong habit of buckling up.
- Follow the manufacturer's instructions and keep them with the car seat.

- Check your vehicle owner's manual for special directions on using car seats with seat belts and air bags.
- Remember: the harness and/or shield holds the child in the car seat and the vehicle seat belt holds the seat in the car. Unless **both** are attached snugly, the car seat may not prevent injury.
- If a lap/shoulder belt does not stay tight, check the car seat instructions about using a metal locking clip.
- Never use a seat that has been used in a crash.

Using Car Seats Correctly

Infant Seats (birth to 20 pounds)

Advantages: Small and Portable. Fits small newborns best.
Disadvantage: Must be replaced by a convertible seat when outgrown.

- Install an infant car seat so the baby faces the back of the car, so that the seat supports both body and head during a crash. Never use an infant-only seat facing forward.
- If your car has a passenger-side air bag, put your baby in the back seat. If the air bag inflates, it could cause serious injuries to a rear-facing infant in the front seat.
- Use the infant car seat until your child reaches 17-20 pounds or until your child's head reaches the top of the car seat. If your baby outgrows it before 20 pounds, use a rear-facing convertible car seat until your child weighs 20 pounds.
- Route the seat belt through the right path on the car seat (see instructions) and pull it tight.
- Adjust the harness to fit snugly over the shoulders and between the legs. Place the plastic harness clip (if provided) at armpit level to keep the straps on the shoulders.
- Keep the shoulder straps in the slots at or just **below** the baby's shoulders.
- To keep a newborn from slouching, pad the sides of the seat and the space between the crotch and the harness with rolled up diapers or receiving blankets.
- If an infant's head flops forward, tilt the seat back a little by wedging padding under the base of the seat, just enough so the head stays upright.
- **Premature infants** should be watched in a car seat before discharge from hospital to see if the semi-reclined position adds to possible breathing problems. If the physician recommends, a car bed may be used for a short period so the baby can lie flat. A premie should ride where an adult can monitor breathing.

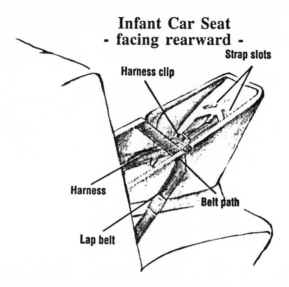

Infant Car Seat
- facing rearward -

Strap slots

Harness clip

Harness

Belt path

Lap belt

Convertible Seats (birth to about 40 pounds)

Advantage: Fits child from 7-8 pounds to about 40 pounds.
Disadvantage: Bulky. Less portable than an infant car seat.

- Use a convertible seat facing the rear for babies up to 20 pounds. Keep it rear-facing as long as possible for the best protection.
- For children over 20 pounds who can sit up well alone, turn the seat to face forward. Use it until your child outgrows it, at about 40 pounds.
- Make sure the seat belt is routed through the car seat correctly in both forward and rear-facing positions (there are usually two different belt paths); pull the belt right.
- Keep the harness snug, and readjust it as your child grows or changes outer clothing. Use a plastic harness clip at armpit level to hold shoulder straps in place, if provided.
- Thread the shoulder straps through the top harness slots in the forward-facing position.
- If you have an older seat that requires a top tether strap when facing forward, be sure to install it. Newer models do not need tethers, although use of an optional tether gives extra protection.

Toddler-Only Seats, Vests (over 20-25 pounds)

- These may take the place of convertible seats where available and appropriate.
- Follow installation and usage instructions with the device. Weight limits will vary.
- Always keep seat belts and harness straps snug.

Convertible Car Seat
- facing forward -

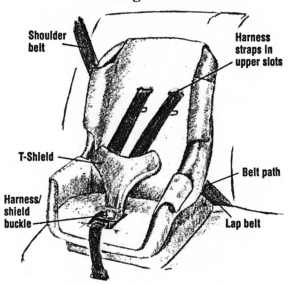

Shoulder belt

Harness straps in upper slots

T-Shield

Belt path

Harness/ shield buckle

Lap belt

Booster Seats (for children who have outgrown convertible seats)

Belt-Positioning Booster Seats (over 30 pounds)

Advantages: Uses vehicle shoulder belt to protect upper body and head. Preferred to shield booster when a lap/shoulder belt is available.
Disadvantage: Cannot be used in seating positions with lap belts only.

- The booster base will raise a child up so lap and shoulder belts fit properly.
- Some models have a separate shield that is added for use when only a lap belt is available (preferably over about 40 pounds). Others (not listed in this pamphlet) have only a base and are sold for children over 50 pounds.

Shield Booster Seats (about 40 to 65 pounds)

Advantage: Provides better protection than a lap belt alone.
Disadvantage: Gives less protection than a convertible seat or belt-positioning booster.

- A shield booster is suitable when a child has outgrown a convertible or toddler seat at close to 40 pounds, even if labeled for use at a lower weight.
- Small shield boosters provide more protection than lap belts alone if the lap belt does not fit very tight and low on the hips or if the child slouches so it rides up dangerously high onto the tummy.
- Never use a booster seat with a lap belt alone unless the booster has a shield.

Booster Car Seat

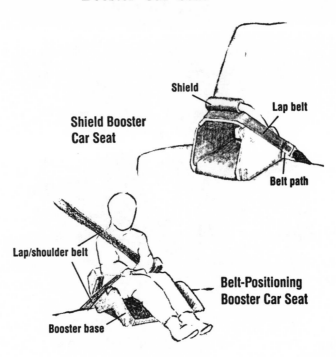

Shield

Lap belt

**Shield Booster
Car Seat**

Belt path

Lap/shoulder belt

**Belt-Positioning
Booster Car Seat**

Booster base

1992 Shopping Guide to Car Seats

All products listed meet current Federal Motor Vehicle Safety Standard 213. New models in italics.

Manufacturer/Name	Harness Type	Harness Adjustment	Special Notes	Price Range
Infant Seats			**(Birth to 20 lbs unless noted)**	
Century 560,565	3-pt harness	One-step	Tilt-indicator; fits in shopping cart.	$30-50
Century 590	3-pt harness	One-step	Tilt-indicator; separate base stays in car; can be used in car without base.	$50-70
Cosco Dream Ride	3-pt harness	One-step	To 17 lbs; use as car bed or reclined, rear-facing.	$59
Cosco TLC	3-pt harness	Manual	Shoulder belt wraps around front of seat.	$29-34
Evenflo Dyn-O-Mite	3-pt harness	Manual	Shoulder belt wraps around front of seat.	$32-49
Evenflo Joy Ride	3-pt harness	Manual	Separate base stays belted in car; seat can be used in second car without base; locks in shopping cart.	$49-69
Evenflo Travel Tandem	3-pt harness	Manual		
Fisher-Price Infant Car Seat	T-shield	Manual	No locking clip; leveling line; locks in shopping cart.	$50
Gerry Guard with Glide	3-pt harness	Manual	Fabric cover for harness clip; use as glider in house.	$50-60
Kolcraft Rock 'N Ride	3-pt. harness	Manual	To 18 lbs; no harness height adjustment.	$29-50
Safeline Sit 'n' Stroll	3-pt harness	Manual	Up to 25 pounds facing rear; converts to stroller.	$129-139
Convertible Seats			**(Birth to 40 lbs. unless noted)**	
Babyhood Mfg Baby Sitter	5-pt harness	Manual	Previously called "Wonda Chair."	$89
Century 1000 STE	5-pt harness	One-step	2 crotch strap positions.	$50-80
Century 2000 STE	T-shield	One-step	2 crotch strap positions.	$60-80
Century 3000, 3500 STE	Tray-shield	One-step	2 crotch strap positions.	$70-90
Century 5000, 5500 STE	Tray-shield	Manual	2 crotch strap positions.	$90-120
Cosco 5-Point	5-pt harness	Manual	Back pads for infant support.	$49-59
Cosco Comfort Ride	Tray-shield	One-step	2 crotch strap positions; adjustable shield; support pads.	$90-120
Cosco Soft Shield	T-shield	One-step	Back pads for infant support.	$69-99
Evenflo Champion, Scout	T-/Tray-shields	Manual	Champion - either shield; Scout - T-shield only.	$79
Evenflo One-Step	Tray-shield	One-step	Back pads for infant support.	$49-69
Evenflo Seven Year	Tray-shield	One-step	Converts to booster (see Evenflo Booster)	$99-120

	Belt Position		Special Notes	Price
Evenflo Ultara I	Tray-shield	One-step		$79-89
Evenflo Premier, Premier V	Tray-shield or 5-pt harness (V)	One-step	Back pads for infant support.	$89-109
Fisher-Price Car Seat	T-shield	Automatic	No locking clip provided.	$78
Gerry Guard SecureLock	Tray-shield	Automatic	Buckle atop hinged stalk that pulls forward to open.	$70-90
Gerry Guardian	T-shield	Automatic	Harness locks on impact; deluxe has infant bolster.	$60-75
Kolcraft Auto-Mate	T-shield	One-step	Harness adjustment on both sides.	$50-70
Kolcraft Traveler 700	Tray-shield	One-step	Harness adjustment on both sides.	$50-85
Nissan Child Safety Seat	T-shield	Automatic	Not tested for aircraft use.	$100
Playskool Carseat (Kolcraft)	Tray-shield	One-step	Inflatable head support for infant.	$70-90
Renolux GT 2000	5-pt harness	Manual	Harness adjusts in back.	$60-80
Renolux GT 5000 Turn-a-Tot	5-pt harness	Manual	Seat swivels on base; harness adjusts in back.	$100-130
Renolux GT 7000	5-pt harness	Manual	Reclines by remote control; harness adjusts in back.	$180-200

Toddler-Only Vests & Integral Seats (20-25 lbs and up)

	Belt Position		Special Notes	Price
Little Cargo Auto Safety Vest (25-40 lbs)	5-pt harness	Manual	Simplified strap-buckle system; auto lap belt attached through padded stress plate.	$39-49
Chrysler Integral Child Seat (20-40 lbs; Booster 40+ lbs)	5-pt harness	Manual	Two build-in seats optional in Minivans; one converts to belt-positioning booster for larger child.	$200
E-Z-On Vest (25+ lbs)	4-pt harness	Manual	Tether strap must be installed in vehicle.	$62

Booster Seats*	**Belt Position**	**Special Notes (Use after convertible/toddler seat is outgrown)**	Price
Century Commander	Wrap-around	**Belt-positioning booster for lap/shoulder belt use;** shield for lap belt use.	$25-35
Century CR-3	Wrap-around	Two seat heights.	$25-40
Cosco Explorer	Wrap-around	Split shield open in middle; belt through base for short child; internal crotch strap.	$25-35
Evenflo Booster Car Seat	Wrap-around or through base		$46-55
Evenflo Sightseer	Wrap-around	**Belt-positioning booster for lap/shoulder belt use;** shield for lap belt use; internal lap strap.	$29-34
Gerry DoubleGuard	Wrap-around or through base		$45-55
Kolcraft Tot Rider Quik Step	Wrap-around	Crotch post; shield pivots down for access to seat.	$20-35

*Belt-positioning boosters without shields for children over 50 pounds not listed.

198

Useful Equivalents
Weights, Measures, and Conversion Tables

Weight	lb.	Kg.	Kg.	lb.	Length	in.	cm.	cm.	in.
	1	0.5	1	2.2		1	2.5	1	0.4
	2	0.9	2	4.4		2	5.1	2	0.8
	4	1.8	3	6.6		4	10.2	3	1.2
	6	2.7	4	8.8		6	15.2	4	1.6
	8	3.6	5	11.0		8	20.3	5	2.0
	10	4.5	6	13.2		12	30.5	6	2.4
	20	9.1	8	17.6		18	46	8	3.1
	30	13.6	10	22		24	61	10	3.9
	40	18.2	20	44		30	76	20	7.9
	50	22.7	30	66		36	91	30	11.8
	60	27.3	40	88		42	107	40	15.7
	70	31.8	50	110		48	122	50	19.7
	80	36.4	60	132		54	137	60	23.6
	90	40.9	70	154		60	152	70	27.6
	100	45.4	80	176		66	168	80	31.5
	150	68.2	90	198		72	183	90	35.4
	200	90.8	100	220		78	198	100	39.4
	1 lb. = 0.454 Kg.		1 Kg. = 2.204 lb.			1 inch = 2.54 cm		1 cm. = 0.3937 inch	

Liquid Measures

1 fluid dram	=	60 minims	=	3.697 ml.
1 fluid ounce	=	8 fluid drams	=	29.573 ml.
1 pint	=	16 fluid oz.	=	473.167 ml.
1 quart	=	32 fluid oz.	=	946.333 ml.
1 gallon	=	128 fluid oz.	=	3,785 ml.

1 milliliter	=	0.061 cubic in.	=	1 cc.
1 centiliter	=	0.61 cubic in.	=	10 cc.
1 deciliter	=	6.1 cubic in.	=	100 cc.
1 liter	=	61.0271 cubic in.	=	1,000 cc.

1 teaspoonful	=	1 fluid dram	=	5 ml.*
1 teacupful	=	4 fluid ounces	=	120 ml.*
1 glassful	=	8 fluid ounces	=	240 ml.*

Linear Measures

1 inch	=	25.4 mm.	=	2.54 cm.
1 foot	=	12 inches	=	30.48 cm.
1 yard	=	36 inches	=	0.9144 meter
1 rod	=	198 in. (16 1/2 ft.)	=	5.029 meters
1 mile	=	5,280 feet	=	1.609 km.

1 mm.	=	0.03937 in.	=	1,000 microns
1 cm.	=	0.3937 in.	=	10 mm.
1 dm.	=	3.937 in.	=	10 cm.
1 m.	=	39.37 in.	=	10 dc.
1 km.	=	3,281 ft. (0.62 mile)	=	1,000 meters

Weights

Apothecary		Apothecary		Metric
1 scruple	=	20 grains	=	1.296 g.
1 dram	=	60 grains	=	3.88 g.
1 ounce	=	480 grains (8 drams)	=	31.1 g.
1 pound	=	5,760 grains (12 oz.)	=	373.24 g.

Avoirdupois		Apothecary		Metric
1 ounce	=	437.5 grains	=	28.35 g.
1 pound	=	7,000 grains	=	453.59 g.
1 ton	=	2,000 lbs. avdp.	=	907.184 kg.

Metric		Apothecary		Metric
1 mg.	=	1/65 grain*	=	0.001 g.
1 cg.	=	1/6 grain*	=	0.01 g.
1 dg.	=	1 1/2 grain*	=	0.1 g.
1 g.	=	15.432 grains	=	0.001 kg.
1 kg.	=	2.2 lbs. avdp.*	=	1,000 g.

* Approximate equivalent.

199

INDEX

I

Ibuprofen, 59
Immunizations, 37, 43
Infant botulism, 49
Infant walkers, 143
Iron, in formulas, 9
Iron deficeincy anemia, 51

J/K/L

Jaundice, 28
Language
    expressive, 126
    receptive, 126
Legs, 83
Lice, 87
Limping, 85

M

Mattering of the eyes, 23
Measles
    disease, 39
    vaccine, 40
Meatitis, 18
Medicine cabinet, 86
Medication rules, 91
Milestones must pass, 118
    growth and development, 116
Minor problems and accidents, 91
MMR vaccine, 40
Mumps, 39
Myths, or old wives tales, 145

N

Naming your baby, 148
Non-toxic products, 129
Nosebleeds, 68
Nursery, 34
Nutrition
    ---see feedings, 47

O/P/Q

Obesity, 85
Office visits, 35
Old wives tales, 150
Oral polio vaccine, 38
Otitis media, 72
Pacifiers, 34
Paraphimosis, 17
Pertussis disease, 36
    --vaccine, 37
Pets, 150
Phimosis, 17
Pink eye, 85
    (see conjunctivitis)
Pinworms, 86
Poisons in the home , 127
Polio disease
    --injectable, killed, 39
    --oral, live, 39
    --vaccine, 39
Pre-natal visits, 3
Precautions, sunbathing, 140
Pregnancy, 1
Propping the bottle, 8, 74

R

Regurgitation, 64

Respiratory syncitial virus,
(RSV), 7
Rubella vaccine, 41
Rules on medications, 94

S

Safety child, 135
safety crib, 4
Schedule feedings, 47
School, return after an illnessn, 62
Seizures, 82
Shoes for children, 84
Sleep, your baby's, 34
Smoking, and pregnancy, 2
Sneezing, 23
Solid foods, 48
Speech , 125
Spitting up, 23
Strep infections, 78
Suffocation, choking and , 141
Sunbathing precautions, 140
Sunscreens, 140
Supplies for baby, 5

T

Tear ducts, clogging of the, 24
Tears, 25
Teething syndrome, 21, 535
Temper tantrums, 112
Tetanus vaccine, 37
Thumbsucking, 118
Tibial torsion, 84
Tips, babysitting, 135
Toeing in, 84
    --out, 84
Toilet training, 99
Tonsillectomy, 79
Tonsillitis, 78
Tooth care, 53, 54
    --re-implantation , 54
    --chart, 191

Torticollis, 78
Toys, 145
TV, children and, 145
Twins and resources
    (see hotlines)
Two year olds
    (the terrible two's), 108

U/V/W

Umbilicus
    --care of, 22
    --hernia, 87
Urinary tract infections, 88
Vaccines,
    (see immunization)
Vaginal discharge, 23
Varicella, 81
    (chicken pox)
Vision, 125
Vitamins, 52
Vomiting, 28
Walkers, infant, 143
Water safety, 138, 139
Weight gain, 16, 98
Well baby check ups, 35
Whole milk, why not?, 50
Whooping cough
    (see pertussis
Witches milk, 23

MAIL ORDER FORM

You can order this book by sending this completed form to:

ABC & F Press
P.O. Box 92
Bedford, Texas 76095

or call toll-free: 1 (800) 528-3975.

Name _____

Address _____

Telephone _____

Credit Card # _____
MC - Visa - Amex - Other:
Expir. Date

Or send check or money order for $ 15.89 to the above address.
($ 12.95, plus $ 0.94 state tax plus $ 2.00 postage and shipping).

This ABC & F book is available at special quantity discounts for bulk purchases for sales promotions, premiums or fund raising. Special books or book excerpts can also be created to fit specific needs.

For more information, write or call the address/phone above.